Diana Brenscheidt gen. Jost

Shiva Onstage

KlangKulturStudien
SoundCultureStudies

herausgegeben von

Lars-Christian Koch
und
Raimund Vogels

Band 6

_____
LIT

Diana Brenscheidt gen. Jost

SHIVA ONSTAGE

Uday Shankar's Company
of Hindu Dancers and Musicians
in Europe and the United States, 1931 – 38

LIT

Cover Picture
Hindu dance group Uday Shankar, in: Hermann & Marianne Aubel, *Die Bedeutung der alten indischen Tanzkultur*, Verlag der Arbeitsgemeinschaft für Natur- und Völkerkunde 1932, p. 9 / Courtesy of Deutsches Tanzarchiv Köln

Gedruckt auf alterungsbeständigem Werkdruckpapier entsprechend
ANSI Z3948   DIN ISO 9706

Bibliographic information published by the Deutsche Nationalbibliothek
The Deutsche Nationalbibliothek lists this publication in the Deutsche Nationalbibliografie; detailed bibliographic data are available in the Internet at http://dnb.d-nb.de.

ISBN 978-3-643-90108-8
Zugl.: Köln, Univ., Diss., 2011

A catalogue record for this book is available from the British Library

©LIT VERLAG GmbH & Co. KG Wien,
Zweigniederlassung Zürich 2011
Klosbachstr. 107
CH-8032 Zürich
Tel. +41 (0) 44-251 75 05
Fax +41 (0) 44-251 75 06
e-Mail: zuerich@lit-verlag.ch
http://www.lit-verlag.ch

LIT VERLAG Dr. W. Hopf
Berlin 2011
Fresnostr. 2
D-48159 Münster
Tel. +49 (0) 2 51-620 320
Fax +49 (0) 2 51-922 60 99
e-Mail: lit@lit-verlag.de
http://www.lit-verlag.de

Distribution:
In Germany: LIT Verlag Fresnostr. 2, D-48159 Münster
Tel. +49 (0) 2 51-620 32 22, Fax +49 (0) 2 51-922 60 99, e-mail: vertrieb@lit-verlag.de

In Austria: Medienlogistik Pichler-ÖBZ, e-mail: mlo@medien-logistik.at

In the UK: Global Book Marketing, e-mail: mo@centralbooks.com

Acknowledgements

There are a number of people to whom I would like to express my gratitude as this work would not have been possible without their support. First of all I would like to thank my supervisor Prof. Dr. Lars-Christian Koch, head of the Musikethnologische Abteilung and the Phonogramm Archiv at the Ethnological Museum in Berlin. He has always supported me in this and in other projects.

As my thesis is strongly based on archival material, my research had been made possible by various people at different institutions. I would here like to thank the staff at the Deutsches Tanzarchiv Köln, the Institut für Zeitungsforschung in Dortmund, the Staatsbibliothek zu Berlin, the Musikethnologische Abteilung at the Ethnological Museum, Berlin, the Dartington Hall Trust Archive and Collection in Totnes, and the British Library (especially the staff at the Newspaper Section in Colindale). Furthermore, I am especially grateful to Brigitte Blockhaus, former librarian at the Institute for Advanced Study in the Humanities, Essen. With her professionalism and profound experience she has made an amazing range of source material on Uday Shankar available to me.

I further wish to thank the project "Humanism in the Era of Globalization. An Intercultural Dialogue on Culture, Humanity, and Values," which was headed by Prof. Dr. Jörn Rüsen and located at the Institute for Advanced Study in the Humanities in Essen between 2007 and 2009. I am very grateful for the confidence the Board of Directors had in me and my work which allowed me to receive a full scholarship by the Gerhardt Mercator Foundation, Duisburg.

I am also grateful to Mr. Chidaram Podder, my Bengali-teacher at the University of Cologne, for his instruction in Bengali language and culture and his encouragement regarding the progress of my work.

Last but not least I would like to thank my parents, Wolfgang and Brigitte Brenscheidt gen. Jost, as well as my grandparents, Hans and Brunhilde Strakosch, who through the entire time supported and believed in me and always will. This also especially applies to my husband, Aarón Grageda Bustamante, as well as to our children Alva and Leo, who literally always keep me running and inspire me to reach for new heights.

Table of Contents

VIII

Introduction

It must have been his younger brother, Ravi, the internationally celebrated *sitar* player, through whom I first heard of Uday Shankar. At that time the once-famous Uday Shankar, who had been probably the first Indian dancer in the 20th century to thrill large audiences in the West and in India, had fallen almost into oblivion. Yet I was immediately captured by the fact that as early as the 1930s a dancer coming from a distant place such as India, whose performances were accompanied by an ensemble of Indian musicians playing Indian music, had fascinated Western audiences, artists and critics to such an extent. In March 2005 in Kolkata, while working in a research project on music teaching in India, I had the opportunity one day of further investigating Shankar's legacy. The address of the Uday Shankar India Culture Centre I had received, however, turned out to be the apartment of his wife Amala Shankar. A widow in her eighties, she kindly invited me in and I was lucky to have a conversation with her about Uday Shankar, his dancing, and the memories she had of their former successes in Europe and the United States. With a sparkle in her eyes she told me about times when she, her husband and the entire company had been received with standing ovations on international art stages. I was further thrilled when Amala Shankar phoned her daughter Mamata, a famous Bengali actress, dancer, and choreographer who I had already known and very much admired for her acting in the films of Satyajit Ray, which I had worked on for my Master's thesis. Later the same afternoon I entered her Kolkata dance institution, Udayan, and was lucky to experience a rehearsal of Tagore's dance drama *Chandalika* as performed by Mamata Shankar's Dance Company. This entire day, especially the warm and open reception by Amala and Mamata Shankar, would remain in my memory and it aroused my curiosity to learn more about Shankar and his international successes. It would, however, take me almost another year until I was able to start an in-depth research project on him and his company of dancers and musicians with a prime focus on their reception in the West.

My inquiry into European and American critics of Uday Shankar not only revealed a tremendous amount of source material starting from the early 1930s and reaching into the 1960s and even to the present. It also showed that the group's most successful years were in the 1930s, more precisely between the company's first opening in Paris in March 1931 and their departure to India in 1938 where Shankar would open up his India Culture Centre in Almora in the following year.[1] During these seven years Shankar nearly continuously performed in most of Europe, the United States, the Middle East, South-East Asia, and India. The close examination of reviews of this time period, especially of his initial tour in the early 1930s, confirms his success mainly with European and American audiences. At the same time it reveals the perceived difference of the performance from what western onlookers were familiar with. As the German writers Herman and Marianne Aubel pointedly pose it: "It is worth the effort to investigate how it has been possible indeed that people from a nation and a culture foreign to us were able to captivate and thrill a large audience to such an extent."[2]

Reviewers of Uday Shankar generally considered India as part of the Orient and they almost unanimously posed Orient against Occident or East against West in regard to their conceptions of dance, music and aesthetics. Only later they distinguished between Indian, Asian, and Oriental arts. The strong dichotomy between Eastern and Western culture and arts, which can be detected in the reviews, explains the use of the generalizing notions "East" and "West" in the context of this writing. Initially critically examined by Edward Said who revealed a structure of domination of the East by the West, the common negative preconceptions about the Orient of the period function as a background for the investigation of the reception of Indian arts in Europe and the United States in the first half of the 20th century.[3] Yet, as John James Clarke has pointed out in *Oriental Enlightenment*, the Western attitude towards the East has for

---

[1] This is also confirmed by Joan Erdman, who identifies the time period between 1931 and 1938 as Shankar's "prime years." See Erdman, "Who Remembers Uday Shankar?" (http://www.mukto-mona.com/new_site/mukto-mona/Articles/jaffor/uday_shanka2.htm last accessed June 21, 2011).

[2] Hermann & Marianne Aubel, *Die Bedeutung der alten indischen Tanzkultur. Betrachtungen und Bilder zum Auftreten der Hindu-Tanzgruppe Uday Shan-Kar*, [Celle:] Verlag der Arbeitsgemeinschaft für Natur- und Völkerkunde 1932: 3; Deutsches Tanzarchiv Köln. This translation and all translations from German and French sources in this book are mine unless indicated otherwise.

[3] See Edward Said, *Orientalism*, New York: Pantheon Books 1978.

long been of an ambivalent nature, bringing forth not only negative but also decisively positive images and stereotypes of the Orient including India.[4] Accordingly, as the detailed examination will show, Uday Shankar's Indian dances and music were mostly perceived favorably, indeed enthusiastically. This reception, having fundamental roots in the Romantic image of India, was strongly influenced by Ananda Kentish Coomaraswamy (1877-1947), probably the most internationally well-known advocate of Indian arts and aesthetics in the 20th century. Reviewers in the 1930s built on Coomaraswamy's aesthetic approach and tried to bring it together with what they saw presented onstage by Uday Shankar. In its focus on the reception of Indian dance and music in the West, this book, from a hermeneutical standpoint, thus reflects the attempt of European and American reviewers and audiences to understand the art and aesthetics of another culture.

Many of the primary sources that are examined here for the first time come from newspapers as well as dance, music, and art journals. They are further complemented by the writings of various modern dancers themselves and a number of monographic works on dance and music dating back to the first half of the 20th century. Additional sources include selected writings by Ananda K. Coomaraswamy, musicological and ethnomusicological writings on Indian music ranging from the British Orientalists up into the discipline of *Vergleichende Musikwissenschaft* in the 20th century, and posthumous reminiscences and biographical works on Uday Shankar. The research was generally restricted to reviews from Germany, France (mainly Paris), England (mainly London) and the United States, as these were the countries or places in which Shankar performed most and most successfully. Readers will, however, notice a focus on German and American sources, the two countries in which the group – according to Ravi Shankar – celebrated their biggest triumphs.[5] This can partly be explained by the origin of modern dance and *Ausdruckstanz* in the United States and Germany, a development which strongly welcomed the reception of Indian dance and music. Prominence is therefore given throughout the entire book to parallels re-

---

[4] See John James Clarke, *Oriental Enlightenment. The Encounter between Asian and Western Thought*, London: Routledge 1997: 3.
[5] See Ravi Shankar, *My Music, My Life*, Vikas Publishing House: New Delhi 1968: 69.

garding the approaches and reception of modern dancers. Shankar, never-theless, initiated his tour in Paris and performed regularly in England (mainly London). As important sites of *expositions universelles* and world fairs these places met the requirements for an Indian ensemble to appear onstage. The British sources are also interesting to examine in re-lation to the British in India and the impact of British Orientalism on the reception of Indian arts.

Most sources accordingly belong to the field of art criticism; few are of a popular nature. The application of the Western term "art" to the Indian performance, as done commonly in the context of this work, how-ever, remains debatable. Although Shankar's presentations are reviewed in the context of Western art criticism, reviewers themselves often de-scribe them as rituals. This shifting attribution between artistic perfor-mance and religious cult is also reflected in the title of this book. By means of Shankar's dances, the mythological figure of Shiva is intro-duced on Western art stages. Dialogue concerning Indian dance and mu-sic and their varied attribution as art, religion, mythology or cult in the 20th century is thus opened.

This book should be understood as a contribution to the history of the Western reception of distinct cultural practices, namely Indian dance and music. It thereby at the same time presents an example of an East-West encounter in the wider field of arts in the 20th century, an encounter which in Europe and the United States would lead to the growing recog-nition of Indian dance and music as of a distinct Indian or Hindu charac-ter, two denominations often used interchangeably without further reflec-tion on the religious implications. This work, moreover, explores the ex-tent of Ananda K. Coomaraswamy's influence on the Western reception of Indian arts and aesthetics in the 20th century. Although his impact on arts and aesthetics in India itself has already been investigated,[6]

---

[6] See in particular Tapati Guha-Thakurta, *The Making of a New 'Indian' Art. Artists, aesthetics and nationalism in Bengal, c. 1850-1920*, Cambridge: Cambridge University Press 1992 and T. Guha-Thakurta, *Monuments, Objects, Histories. Institutions of Art in Colonial and Postcolonial India*, New York: Columbia University Press 2004.

Coomaraswamy's role in their international propagation, especially re-garding the field of dance, needs to be examined in more detail.[7]

The first chapter focuses on the reception of the music employed in Shankar's performances. Shankar brought with him an ensemble of musicians from India playing on various Indian instruments which al-ready by themselves, because of their perceived exoticism, aroused a great deal of enthusiasm in audiences. Due to the fact that the musicians not only accompanied the dances, but also presented musical interludes, reviewers understood the musical part as equally important as the dances. The sources are here examined in their relatedness to distinct anthropo-logical approaches of the time, such as is apparent in the emerging branch of Comparative Musicology at the beginning of the 20th century. A closer look at earlier writings on Indian music since British Oriental-ism will further explore the rootedness of the discussion on Shankar in British Orientalist approaches to Indian art and culture. It also takes into consideration a small number of Indian responses, such as those of S.M. Tagore and Coomaraswamy. An investigation into the company's self-presentation included at the end of the chapter examines how the recep-tion of music was influenced by the accompanying programs and the company's advertizing.

The second chapter takes up again the close link between dance and music in the Indian performance and brings it into relation with unifying approaches to the arts as they have been conveyed into the 20th century. The two main approaches followed are those of Wagner and Nietzsche. Following the reviewers, I will review Shankar's dance drama *Tandava Nrittya* as an example of a united artwork, an ideal at which modern dancers in Germany and the United States from the beginning of the 20th century onwards were still striving. This chapter will further in-vestigate the link between unifying artistic approaches as perceived in the Indian performance, and notions of primitivism.

The third chapter predominantly deals with the study of dance movements and the use of the body in dance in both the East and the

---

[7] In the beginning of 2005, during my work in a research project on music teaching in India conducted at the *Gandharva Mahavidyalaya* in New Delhi, I asked the school's librarian about information on Indian dance and music, especially regarding theoretical and aesthetic aspects. He directly referred me to the writings of Coomaraswamy.

West. The reception of Shankar here initially put him into the field of Oriental dance, a genre which will be investigated and further specified. A closer consideration of the sources on Uday Shankar as well as of other dance writings of the time will then inquire into the increasing distinction between Oriental and Asian or, more explicitly, Indian dance and dance movement from the 1920s onwards. A final aspect of the examination here builds on Shankar's bodily presence onstage and the critics' discussion of his perceived beautiful, androgynous appearance.

The fourth and final chapter is concerned with a topic which looms in the background over the course of the entire work, namely the question of the religious or mythological background of Shankar's Indian performances. In times of spiritual discontent in the West, reviews show that Shankar's dances were perceived as deeply rooted in religion and mythology, a perception which needs to be investigated and further specified. One main point of interest here is the role of Coomaraswamy in shaping the image of Indian religious or spiritual arts in the West, including his propagation of the figure of Shiva incarnated as the dancing god *Natarāja*. Following an outline of Coomaraswamy's intellectual background and his theoretical approach to Indian arts and aesthetics, the investigation will once more return to the sources on Shankar and focus on the efforts of the reviewers and their apparent difficulties in understanding the deeper significance of the Indian dance and music performance.

Before commencing with the main investigation, however, readers will be given a brief overview of the personal and artistic background of Uday Shankar. This will serve as a starting point for the discussion on Shankar and the reception of the company in the West.

As a matter of fact, when the *Compagnie d'Uday Shan-Kar Hindoue Danses et la Musique* débuted on March 3, 1931 at the *Théâtre des Champs-Elysées* in Paris, Uday Shankar (1900-1977) had already gleaned experience as a dancer in Europe for several years. He was the first child of Shyam Shankar, a teacher and later the Prime Minister of Jhalawar, and his wife Hemangini Devi and he was named after his city of birth, Udaipur, which is located in today's Rajasthan. Shyam Shankar showed a keen interest in Western as well as Indian literature, music, and drama. He had also spent a significant amount of time in Europe while

training to become a barrister-at-law in London and subsequently working on a doctorate in political science in Switzerland.[8] At the age of
seventeen or eighteen Uday Shankar was sent to Bombay to become a
student of painting at the J.J. School of Arts. During this time, he took
music lessons on the side at Vishnu Digambar Paluskar's music school,
Gandharva Mahavidyalaya. Shankar graduated in 1920 and soon after
went to London to join his father who had started to organize and present
shows for Western audiences in order to raise funds to aid Indian soldiers
who had been wounded in the First World War. One of these shows was
named *The Great Moghul's Chamber of Dreams* and performed in
Covent Garden in March 1924. Uday Shankar here prepared slides and
presented magical effects, whereas for other earlier stage events he had
already choreographed brief dances and played Indian and Western instruments.[9] His father introduced him to William Rothenstein, the British
painter and Principal of the Royal College of Art in London and Shankar
secured a scholarship and started his advanced studies in painting under
Rothenstein. Rothenstein who had formed a friendship with Ananda K.
Coomaraswamy, urged Uday Shankar not to imitate the style of European paintings but rather to find an "Indian" style – advice Anna Pavlova
would repeat soon after in reference to dancing.[10] Shankar himself acknowledged the initial role the English painter played for his decision to
dance: "William Rothenstein had a perfect understanding of what I was
doing. He was the first to open my eyes to the greatness and beauty of
India and her arts".[11] At that time Indian dance, which was traditionally

---

[8] See Joan L. Erdman, "Performance as Translation. Uday Shankar in the West," *The
Drama Review* (New York), vol.31 no.1, spring 1987: 64-88; here 69ff; as well as
Mohan Khokar, *His Dance, His Life. A Portrait of Uday Shankar*, New Delhi:
Himalayan Books 1983: 13ff.

[9] See Erdman, "Performance as Translation" 71; J. Erdman, "Performance as Translation II: Shankar, the Europeans, and the Oriental Dance," S. Hoeber Rudolph et al
(ed.), *Institute For Culture and Consciousness. Occasional Papers I*, Chicago:
University of Chicago 1993: 34-47; here 35, 41; J. Erdman, "Towards Authenticiy:
Uday Shankar's First Company of Hindu Dancers and Musicians," in: D. Waterhouse
(ed.), *Dance of India*, Mumbai: Popular Prakashan 1998: 69-97; here 75ff.

[10] See Roger Lipsey, *Coomaraswamy. Vol.3: His Life and Work*, Princeton: Princeton
University Press 1977: 48.

[11] Khokar, *His Dance, His Life* 25.

either associated with folk dance or linked to the temple, had been regarded as corrupt since the arrival of the British in India. This is true at least for its later form.[12] Temple dance, known in Tamil as *sādir āttam* and in its anglicized version (from the Hindi *nāc*) as nautch, was performed by female dancers who had been dedicated and married to a god. During British rule their position was mainly associated with common prostitution which at the turn of the century led to the so-called "'anti-nautch' campaign,"[13] the advance by British rulers as well as Indian social reformers to prohibit temple dancing as a whole. This would lead almost to the extinction of or at least the marginalization of Indian dance.

In June 1922 Uday Shankar appeared in a performance at a garden party given by the League of Mercy at Regent Park in London, where King George V showed himself very impressed by his dance.[14] As it happened, Shankar eventually came into contact with the Russian ballerina Anna Pavlova.[15] Pavlova, who had just toured and traveled in India and unsuccessfully tried to witness Indian dance performances, was interested in creating more authentic Indian dances. This led to her cooperation with Shankar regarding the choreography and the performance of two Indian ballets called *A Hindu Wedding* and *Radha-Krishna* to music from the Indian musician Comolata Banerji. Together with a third miniature piece named *Dance of Japan* the works were announced under the title *Oriental Impressions*. Mohan Khokar, biographer of Uday Shankar, described the outlook of the ballets, their décor and the accompanying music as follows:

> *A Hindu Wedding* was of fourteen minutes duration; *Krishna and Rhada*, ten. The music was played by the orchestra, on Western instruments, by some eighty hands. Miss Banerji simply provided the melody and rhythm, they did the rest. In *A Hindu Wedding*,

---

[12] Judith L. Hanna, "Feminist Perspectives on Classical Indian Dance: Divine Sexuality, Prostitution, and Erotic Fantasy," in: D. Waterhouse (ed.), *Dance of India*, Mumbai: Popular Prakashan 1998: 193-231; here 210.
[13] Ibid. 213.
[14] See Khokar, *His Dance, His Life* 13.
[15] Regarding the discussion on who introduced Shankar to Anna Pavlova see Erdman, "Towards Authenticity" 93ff.

Shankar drew upon his memories of the colourful ceremony he had seen in Rajasthan. For *Krishna and Rhada* he did not weave any story, nor was there mime to suggest narrative. He just made a decorative sequence, with the performers standing, sitting, swaying, turning, to the accompaniment of assorted hand and arm movements. But for the flute he was holding, not very perfectly either, the dance could have been a duet. The *gopis* for the most part swirled in their ample, flounced skirts and deposited themselves staring glassy-eyed at the haloed pair. Costumes and decor for the two ballets were based on miniatures in the Victoria and Albert, and designed by Allegri. This had been done soon after it had been decided to produce the ballets, and before Miss Banerji and Uday Shankar were discovered. The fabric for the costumes was genuinely Indian, which Pavlova had brought with her from India.[16]

It is important to have a closer look at the presentation and reception of these dances as they built up a background for Uday Shankar's later choreographies as well as for his Western reception. As Khokar's description shows, the two pieces were based on Indian themes: first, a wedding which opened up the opportunity to present a colorful and decorative side of India; second, the mythological story of Krishna and Radha whose content was not further developed, but gave spectators at brief glimpse into the mythological world of the Hindu pantheon. As the reviews of their London performances beginning on September 10, 1923 at the Royal Opera House, Covent Garden made clear – *Oriental Impressions* was only included since Thursday, September 13 – audiences were primarily impressed by the use of costume and décor. One writer for the *Daily Telegraph* mentioned the "gorgeous costume."[17] Another critic writing in *The Morning Post* noticed: "There was little movement, but a wonderful display of colour. The Nautch girls wore dresses of ravishing beauty."[18] A reviewer in *The Times* further stressed the authentic charac-

---

[16] Khokar, *His Dance, His Life* 29.
[17] *The Daily Telegraph* (London); quoted in: ibid. 34.
[18] *The Morning Post* (London); quoted in: ibid. 30.

ter of the depictions: "It was difficult to get back to the frame of mind necessary to enjoy more oriental realism in the two Hindu scenes which followed."[19] The same reviewer in this context also mentioned the music of Comolata Banerji which was – although presented by a Western orchestra – received as typical Eastern or Indian. The Oriental or even Indian character of the music was explained by the use of "long and wandering dance tunes with percussive accents and drones cleverly devised in Western orchestration" which in their combination "produce effects which belong to the East."[20] Another reviewer in the *Daily Mail*, more deprecatory in his account, even describes the musical accompaniment as "typically monotonous Indian music."[21] A critic writing for *The Daily Telegraph* even went so far as to state that the presentation of Indian tunes before a Western audience as well as the mixing of Indian and Western elements in music would not be advisable due to the incompatibility of Eastern and Western art:

> But, perhaps, it was not wholly wise to go to the East for music. In that field East is East and West is West. No doubt the tunes we heard were genuine enough and beautiful. But there are artistic products which cannot be exported without losing their characteristic flavour. But, perhaps, this is a matter of taste, and others may prefer Eastern music undiluted.[22]

Only marginally mentioned in the British reviews, the cooperation with Pavlova led Uday Shankar on a tour through the United States starting on October 9, 1923 at the Manhattan Opera House in New York. In the course of this tour Uday Shankar would meet Ananda K. Coomaraswamy and receive a copy of *The Dance of Shiva* by the author himself, a book which should strongly influence his presentations.[23]

---

[19] *The Times* (London); quoted in: ibid.
[20] Ibid.
[21] *The Daily Mail* (London); quoted in: ibid. 34.
[22] *The Daily Telegraph* (London); quoted in: ibid.
[23] See ibid. 42.

10

Following his collaboration with Anna Pavlova, during which she encouraged him to return to an Indian style of dancing instead of learning Western ballet, Uday Shankar stayed for a while in London, where he, with the help of Lady Meherbai Dorabij Tata, performed at the Empire Exhibition at Wembley in 1924. In August 1924 he moved to Paris, the city where celebrated exotic dancers such as Mata Hari or Josephine Baker had started their career.[24] For a few years he appeared in cabarets, revues, and vaudeville shows with changing female partners, such as the sisters Rachel and Adelaide Lanfranchi, themselves former members of Pavlova's company, and Michèle Damour.[25] At the end of the 1920s he met the French pianist Simone Barbier who, renamed as Simkie, would soon after become his dancing partner until the 1940s. As an announcement printed in the biography of Uday Shankar by Mohan Khokar shows, the two had a performance together in Paris at the Salle d'Iena on April 18, 1929 accompanied on the piano by M. de Moor.[26] In the same year he also got to know the Swiss painter and sculptress Alice Boner (1889-1981), whom he had first met in Zurich in 1926. She would join him on a trip to India starting in January 1930 during which they tried to gain financial support by Indian Maharajas with the help of letters of recommendation written by Shyam Shankar. Uday Shankar was hoping to be able to build up a troupe of Indian dancers and musicians in order to bring them to Europe and present solo, duet and group dances accompanied by live music. Alice Boner supported his plan and would soon be his major patron. While in India they visited a number of temples and caves and were able to see a few dancers perform, but they were especially impressed by a performance of the South Indian dance drama *Kathakalī*, which they witnessed in Guruvayur under the auspices of the poet Vallathol.[27] Uday Shankar himself performed before different

---

[24] See Erdman, "Performance as Translation II" 43.

[25] See Khokar, *His Dance, His Life* 40ff.

[26] See ibid. 40. It is possible that the pianist accompanying Uday and Simkie was Michèle Damour, sometimes spelled d'Amour, as Uday Shankar listed her in an unpublished biography under the name "de Moor." See Joan L. Erdman, "Performance as Translation II" 44.

[27] See Alice Boner, *Indien, mein Indien. Tagebuch einer Reise*, ed. by G. Boner & H. David, Zürich: Werner Classen Verlag 1984: 77ff.

Maharajas and gave a very successful dance recital at the Oriental Society in Calcutta on July 8, 1930 in the presence of the painter and nephew of Rabindranath Tagore, Abanindranath Tagore. This was followed by more performances at the Empire Theatre in Calcutta starting from August 5, 1930. In his personal reminiscences Uday Shankar's brother Rajendra quoted Abanindranath Tagore as follows:

> "when I heard that a dancer, a male, coming after years in the West was going to dance, I came prepared to suffer some kind of 'khichri' [mixed or mish-mashed] performance. But what I saw created a strange effect. It is nothing like what we see or know of and yet its soul seems Indian and very stirring."[28]

This comment was also noted down in the diary of Alice Boner.[29] With financial support still lacking, Boner finally decided to sponsor the whole troupe with her own money and became its manager. The company was then formed with several members of Shankar's family, including his three brothers Rajendra, Debendra and Ravi (later the internationally famous *sitar* player), his cousin Kanaklata, and a friend of Ranjendra. These performed as dancers, though they were at that point untrained. Also included were two uncles who served as musicians. Furthermore, the *sarod* player Timir Baran Bhattacharya, whom Shankar got to know in the course of a performance in Calcutta in 1930, became the music director. He was accompanied by Vishnudass Shirali, an instrumentalist Shankar had met in Paris shortly before his trip to India.[30] In October 1930 they all, including Shankar's mother Hemangini Devi, went to Paris and moved into a house where they started to rehearse and make costumes out of fabric brought from India. Only a few months later the ensemble of Indian dancers and musicians would start their international tour, a tour outstanding in the history of Indian performances in the West and which would make them highly successful.

---

[28] Rajendra Shankar, "Uday Shankar – Personal Reminiscences," in: *Nartanam* (Mumbai), no.4, October – December 2001: 12-28; here 23.
[29] See Boner, *Indien, mein Indien* 127.
[30] See Khokar, *His Dance, His Life* 45-52.

This book was written within the framework of the Graduate School sponsored by the research project "Humanism in the Era of Globalization. An Intercultural Dialogue on Culture, Humanity, and Values" located between 2007 and 2009 at the Institute for Advanced Study in the Humanities in Essen, Germany. The study on Uday Shankar accordingly also understands itself as an example of an intercultural dialogue between Western and Indian artists, art experts, critics and audiences in the first half of the 20th century, a dialogue on Indian arts and aesthetics which should wield its influence on the perception of Indian arts in the West as well as partly in India for a time to come.

1. Music and the Musical Instruments

1.1 Music and Its Reception in Uday Shankar's Early Performances

La Compagnie d'Uday Shan-Kar Hindoue Danses et la Musique débuted at 9 p.m. on March 3, 1931 in the Théâtre des Champs Élysées in Paris.[1] This evening marked the starting point of the performance's first European tour. In addition to France, the tour would lead the company throughout countries such as Germany, Switzerland, Austria, Italy, Hungary, Czechoslovakia, and the Netherlands; this inaugural tour was quickly followed by an American tour starting in New York in December 1932.[2]

The first night's program in Paris included Uday Shankar's solo dances *Indra* and *Wedding Dance*; *Gandharva*,[3] *Temple Dance* and *Spring Dance* by Simkie; the duets *Peasant Dance*, *Radha and Krishna* and a *Sword Dance* presented by Shankar and Simkie, and the dance-drama *Tandava Nrittya*, in which Shankar and Simkie were joined by Debendra and Kanaklata. The pieces were accompanied with music and, furthermore, musical interludes entitled as Ragas (Raga Pahari, Raga Kafi) were included between the dances. Although not directly mentioned in the French reviews, early printed programs indicated that the performance also included rhythmical solo-pieces, such as a piece by Vishnudass Shirali on the *tablā tarang*, following Ravi Shankar a "set of ten or twelve tablas, each tuned to a different pitch for a particular raga, arranged in a semi-circle and played with both hands."[4] A program listing in the German *Stuttgarter Neues Tageblatt* from November 1931 entailed a schedule similar to the one presented in Paris. It included the dance pieces *Indra*, *Ländlicher Tanz* (probably *Peasant Dance*), *Radha*

---

[1] See the announcement "Spectacles," *L'Oeuvre* (Paris), March 3, 1931: 6.

[2] Ravi Shankar mentions additional tours to Belgium, Yugoslavia, Romania, Bulgaria, Estonia, Lithuania and Latvia. See R. Shankar, *Raga Mala. The Autobiography of Ravi Shankar*, Edited and introduced by George Harrison, New York: Welcome Rain Publishers, 2nd edition, 1999: 41.

[3] Joan Erdman doesn't mention the dance piece *Gandharva* as part of the company's early Parisian program. See Erdman, "Towards Authenticiy" 87 (see Introduction, footnote 9).

[4] Ibid.; Shankar, *Raga Mala* 64.

and *Krishna*, *Frühlingstanz* (*Spring Dance*), *Gandharva*, *Schwert Tanz* (*Sword Dance*) and two other dances named *Tanz zum Ramchandra-Fest* and *Ganga-Puja-Tanz*. The latter apparently was a solo by Simkie which seems either analogous or a counterpart to the *Temple Dance* presented in Paris. The performance ended once again with the dance-drama *Tandava Nrittya* and included musical interludes, namely *Rag Bhairavi, Sindha Bhairavi, Rag Lalit, Kaphi-Tritala*, a drumming part presenting *Maha-Mrdanga* and *Khol* and another *raga* here named *Rag Schini*.[5] Another program from Berlin, dated April 1932 and announcing the subsequent year's schedule, essentially repeats the Stuttgart performance with the supplemental additions of a *Danse des Santals*, a *Tanz des Schlangenbe-zauberers* (*Dance of the Snake Charmer*) and the duet *Shnanum* (*Sna-num*) presented by Simkie and Kanaklata. Again, the performance uti-lizes various musical interludes – this time *Rag Multani, Rag Lalit, Tilak Kamode-Tritala, Kaphi-Tritala* and *Rag Sohini*. These program notes fur-ther provided the audience with information on the Ragas used as musi-cal accompaniment for the dances, including the times of the day of their performance and the aesthetic moods or *rasas* they were connected with.[6]

An initial examination of the programs easily reveals the impor-tant position music held in the performances. This is further reflected in the early French and German reviews. In France, the daily journal *L'Oeuvre* printed a long review in the musical section named "Les con-certs" with almost three quarters of the text concerned with musical as-pects of the performances.[7] Similarly the journal *Candide* included a re-view in the section "Les événements musicaux" that solely focused on the musical portion of the performance.[8] And while *Le Figaro* was alone in discussing the evening in the section "Concerts et recitals" under the title "La danse – Uday Shan-Kar et sa compagnie," it still ended up put-

---

[5] See the announcement "Württ. Landestheater. Großes Haus," *Stuttgarter Neues Tageblatt* (Stuttgart), morning edition, November 20, 1931: 4.
[6] See "Gastspiel der Brahmanischen Inder (Hindus) mit Uday Shank-Kar," Theater des Westens, Berlin, April 1932; Deutsches Tanzarchiv Köln.
[7] Jules Casadesus, "Les Concerts," *L'Oeuvre* (Paris), March 6, 1931: 5.
[8] Emile Vuillermoz, "Les événements musicaux," *Candide* (Paris), March 12, 1931: n.p.

ting music above dancing in the review.[9] Further, the newspaper reviews preceding and following Uday Shankar's performances in Germany between September 1931 in Hamburg and November 1932 in Munich did include the word "dance" in their titles, but they similarly focused strongly on musical elements. This weight on music might be explained by the fact that newspaper reviews on dance at this time seem to have generally been written by music critics.[10] Yet in the course of the emergence of modern dance in the United States, whose forerunners Loie Fuller, Ruth St. Denis and Isadora Duncan had their first successes in Paris and Berlin, critical interest in dance was growing. From the end of the 1920s on, various dance magazines were founded, such as *The American Dancer* first published in New York in 1927 and the German magazine *Der Tanz* edited by J. Lewitan in Berlin in 1928.[11] The *Figaro Artistique Illustré* published an entire issue on dance in 1931.[12] In 1931 *Les Archives Internationales de la Danse*, an archive solely concerned with dance, was opened in Paris by Rolf de Maré. From 1933 onwards, the archive published the *Revue Trimestrielle* which included articles on the history and aesthetics of dance being concerned with classical, modern as well as non-European dance.[13]

Yet the occupation with the music and the instruments utilized in Shankar's performances corresponds primarily with a rising anthropological interest in foreign or exotic music cultures at the beginning of

---

[9] Georges Mussy, "Concerts et récitals. La danse: Uday Shan-Kar et sa compagnie," *Le Figaro* (Paris), March 13, 1931: n.p.

[10] For the situation of newspaper dance criticism in the USA see Lynne Conner, *Spreading the Gospel of Modern Dance: Newspaper Dance Criticism in the United States, 1850-1934*, Pittsburgh: University of Pittsburgh Press 1997.

[11] The first monthly dance magazine to have emerged internationally apparently was the *Dancing Times* which was first published in London in 1894 and became independent in 1910. See the information on *Dancing Times* and *Dance Today* on the website of the Tanzarchiv Leipzig (http://www.tanzarchiv-leipzig.de/?q=de/node/163; last accessed June 21, 2011).

[12] See "La danse," *Figaro Artistique Illustré* (Paris), November 1931: n.p.

[13] See Franz Anton Cramer, "Die Erfindung der Tanzwissenschaft. Die Archives Internationales de la Danse in Paris," *tanz journal* (München), no.5, October 2006: 11-13; and also Inge Baxmann (ed.), *Körperwissen als Kulturgeschichte. Die Archives Internationales de la Danse (1931-1952)*, München: Kieser 2008.

the 20th century, as seen in the emergence of comparative musicology, one predecessor of today's ethnomusicology.

1.2 Counting and Measuring. Shankar and German Comparative Musicology

At a time when audiences in Europe had already witnessed Western dancers and popular vaudeville stars such as Ruth St. Denis or Maud Allen presenting oriental or exotic theme dance and music, the performances of Uday Shankar, the dancing as well as the musical part, were described by early critics as authentic Indian depictions. This is already acknowledged in one of the first French reviews written by Jules Casadesus and published in *L'the first time that a group of a Oeuvre*. Casadesus begins his article with the statement: "This is, I think, uthentic instrumentalists and dancers from India visits us in France."[14] This is also repeated by Franc Scheuer writing about the Parisian performance in the London dance magazine *Dancing Times*. He ascribes the company's success "to Shan-Kar's own simplicity of taste" as well as "to the authentic Hindu orchestra imported by him from India for the first time."[15] Many reviewers obviously linked authenticity with the Indian origin of the instruments used as well as – what seems more prevalent – with the question of racial or religious affiliation of the musicians and dancers. From the very outset, the Indian, or more precisely, the Hindu background of the group members had been a main concern in its marketing. In an early document which emerged in the course of the company's formation and its search for sponsors, Alice Boner had stressed the importance of an authentic Indian musical ensemble to accompany Uday Shankar's dancing:

> Mr. Shankar has been up till now the only authentical Hindu dancer who ever went out of his country to show to the public in Europe and America the original art of Indian dancing as it has been elaborated through centuries of evolution and whose remainders have

---

[14] Casadesus 5.
[15] Franc Scheuer, "Uday Shan-Kar and Simkie. At the Théâtre des Champs-Elysées," *Dancing Times* (London), April 1931: 15.

still a part in all Hindu life, its religion, philosophies, ceremonies, enjoyment and daily occurrences. [... He] ought not to be contented any longer with the European musicians but back himself with a set of good Indian artists. With their help only he could bring his shows to the utmost possible perfections and convey to the western public the true soul of our art.[16]

At world's fairs and colonial exhibitions both the European as well as the American public had already gotten used to the display of foreign or exotic peoples in settings that supposedly equaled authentic living situations in their home countries. These displays, which Paul Greenhalgh calls "human showcases," also included performances of religious rituals as well as demonstrations of their arts and crafts, strongly focusing on dance and music.[17] At the beginning of the "age of the museum" authenticity was strongly linked to the object; and in the anthropological and popular context of the time the displays included people as well as their artistic output.[18] As described by Charlotte Brinkmann, early comparative musicologists (interested in foreign music cultures) used these kinds of presentations as sources for their research and started to make phonograph recordings in order to build up vast collections of foreign musicological material for further classification and comparison.[19] Shankar also performed in this context, first at the *British Empire Exhibition* in Wembley near London in 1924 and later at the *Exposition Coloniale* in Paris in the autumn of 1931, appearing with his group of dancers and musicians in sixteen shows.[20] Encouraged by the widespread presentation

---

[16] From the foreword of the Project for the Constitution of a Company of Hindu Stage-artists under the direction of Mr. Uday Shankar, draft document in the Alice Boner Collection, Zürich, dated 1930 by Georgette Boner; quoted in: Erdman, "Towards Authenticity" 82ff.

[17] Paul Greenhalgh, *Ephemeral vistas: The Expositions Universelles, Great Exhibitions and World's Fairs, 1851-1939*, Manchester: Manchester University Press 1988: 82.

[18] See ibid. 83; 88.

[19] See Charlotte Brinkmann "Claire Holt und die Anfänge einer modernen Tanzethnologie im Umfeld der A.I.D.-Expeditionen nach Niederländisch-Indien," in: Baxmann 116-136; here 123.

[20] See Khokar, *His Dance, His Life* 41; 64 (see Introduction, footnote 8). In November 1931 the French *L'Oeuvre* announces a performance of Uday Shankar's company in the

of exotic dancers and musicians at various world's fairs at the beginning of the 20th century, non-European dancers and musicians began to appear in contexts other than world exhibitions. And from March 1931 onwards, Uday Shankar and his group, likely aided by his former collaboration with Anna Pavlova, performed primarily on regular stages where they were received by audiences and critics who were familiar with current Western Oriental theme dance and music which they had to compete with.

Critics first of all reviewed the Indian presentations in reference to Western musical parameters. Jules Casadesus, writing for the Parisian journal *L'Oeuvre*, for example, presents the reader with a detailed description of the instruments and the scales as used by what he calls the "L'orchestre hindou."[21] He begins by differentiating the instruments seen on stage into cords, winds, and percussions, then classifying them according to the material from which they are constructed, and finally classing them by the manner in which they are played. At the time, this common way of instrumental taxonomy had however already been challenged by a new classification into four categories – idiophones, aerophones, membranophones and chordophones – a classification presented by Erich M. von Hornbostel and Curt Sachs in the German *Zeitschrift für Ethnologie* in 1914. In order to integrate the Indian instruments and modes into a system, Casadesus further compares them to their European counterparts. He thereby gives his readers a more vivid impression of the performance, such as in the case wherein the Indian *sitar* and *sarod* are described as lutes:

> The play of the lute (*sarod, sitar*) corresponds to that of the guitar or even more of the mandolin; one will observe, however, that the instrumentalist now plucks the string bluntly, with clarity, now slides the finger throughout pressing strongly in fixed points, which produces, slightly blurred effects which come somewhat close to those of the Hawaiian guitar. Besides, the majority of these instru-

---

context of "Le Monde Colonial qui chante et qui danse" together with other international performers such diverse as the Maori dancer Djemil Anik and the Mangan Tiller Girls. See "Petites nouvelles," *L'Oeuvre* (Paris), November 7, 1931: 6.

[21] Casadesus 5.

ments is built in the same way as our ancient violas and have congenial strings.[22]

Casadesus continues in this evaluative vein when he compares the Indian *rāgas* with the Chinese, the ancient Greek, or even the minor mode of the European tempered system:

> The scales come close, now to the Chinese scale, now to the Greek modes; the one which seemed to me the most ordinary consists of five notes, like the Chinese, and the impression which it produced in our European ears is quite similar to our minor mode.[23]

In a German review in the *Hamburger Fremdenblatt* in September 1931, the critic describes the "original Indian orchestra" by trying to classify the various instruments, such as the drums. He then refers to the Indian chordophones – here *sitar* and *sarod* – as possible prototypes of Western stringed instruments such as viola, guitar and mandolin:

> The Indian orchestra contains a very large number of other drums made of metal, wood, and burnt clay, all with diverse timbres and nuances. The stringed instruments appear to be the prototype of our old violas, guitars and mandolins. In addition to the strings which are struck or plucked, they contain numerous other strings used for their vibration.[24]

Similarly, another German critic writing for the *Hamburger Anzeiger* seeks to group the fifty-six instruments presented by Shankar's musicians according to the common system of classification. Here he also draws parallels with western instruments from past and present:

---

[22] Ibid.

[23] Ibid.

[24] "Zum Gastspiel des Indischen Balletts," *Hamburger Fremdenblatt* (Hamburg), September 26, 1931, evening edition: 3.

Aside from a flute and a cornet-like wind instrument, this orchestra consists solely of stringed and percussion instruments. The former are constructed with valuable finishing and in fantastical forms somewhere between mandolins and antique viola da gamba and they are struck and plucked in manifold ways; the drums, made of wood, Bengali metal, and terracotta, are classified as vocal instruments, since their function is seldom tone and sound, but primarily melody.[25]

The reviewers' approaches to the musical aspects obviously fit into the musicological debates of their time. At the beginning of the 20th century musicological research and writing on the music of non-European – often referred to as "exotic" or "primitive" – cultures concerned itself to a large extent with problems of classification involving scales, tone systems, and instruments. Musicology strongly relied on collecting and measuring empirical data for systematization, an approach which had its basis in the positivism of natural science. Led by the aim of developing a universal scheme wherein all the world's musical cultures would find their appropriate place, its practitioners strongly tended towards comparison, a method which – if one thinks of the development of the discipline of comparative studies in literature – had its origin in Romanticism.[26] One branch, which even incorporated the comparative approach into its name, was the Berlin School of Comparative Musicology, one of the forerunners of today's ethnomusicology.[27]

---

[25] Sdt., "Indische Musik, indischer Tanz. Uday Shan-Kar und Simkie mit indischem Orchester. – Abend der Hamburger Bühne," *Hamburger Anzeiger* (Hamburg), September 30, 1931: n.p.

[26] See A. Leslie Willson, *A Mythical Image: The ideal of India in German Romanticism*, Durham, N.C.: Duke University Press 1964: 72ff.

[27] Stephen Blum describes four different branches which conducted early ethnomusicological research: cultural anthropology in the USA, musical ethnography in the Russian Empire and Soviet Union, comparative musicology in Germany, Austria and partly France as well as musical folklore and programs of national musical research in other European countries and Latin America, each branch having its own distinctive vocabulary. They all are here regarded as forerunners of what was after the Second World War in the English context generally termed ethnomusicology (in German *Musikethnologie* and in French *ethnologie musicale*). See Stephen Blum, "European Musical

The German School of Comparative Musicology or *Verglei-chende Musikwissenschaft* was initiated by the psychologist and philosopher Carl Stumpf (1841-1936). It originated and flourished mainly in Berlin and Vienna, and it was popular to a lesser extent in Paris as *musicologie compare*.[28] As director of the Psychological Institute of the Friedrich-Wilhelms-University in Berlin, Stumpf showed a "psychological interest in the sensual experience of tones and intervals and their ordering into tone systems," mainly in order to test his hypothesis about the fusion of tones, (known in German as *Verschmelzungstheorie*).[29] As early as 1886 he had presented empirical data in an article on the songs of the Bellakula-Indians, followed a few years later by writings on Siamese music and the Siamese tonal system.[30] In 1901 Otto Abraham, a medical doctor, and Erich Moritz von Hornbostel (1877-1935), who was trained in philosophy and sciences, were assigned with the task of building a collection of phonograph recordings for further psychological research. This task in turn led to the installation of the *Phonogrammarchiv* in 1904.[31] It was Hornbostel who would later expand the project so that it transcended the bounds of psychology to comparative musicology. It is, however, due to Stumpf that systematic musicology, which then encompassed comparative musicology, was accepted as an independent academic discipline at the Friedrich-Wilhelms University in Berlin.[32]

Terminology and the Music of Africa," in: B. Nettl. & P.V. Bohlman (eds.), *Comparative Musicology and Anthropology of Music*, Chicago: University of Chicago Press 1991: 3-36; here 3; 27.

[28] Albrecht Schneider mentions Fétis as an early forerunner of *musicologie comparée* in France, especially his classification of the peoples of the world according to their tonal system. See Fétis, "Sur un nouveau mode de classification des races humaines d'après leurs systèmes musicaux," *Bulletins de la Société d'Anthropologie*, N.S. 2, 1867: 134-143; quoted in: Albrecht Schneider, *Musikwissenschaft und Kulturkreislehre. Zur Methodik und Geschichte der Vergleichenden Musikwissenschaft*, Bonn: Verlag für systematische Musikwissenschaft 1976: 67.

[29] Dieter Christensen, "Erich M. von Hornbostel, Carl Stumpf, and the Institutionalization of Comparative Musicology," in: Nettl & Bohlman 201-209; here 204.

[30] See Carl Stumpf, "Lieder der Bellakula-Indianer," *Vierteljahrsschrift für Musikwissenschaft* (Leipzig), vol.2, 1886: 405-426 and C. Stumpf, "Tonsystem und Musik der Siamesen," *Beiträge zur Akustik und Musikwissenschaft* (Leipzig), vol.3, 1901: 69-138.

[31] See Schneider, *Musikwissenschaft und Kulturkreislehre* 73.

[32] See Christensen 205.

Comparative musicology did emerge in opposition to unilineal evolutionary fundamentals in Western music theory and history, as in the German context strongly represented by Hugo Riemann (1849-1919). Exhibiting a Eurocentric stance, "many scholars shared Hugo Riemann's belief that adequate description of most tone systems would show them to be special developments of the universal principles known to Western musicians and theorists."[33] Hermann von Helmholtz (1821-94), originally a physician and physicist, was one of the first who would counter this opinion by stating that "the same properties of the ear could serve as the foundation of very different musical systems."[34] In 1884-85 Alexander John Ellis (1814-1890), a British mathematician and philologist who had studied Helmholtz's work and translated it into English, compared different tuning systems and scales from ancient Greece and a number of non-European countries in an essay named "On the musical scales of various nations" to show that there existed a variety of systems based on principles that were distinct from Western European ones. He concluded:

> The final conclusion is that the musical scale is not one, not 'natural' nor even founded necessarily on the laws of the constitution of musical sound, so beautifully worked out by Helmholtz, but very diverse, very artificial, and very capricious.[35]

Here Ellis referred to one of the conclusions on the arbitrariness or artificiality of scales described by Helmholtz first in 1862 in *On the Sensations of Tone*:

> I have done my best ... to prove that the construction of scales and the harmonic texture are a product of artistic invention and by no

---

[33] Blum 11.

[34] Hermann L.F. von Helmholtz, *Die Lehre von den Tonempfindungen als physiologische Grundlage für die Theorie der Musik*, Braunschweig: Friedrich Vieweg 1877, 4th edition, Engl. transl. by A.J. Ellis, London: Longmans 1885; quoted in: Blum 10ff.

[35] Alexander J. Ellis, "On the musical scales of various nations," *Journal of the Society of Arts* (London) 33, 1885: 526; quoted in: Schneider, *Musikwissenschaft und Kulturkreislehre* 74.

means instantaneously given by ways of the natural structure or natural function of our ear, as has hitherto been generally maintained.[36]

In this context he also established the Cent-system, an "arbitrary division of the tempered octave into 1,200 parts or 'cents'" as a new method of comparison. [37] The Cent-system opened up the possibility for the exact measureing of intervals and therefore was in accordance with the positivistic approach of comparative musicology, in Helmholtz words, that "counting and measuring are the bases of the most fruitful, secure, and exact methods of which we have a thorough understanding."[38] Hornbostel, who translated Ellis' essay into German and included it at the beginning of the first volume of the *Sammelbände für vergleichende Musikwissenschaft* (1922), introduced him as the founding figure of comparative musicology:

> Ellis emerged as the very founder of comparative musicology; while even though before him the music of individual peoples and nations had been dealt with monographically, he was the first one who brought together all material available and drew up a cross section which already covered a huge part of the musical world map.[39]

---

[36] Hermann v. Helmholtz, *Die Lehre von den Tonempfindungen*, Vieweg: Braunschweig 1870, 3rd edition: 568; quoted in: Scheider, *Musikwissenschaft und Kulturkreislehre* 74.

[37] Mantle Hood, "Ethnomusicology," in: Willi Apel (ed.), *Harvard Dictionary of Music*, Cambridge: Harvard University Press 1969²: 298; printed in: K. Kaufman Shelemay (ed.), *Ethnomusicology. History, Definitions, and Scope*, Garland: New York & London 1992: 134ff.

[38] H. von Helmholtz, "Zählen und Messen, erkenntnistheoretisch betrachtet," in: *Philosophische Aufsätze. Ed. Zeller zu seinem 50jährigen Doktorjubiläum gewidmet*, Leipzig 1887: 17; quoted in: Schneider, *Musikwissenschaft und Kulturkreislehre* 101.

[39] Erich Moritz von Hornbostel, "Vorwort des Übersetzers," in: C. Stumpf & E.M. von Hornbostel (eds.), *Sammelbände für vergleichende Musikwissenschaft*, vol.1, Georg Olms Verlag: Hildesheim & New York 1975 (Reprint from the original, 1922-23): 3.

Challenging the Eurocentric approach in musicology, early comparative musicologists such as Hornbostel were eager to prove that a variety of different musical systems existed (one might also say tone systems), with each one being a product of a different strata of cultural history and, for that reason, not sufficiently explicable by the standards of Western music theory.[40] Hugo Riemann criticized this cultural relativist approach:

> It is, however, utterly misguided to doubt the general validity of our musical system's fundamentals on the basis of the examination of the musical performance of tribes remote from European culture.[41]

Acknowledging the importance of Western music and musicology, Hornbostel and Stumpf aimed at an equal recognition of the entire world's music as they announced in their introduction to the first volume of the *Sammelbände*. The recognition of other musical cultures, however, also served the intention of gaining more knowledge about the beginnings of music in general, including Western art music:

> The purely historical insight into the origins and destinies of our own music surely deserves the most considerate care in the future as well, since the occidental music of past centuries is the valuable property of humanity and the German contribution in its development one of the finest titles of fame of our people. Yet the appreciation of European art music itself can never ever be based on the grounds of itself alone. And finally one has to admit that, after all, we Europeans are not the only people and that we can occasionally learn something from others.[42]

---

[40] See Blum 10.

[41] Hugo Riemann, *Grundriß der Musikwissenschaft*, Quelle & Mayer: Leipzig 1914[2]; quoted in: Barbara Boisits, "Hugo Riemann – Guido Adler. Zwei Konzepte von Musikwissenschaft vor dem Hintergrund geisteswissenschaftlicher Methodendiskussionen um 1900," in: T. Böhme-Mehner & K. Mehner (eds.), *Hugo Riemann (1849-1919). Musikwissenschaftler mit Universalanspruch*, Köln: Böhlau 2001: 17ff; here 22ff.

[42] Hornbostel, "Vorwort des Übersetzers" 3.

Although Hornbostel obviously challenged the Eurocentric stance of Hugo Riemann and other historically oriented musicologists, comparative musicology was strongly concerned with questions of the origin of music and its development throughout the world. The idea was to find universals in music, so called anthropological constants, by closely examining different musical cultures. In Hornbostel's words: "we would like to uncover the remotest, darkest past and unveil, in the wealth of the present, the ageless universal in music; in other words: we want to understand the evolution and common aesthetic foundation of the art of music."[43] He was, however, at least careful how to integrate his empirical findings into the evolutionary models of the time:

> We may draw parallels – if with some caution – between the condition of 'primitive' peoples and earlier stages of our own culture. We would then have to seek analogies in primitive music to the music of our ancestors. Such analogies can actually be found, for instance, between Oriental and ancient Greek music. However, we should never forget that even the most primitive of today's cultures can look back on a long development, and when one sees, or rather hears, how sophisticated in its monophony a Japanese, Indian, or Arabic musical composition is, one has to acknowledge the presence of a highly developed art, which, although perhaps originating from the same source, has undoubtedly grown in climates and directions different from our own. The more extensive the data that we submit for comparison, the sooner we may hope to be able to explain a posteriori the archetypal beginnings of music from the course of its development.[44]

In 1959, the German musicologist and Berlin School adherent Curt Sachs (1881-1959) still stood firmly for an evolutionary approach

---

[43] Erich Moritz von Hornbostel, "The Problems of Comparative Musicology," transl. by Richard Campbell, in: K.P. Wachsmann et al. (eds.), *Hornbostel Opera Omnia*, vol. 1, Martinus Nijhoff: The Hague 1975: 247-270; here 269; in German original entitled "Die Probleme der Vergleichenden Musikwissenschaft," *Zeitschrift der Internationalen Musikgesellschaft* (Leipzig), vol.7 no.3, 1905: 85-97; here 85.
[44] Ibid. 269ff.

with Western composition at its highpoint. He was clearly furthering the notions behind his own influential systematization of musical instruments that he had developed together with Hornbostel when he wrote:

> Because what the science of foreign culture music reveals is both the fate which has led and will lead us and the path which we have followed. The thousandfold expressions of human life which are spread over all continents like a multicolored blanket are only residues of a development which our own ancestors have undergone.[45]

In 1933 Curt Sachs had already published *Eine Weltgeschichte des Tanzes* in Germany, which was translated into and published anew in English under the title *World History of the Dance* in 1937.[46] This book represented the first written approach to dance as an independent and universal phenomenon.[47] Sachs' writings on dance as well as his musicological work were developed in the context of the German anthropological branch of *Kulturkreislehre*. Here a "Kulturkreis" (culture circle) signified "a complex of culture traits which originally developed together in a specific geographical area and then spread as a unit to other areas, usually by means of the mass migration of peoples."[48] This approach also favored the search for a universal origin of all the world's cultures. As Suzanne Youngerman stresses, *Kulturkreislehre*, which influenced the whole branch of comparative musicology, originally evolved in opposition to nineteenth-century evolutionist approaches, but could not, however, escape developing its own evolutionist scheme.[49] Youngerman de-

---

[45] Artur Simon, "Probleme, Methoden und Ziele der Ethnomusikologie," in: *Jahrbuch für Musikalische Volks- und Völkerkunde* (Köln), vol. 9, 1978: 11; printed in: K. Kaufman Shelemay (ed.), *Ethnomusicology. History, Definitions, and Scope*, Garland: New York & London 1992: 252-296; here 255.

[46] See Curt Sachs, *Eine Weltgeschichte des Tanzes*, Dietrich Reimer & Ernst Vohsen: Berlin 1933 and *World History of the Dance*, translated by Bessie Schönberg, New York: W.W. Norton & Company 1937.

[47] See Brinkmann 125.

[48] Suzanne Youngerman, "Curt Sachs and His Heritage: A Critical Study of 'World History of the Dance' with a Survey of Recent Studies That Perpetuate His Ideas," *CORD News*, vol.6, 1974: 6-19; here 10.

[49] See ibid.

scribes the differences in these two models and then names their shared evolutionist conclusions:

> In unilineal evolutionary theory, cultures must pass through a series of progressively more advanced stages, although some societies may lag behind others or become 'frozen' at any point along this sequence. In <u>Kulturkreislehre</u>, a cultural strata [sic] remains unchanged until another culture circle come into contact with it. Therefore, those older culture circles which have been forced into marginal regions untouched by subsequent migrations remain stable and are, therefore representative of an earlier migration or strata in culture history. The resulting conclusion from both theories is [...] that modern 'primitive people' represent earlier stages of Western civilization.[50]

The value and use Western music history therefore assigned to the research on non-European music is accordingly directly described by Sachs in the following comment on a new name for the discipline of comparative musicology:

> The science of the music of foreign cultures deals with the musical expressions of the non-European peoples regardless of their level of civilization. On European ground it ventures only into those places where, far removed from the very occidental forms of musical life, remains of ancient musical practice resembling the non-European ones have survived. Its former name 'Comparative Musicology' is misleading and has generally been abandoned. It "compares" no less and no more than any other science: over time, it begins to divide and lays bare the main characteristics of a development which ascends from the bare beginnings up to the level where

---

[50] Ibid. 10ff.

29

the high mountains of modern European musical art are established.[51]

Kulturkreislehre was based in culture history and diffusionism.[52] These approaches in German anthropology mainly go back to Friedrich Ratzel and similarly emerged in opposition to unilineal evolutionism. As such, they explained the similarities between cultures as a result of the spread or diffusion of ideas, innovations or cultural items throughout different geographical cultures in history. This was mainly seen to have been inaugurated by means of cultural contacts, such as migration and trade. Accordingly, in search of the pure forms or the shared historical origin of cultural assets, the study of the world's material culture gained importance and huge ethnographic collections of artifacts were built up in museums for systematic evaluation.[53] Hornbostel and Sachs's *Systematik der Musikinstrumente* with its universalistic approach of cultural history emerged in this tradition. However, the authors stress the problems they are faced with in applying a universal system:

> In addition to a practical use, a classification can also be of theoretical use. Things which otherwise appear to have little in common often move closely together and lead to the observation of new genetic and cultural-historical links. And this will always be the most prevalent criterion for the value of the characteristics which have been used for the classification. The difficulties which oppose an eligible system of instruments are enormous, because what applies

---

[51] Curt Sachs, *Vergleichende Musikwissenschaft: Musik der Fremdkulturen*, Heidelberg: Quelle & Meyer 1959: 5; quoted in: Artur Simon, *Ethnomusikologie: Aspekte, Methoden und Ziele*, Berlin: Simon Verlag für Bibliothekswesen 2008: 17ff.

[52] The English translation "culture history" for German "kulturhistorische Schule" is taken from Martin Rössler, "Die deutschsprachige Ethnologie bis ca. 1960: Ein historischer Abriss," *Cologne Working Papers in Cultural and Social Anthropology*, no. 1, April 2007: 3 (http://kups.ub.uni-koeln.de/volltexte/2007/1998/pdf/kae0001.pdf; last accessed June 21, 2011).

[53] See Brinkmann 121ff and Rössler 4ff.

for instruments of a certain time or nation for this reason does not have to be adequate as a basis for all peoples and all times.[54]

Sachs, as well as Abrahams and Hornbostel, obviously didn't conduct field research in non-European countries, but instead made phonograph recordings of presentations by foreign musicians who happened to visit or live in Germany. This was also the case with their Indian recordings on which they commented and presented transcriptions in Western staff notation in 1904.[55] In this same article they also transcribed recordings of a Bengali orchestra taken at popular theatre shows by the *Deutsche Grammophon Gesellschaft* in Calutta.[56] As was the case with the early so-called armchair-anthropologists who based their anthropological writings on observations of others, (such as from travel journals) their culture historical approach meant bringing together as much previously collected data for evaluation and systematization as possible.[57] Accordingly, Uday Shankar's presentations, which included music and were perceived as authentic Indian depictions, fit well into the current musicological research. This might explain the number of musicological reviews written about his performances at this time.

Although they still follow a somewhat evolutionary approach, comparative musicology and *Kulturkreislehre* should be seen in the context of the beginning of cultural relativism. Cultural relativism would then however be identified first of all with the American strand of cultural anthropology initiated by the work of Franz Boas in the 1920s.[58] Opposing the

---

[54] Erich Moritz von Hornbostel & Curt Sachs, "Systematik der Musikinstrumente," *Zeitschrift für Ethnologie* (Berlin), vol.46 no.4-5, 1914: 553-590; here 554.

[55] See Otto Abraham & Erich Moritz von Hornbostel, "Phonographierte Indische Melodien," in: Stumpf & Hornbostel, *Sammelbände für Vergleichende Musikwissenschaft*, vol. 1: 251-290; English translation entitled "Indian melodies recorded on the phonograph" by Bonnie Wade in: Wachsmann 115-182.

[56] "Finally, we had at our disposal a series of discs, made by the Deutsche Grammophon Gesellschaft in Calcutta, of musicians of the Corinthian Theater and the Classic Theater, and of a Bengali orchestra." Ibid. 122.

[57] See Youngerman 7 and Rössler 5.

[58] See Franz Boas, *The Mind of Primitive Man*, New York: The Macmillan Company 1911.

ethnocentrism of German anthropology as well as its methodology consisting of the classification or artifacts without considering their provenance, Boas supported extensive field work as he regarded every culture as unique and only understandable out of itself.[59]

As the reviews have shown, musical aspects in the early presentations of Uday Shankar's company of dancers and musicians were received in accordance with current trends of comparative musicology's systematic approach to foreign music cultures. Indian scales and instruments were thereby regularly compared with those of ancient Greece. Indian music seemed to have come directly out of antiquity and therefore partly stirred European musicologists' interest in the origin of music. But the link between India and classical antiquity and India's important role in the search for cultural origins emerged long before comparative musicology came into existence. Having its roots in 19th-century Romanticism and British Orientalism, such links from early on entered the discourse on Indian music and here had their impact up into the 20th century. The following subchapter will examine the main musicological writings on Indian music as they emerged under and in the wake of British Orientalism in India. These writings serve as an important background for Uday Shankar and will help to identify the main ideas associated with Indian music as they still affect both the reception and the self-presentation of Shankar and his company in the 20th century.

1.3 From "Hindu Music" to "Indian Music." British and British-Indian Musicological Writing from William Jones to Ananda K. Coomaraswamy

In his *Essay on the Origin of Language* (1770), Johann Gottfried Herder referred to the Orient as the place where language originally developed.[60] A few years later in *This Too a Philosophy of History for the Formation of Humanity* (1774) he claimed the Orient was the cradle of all mankind, of all human inclinations and of religion.[61] And it would be in *Outlines of a Philosophy of the History of Man* (1785-87) that Herder

---

[59] See Brinkmann 130.
[60] See Willson 50.
[61] See ibid. 51.

explicitly named India as the place of origin of all peoples and thereby stirred the early Romanticists' image of India. Following his predecessor Voltaire (1694-1778) by relying on early travel books, essays, and translations of Sanskrit works, Herder located "the area of inception of human culture near the Ganges, a region which was the primordial garden where the first flicker of human wisdom was nourished."[62] The emergence of Romantic fascination with Indian culture competed with and partly replaced the already established German "image of Greece as the birthplace of classical civilization."[63] Herder not only made a link between India and Greece due to their antiquity and cultural achievements, but he also gave priority to India by praising its arts, mythology, religion and philosophy. Others, such as Sir William Jones, a British official in India and early translator of Sanskrit works (who thereby delivered the Romanticists with material for their mythical view of India), repeated the connection between India and Greece. In his essay entitled "On the Gods of Greece, Italy and India" (1784), he describes correspondences between Indian mythological figures on the one hand and Greek and Roman figures on the other. However, he doesn't raise the question of origin.[64]

The theme of the antiquity of Indian arts and culture also engages Uday Shankar's critics. In the reviews, Indian dancing and music, and seemingly even the Indian artists themselves, are often regarded as deriving directly from ancient times. On the musical level, the reference is further concretized in a comparison between Indian and Greek music, mainly regarding instruments and modes. This is exemplified in Jules Casadesus's descriptions of the Indian *rāgas* as similar to the Greek modes and the construction of *sitar* and *sarod* as resembling the antique viol.[65] The same topic is taken up by other reviewers, such as by Georges Mussy who published a review in *Le Figaro* and also related the Indian *sitar* and *sarod* to Greek instrumental culture by describing them as

---

[62] Ibid.
[63] Nicholas A. Germana, *The Orient of Europe: The Mythical Image of India and Competing Images of German National Identity*, Newcastle upon Tyne: Cambridge Scholars Publishing 2009: 11.
[64] See Willson 40.
[65] Casadesus 5.

"relatives of the ancient viol."[66] Raoul Brunel, writing for the French *L'Oeuvre* after a performance of the group in May 1932, also states the similarity between the presented Indian and ancient Greek modes: "The modes employed are, in the depths, of the same type as our Greek modes."[67] Critics seemed to be sure that the music and instruments themselves had been unchanged since antiquity. This is evident, for example, in the description of the *rāgas* as "unchanging, ancient themes" or the instruments as authentic and antique: "The archaic instruments of strange forms and tones come directly from India."[68] This view is also expressed by a German reviewer in the *Hamburger Fremdenblatt*: "The Indian instruments are age-old; they have hardly changed in the course of millennia; and some – which are depicted in the oldest sculptures and already mentioned in the Vedas – are still in use today."[69]

Soon after Uday Shankar's first performance in Paris, Emile Vuillermoz writes in *Candide* that it opened up "the occasion to hear some pieces of Indian classical music performed on about sixty instruments forming an orchestra of a striking originality and novelty."[70] Vuillermoz who at the same time stresses the antiquity and originality of the Indian music and instruments and their novelty for Western audiences goes on by stating:

> These instruments are closer to nature than ours. They produce sounds which recall those of the headwaters of fast-flowing streams or small rivers. They roar like the thunder or whine like the wind. These are tamed natural forces.[71]

The theme of the close relationship between the Indian instruments and nature is also repeated and even surpassed in later French reviews.

---

[66] Mussy n.p.

[67] Raoul Brunel, "Danses et musique hindoues d'Uday Shan-Kar," *L'Oeuvre* (Paris), May 16, 1932: 5.

[68] Mussy n.p.; Henry Malmerse, "Au Théatre des Arts: danses hindoues de M. Unday [sic] Shankar et de Mlle Simkie," *Le Temps* (Paris), June 10, 1931: 3.

[69] "Zum Gastspiel des Indischen Balletts" 3.

[70] Vuillermoz n.p.

[71] Ibid.

Gérard d'Houville not only gives detailed descriptions of the instruments made of or resembling strange fruits, but goes one step further and compares the instrumentalists' hands with insects: "these hands, now and then, have the agility of big insects."[72] The "similarity of all these instruments with various fruits and insects or at times flowers" is also repeated in the German press.[73] Another German reviewer describes the instruments mainly by referring their apparently strange and unknown sounds to those occurring in nature and thus following natural laws:

> Never has anything been heard like this nonsensory-extrasensory sound of the narrow flutes, the gentle slender tone of the low-pitched violin, the chirring and whining of the guitars, the cymbaling of the metallic batons, the rattling of the bells and the thousand-fold gurgling, rumbling, stomping and wiping, the dripping and slurping, the breathing and stertorousness of the timbals and drums in their highly visible abundance. [...] This entire ocean of sounds then rises and decays like wind in the trees, ascending to luminous broad sound and dying down like a summery evening; it lives and breathes in accordance with the laws of nature.[74]

These comments, especially in the French context, might be linked to Jean-Jacques Rousseau's ideal of the "noble savage" in reference to the Indian people. On the musical level they are reminiscent of Rousseau's differentiation between two types of musical systems, "one emphasizing artifice and theory, the other nature and practice."[75]
In the newspaper reviews the supposed closeness between Indian culture and nature is combined with common ideas of primitivism. This view is also affirmed by Houville's descriptions of Uday Shankar's costume as

---

[72] Gérard d'Houville, "Chronique des Théatres de Paris. Théatre des Arts: Salomé, drame en un acte d'Oscar Wilde. Représentations de la Compagnie Pitoëff. – Danses hindoues," *Le Figaro* (Paris), June 8, 1931: n.p.
[73] a.l., "Indischer Tanzabend," *Hamburger Fremdenblatt* (Hamburg), September 30, 1931, evening edition: 3.
[74] R. Mk., "Indischer Tanz. Hamburger Bühne (Besprechung beim ersten Auftreten der Inder in Deutschland)," *Hamburger Nachrichten* (Hamburg), September 29, 1931: n.p.
[75] Blum 13.

"at a time primitive and complicated."[76] However, his comment describing Shankar's dancing as "wild and refined, barbaric and delicate" also indicates that he placed the performance between primitive and high art.[77]

A German reviewer writing for the *Fränkische Tagespost* shows himself convinced of the lower, comparatively primitive status of Indian music. His main argument is its apparent lack of harmony. He nevertheless acknowledges the artistic use of musical embellishment and rhythmical variation:

> The music played by this orchestra is, despite all virtuosity, primitive in comparison with ours. Above all because it completely lacks the concept of harmony, which is at the very most, only occasionally hinted at by means of one or two long-carried tones. The melodic instruments always play in unison in the same manner: mostly relatively short and plain motives whose melodics sound our old ecclesiastical modes. These are, however, almost always embellished and modified by one or another player through the use of artistic trills, embellishments, or rhythmical variations. To this is added the important element of the counterpoint of the percussions which produce, in most refined combination of sounds, very complicated rhythms which often have a sweeping effect.[78]

The critics' focus on melody and melodic variation in the musical performance of the company is sometimes combined with its description as monotonous, a characterization – as will be seen further on – already made use of in early British writings on Indian music. Eduard Szamba, for example, refers to the instrumental performance as tiresome and only loosely linked to the dance part:

---

[76] Houville n.p.

[77] Ibid.

[78] Brunck, "Gastspiel indischer Tänzer und Musiker im Opernhaus," *Fränkische Tagespost* (Nürnberg-Fürth), November 7, 1932: n.p.

Even though it is so compelling to get to know the sixty different instruments, their bizarre appearance from time to time, and their use which demands technical skills, they nevertheless have a tiring effect on European ears and appear to support the course of the dances less efficiently than a piano which can be provided at a lower cost.[79]

Most reviewers, however, directly oppose the common presumption of Indian music's monotony and instead stress its range of melodic and rhythmical variation as well as its variety of movements regarding the dancing. Raoul Brunel writes for the French *L'Oeuvre*: "However, all monotony is thereof banned, thanks to *decrescendo*, to *rinforzando*, to alterations of movement which permit to present the same themes out of very different perspectives."[80] In the New Yorker *Time* magazine the reviewer mentions that it is only due to the drummers' and Uday Shankar's expertise that the performance could avoid the common catch of Indian music's monotony: "It was delicate, highly refined music for the most part which, with its single thread of melody, might have sounded monotonous to Occidental ears but for the drummers tapping and slapping a swift, intricate counterpoint, and for Shankar."[81]

If we have a look at ethnomusicological writing of the early twentieth century as occupied with India we can see that the theme of antiquity, the supposed affinity between Indian music and nature as well as the question of its status as primitive or high art concerned its practitioners. As quoted before, the comparison between Oriental – including Indian – and ancient Greek music had been made use of by Hornbostel.[82] In

---

[79] Eduard Szamba, "Tanzbriefe: Paris," *Der Tanz* (Berlin), vol.4 no.4, April 1931: 14.

[80] Brunel 5.

[81]"Music: Radio Favorites … Dancer from Hindustan," *Time* (New York), January 9, 1933 (http://www.time.com/time/magazine/article/0,9171,753594,00.html; last accessed June 21, 2011).

[82] In their article "Indian Melodies Recorded on the Phonograph" Abraham and Hornbostel use the phrase: "As a true Oriental, the well-educated Indian […]." They hereby state, that they regarded – in accord with the general view of their time – India as part of the Orient. Ibid. 118.; See Hornbostel, "The Problems of Comparative Musicology" 269.

the course of their transcription of Indian melodies, he and Abraham stated that the scales used in Indian music represent "successive tones [...] corresponding to the ancient Greek and medieval octave-species (church tones)."[83] This link already had its history. From the end of the 18th century on, starting with the writings on Indian music by British Orientalists such as Sir William Jones, it not only reached German comparative musicology, but also found its way into Indian musicological writing which emerged in reaction to the debates held by the British. The following subchapters will follow the development of certain ideas or clichés about Indian music that still come up in the reception of Uday Shankar. I will here examine writings of British and Indian authors ending with Ananda K. Coomaraswamy who, as one of the most famous modern Indian art experts, strongly shaped the reception of Indian arts in the 20th century and accordingly must be considered in the context of Uday Shankar.

1.3.1 The British Orientalists: In Search of Classical Origins

Musicological writing on India emerged in the 18th and mainly 19th century under British colonial rule and would in the beginning be identified with the so-called British Orientalists. British Orientalism more explicitly refers to a civil service elite consisting of officials employed at the East India Company which, in the 1770s, was put together by Governor-General Warren Hastings as part of a new administrative and cultural policy in India. In 1784 Hastings further founded the Asiatic Society of Bengal with the aim of "establishing an Orientalized service elite competent in Indian languages and responsive to Indian traditions."[84] This was followed by the establishment of the College of Fort William, an institutional training center for British civil servants in 1800 that included Indians as faculty members. The establishment of the College led to further research on Indian philology, history and archaeology by officials such as William Jones, H.T. Colebrooke, Charles Wilkins or H.H. Wilson. These officials would combine their administrative and scholarly

---

[83] Abraham & Hornbostel, 156.
[84] David Kopf, "Hermeneutics versus History," in: A.L. Macfie (ed.), *Orientalism. A Reader*, New York University Press: New York 2000: 194-207; here 199ff.

interests and start their investigation into Indian law, politics, society, re-ligion, lan-guage and arts.[85] The Orientalists further showed a special interest in a Hindu classical age conducting research on Vedic India and the Indo-Aryan period.[86]

As early as 1784 Sir William Jones, at that time president of the Asiatic Society of Bengal, wrote a first shorter version of his treatise "On the musical modes of the Hindoos" which would be first published in a longer version in Calcutta in 1792.[87] Together with Francis Fowke's article "On the Vina or Indian Lyre," published in *Asiatick Researches* in 1788, Jones's treatise is generally regarded as one of the first works on Indian music which is "academic in form, content and methodology."[88] It would be followed by a number of writings by other British officials discussing and defining the theoretical and practical principles of music in India. Jones's writing on music is also included in a compilation published a century later, in 1875, by Sourindro Mohun Tagore, a cousin of the poet and Nobel prize winner Rabindranath Tagore, under the title *Hindu Music from Various Authors*. In 1904 Abraham and Hornbostel still mention this compilation as an influential work of reference for their research on Indian music.[89]

Among his contemporaries, William Jones was mainly known for his philological work on Sanskrit including his discovery of the family of Indo-European languages by postulating the link between Sanskrit and European languages.[90] In his treatise Jones accordingly follows a strongly text-based approach and describes and explains Indian music mainly in

---

[85] See Romila Thapar, "Ideology and the Interpretation of Early Indian History," in: R. Thapar, *Cultural Pasts. Essays in Early Indian History*, New Delhi: Oxford University Press 2000: 3-20; here 4.

[86] See David Kopf, *British Orientalism and the Bengal Renaissance. The Dynamics of Indian Modernization 1773-1835*, Calcutta: Firma K.L. Mukhopadhyay 1969: 22; 39ff.

[87] See Benett Zon, "From 'very acute and plausible' to 'curiously misinterpreted': Sir William Jones's 'On the Musical Modes of the Hindus' (1792) and its reception in later musical treatises," in: M.J. Franklin, *Romantic Representations of British India*, London & New York: Routledge 2006: 197-219; here 199.

[88] Ibid.

[89] Abraham & Hornbostel 118ff.

[90] See Gerry Farrell, *Indian Music and the West*, New York: Oxford University Press 2004: 18; 23.

reference to Sanskrit sources, such as Somnātha's *Rāgavibodha* from the early seventeenth century and Sārngadeva's *Sangītaratnākara* which was written in the first half of the thirteenth century.[91] He hereby almost completely neglects the Indian music practice of his period with its strong Persian influence in North Indian or Hindustani classical music. Beyond that, being one of the first serious writers on music in the subcontinent, he would be the one "introducing European terms of reference to explain the distinctive features and technicalities of Indian music."[92]

In his treatise Jones not only draws a sharp line between the current Indian and European musical system, but at the same time he establishes a connection between Indian and ancient Greek music. This connection is indicated when he names the "astonishing effects ascribed to music by the old *Greeks*, and in our days, by the *Chinese, Persians*, and *Indians*."[93] Whereas Jones, who here attributes animal reactions to music, describes these effects as having "probably been exaggerated and embellished," he however partly acknowledges them and from here on hints at another link between all these musical cultures, the unity of the different arts:[94]

> [I]t may, therefore, be suspected (not that the accounts are wholly fictitious, but) that such wonders were performed by music in its largest sense, as it is now described by the *Hindoos*, that is, by the union of *voices, instruments*, and *action*; for such is the complex idea conveyed by the word *Sangita*, the simple meaning of which is no more than *Symphony*.[95]

---

[91] See Zon 200.

[92] Lakshmi Subramaniam, "Negotiating Orientalism: The *Kaccheri* and the Critic in Colonial South India," in: Martin Clayton & Bennett Zon (eds.), *Music and Orientalism in the British Empire, 1780s-1940s: Portrayal of the East*, Hampshire: Ashgate Publishing Limited 2007: 189-206; here 192.

[93] Sir William Jones, "On the Musical Modes of the Hindoos," (1784) in: Sourindro Mohun Tagore (compiler/ed.), *Hindu Music from Various Authors* (1875/1882), Chowkhamba Sanskrit Series Office: Varanasi 1965: 123-160; here 128.

[94] For a detailed examination of the relatedness of the arts in India see Chapter 2.

[95] Jones 128ff.

Soon after, when he comes to the concept of mode or *rāga*, the Indian-Greek connection which Hornbostel and Abraham also referred to, is established: [96]

> [W]e must not confound them [the Indian *rāgas*] with our modern modes, which result from the system of accords now established in *Europe*; they may rather be compared with those of the *Roman* Church, where some valuable remnants of old *Grecian* music are preserved in the sweet, majestic, simple, and affecting strains of the Plain Song.[97]

In spite of the connection drawn, Sir William Jones also differentiates between antique Greek and Indian music due to their scientific and imaginative approach. Whereas he describes most of the Greek experts or writers on music as "professed men of science, who thought more of calculating ratios than of inventing melody," Jones seems to prefer the ancient Indian authors' approach to music, "who leave arithmetic and geometry to their astronomers, and properly discourse on music as an art confined to the pleasures of imagination."[98] That Jones indeed favors the (Indian) imaginative over the (Greek) scientific approach is proven by the opening remarks of his treatise. He here opposes music as a science to music as a fine art distinguished by its link to imagination and the expression of emotion and thus sets himself in the Romantic tradition:[99]

> Music belongs, as a *science*, to an interesting part of natural philosophy, which, by mathematical deductions from constant phenomena, explains the causes and properties of sound, limits the number of mixed, or *harmonic*, sounds to a certain series, which perpetually recurs, and fixes the ratio, which they bear to each other or to one leading term; but, considered as an *art*, it combines the sounds, which philosophy distinguishes, in such a manner as to gra-

---

[96] Jones equates mode and Raga: "Rága, which I translate as mode". Ibid. 142.
[97] Ibid. 130ff.
[98] Ibid. 132; 135.
[99] On Jones's link with Romantic philosophy see Zon 202ff.

tify our ears, or effect our imaginations; or, by uniting both objects, to captivate the fancy, while it pleases the senses; and speaking, as it were, the language of beautiful nature, to raise correspondent ideas and emotions in the mind of the hearer; it then, and only then, becomes what we call a *fine art*.[100]

This would mean that Jones regards Indian music as a respectively fine art, or at least ancient Indian music, as he clearly differentiates between music described in Sanskrit sources and Indian music of his time, which he sees as in a state of degeneration: "although the *Sanscrit* books have preserved the theory of their musical composition, the practice of it seems almost wholly lost (as all the *Pandits* and *Rájas* confess) in *Gaur* and *Magarha*, or the provinces of *Bengal* and *Behar*."[101] According to Jones, the theory of Indian music supposedly has even more ancient roots than Greek theory. This is exemplified in reference to a translation of Plutarch by a Dr. Burney who described how the omission of tones from the descending diatonic scale produced new, beautiful effects of expression.[102] Jones, in reference to his then following systematization of Indian *rāgas*, including *rāgas* consisting of no more than five tones, claims: "This method then of adding to the character and effect of a mode by diminishing the number of its primitive sounds [...] must have been older still among the *Hindoos*, if the system, to which I now return, was actually invented in the age of RÁMA."[103] Jones furthermore finds a culprit for the state of loss and degeneration in Indian music. At some other part in the essay just generally hinting at "the revolutions of their [= the Indians'] government since the time of ALEXANDER,"[104] he then names the Persian or Muslim influence in India, namely their inexpert translations of Sanskrit sources, as a cause for impureness:

---

[100] Jones 125.

[101] Ibid. 155f.

[102] See ibid. 147. Jones here probably refers to a monograph named *General History of Music from the earliest ages to the present period* by a Dr. Charles Burney published at the end of the 18th century.

[103] Jones 148.

[104] Ibid. 155.

[M]y experience justifies me in pronouncing that the *Moghols* have no idea of accurate translation, and give that name to a mixture of gloss and text with a flimsy paraphrase of them both; they are wholly unable, yet always pretend, to write *Sanscrit* words in *Arabic* letters; that a man, who knows the *Hindoos* only from *Persian* books, does not know the Hindoos; and that an *European*, who follows the muddy rivulets of *Mussalman* writers on *India*, instead of drinking from the pure fountain of *Hindoo* learning, will be in perpetual danger of misleading himself and others.[105]

British Orientalists such as Jones accordingly understood themselves as coming to the rescue of the original authentic Indian or "Hindu" arts and language. Gerry Farrell points out how Jones's text is "written in the spirit of the times, with Europeans in the act of discovering the 'real' culture of India, embodied in Sanskrit texts and Hindu thought" and thus still unaffected by Persian influences.[106] Farrell further identifies the "Western veneration of India's Hindu past" as one dimension of orientalism with Western scholars setting on themselves the task to "rediscover, preserve, and interpret the greatness of this past, and on numerous occasions contrast it with the 'muddy rivulets' of Muslim thought."[107] In times of Western classicism with its admiration for ancient Greece, India's Sanskrit musical writing would be referred to and compared with ancient Greek music theory in order to be systematized and thus understood. In the course of a Western search for cultural origins, the cultivation of Indian arts seemed to propose a contemporary return to a European past. As Farrell concludes:

India became, with Greece, Rome, and Egypt, an ancient civilization to be studied, discussed, and dissected in detail, an Asian adjunct to the classicism that was a basic tenet of European philosophical and artistic thought. But, unlike the other great civilizations of the past, India was a living culture, even though, as will become

---

[105] Ibid. 136.
[106] Farrell 26.
[107] Ibid. 19; Ibid. Quote from Jones 136.

apparent in relation to music, its living manifestations were seldom the focus of Western scholarly attention.[108]

It is this line of investigation regarding India's connection with western classicism which is taken up again by Captain N. Augustus Willard in "A Treatise on the Music of Hindoostan" (1834), which is also included in S.M. Tagore's compilation. Willard regularly refers to Jones and obviously builds on the topics established by the former with the aim to develop them further. However, Captain Willard's approach differs from Jones's in so far as, following Bennett Zon, it relies on information from living musicians instead of solely written works. Willard strives to combine the theory on ancient Sanskrit music with current musical practice; thus he does not restrict himself solely to Hindu performers, but he is able to include Muslim musicians as well:

> I have not confined myself to the details in books, but have also consulted the most famous performers, both Hindoos and Mussulmans, the first Veenkars in India, the more expert musicians of Lucknow, and Hukeem Sulamut Ulee Khan of Benares, who has written a treatise on music. The reader will not find this work a translation of any of the existing treatises on music, but an original work, comprehending the system of Hindoostanee music according to the ancient theory, noticing as much of it as is confirmed by the practice of the present day.[109]

His strong reliance on current musical performance in India leads him to the conclusion that "even so able and eminent an Orientalist as Sir William Jones has failed" due to his mere focus on text and theory which separated itself from practice and left the latter to the illiterate.[110]

---

[108] Farrell 18.
[109] Captain N. Augustus Willard, "A Treatise on the Music of Hindoostan, Comprising a Detail of the Ancient Theory and Modern Practice," in: Tagore, *Hindu Music from Various Authors* 1-122; here 12.
[110] Ibid. 3.

Willard obviously uses the connotation "Music of Hindoostan" as a general reference to music in India without further differentiating between the North Indian Hindustani and the South Indian or Carnatic music tradition. Already presupposing a link between Indian and ancient Greek music, he describes his main intentions in the preface as "The similitude between the music of the classical nations and that of Hindoostan has never, I believe, been traced, and the following labour will, I presume to hope, be productive of some fruit."[111] In the introductory part of his paper, Willard returns to the topic and presents a number of points of reference between the Indian and the ancient Greek musical systems namely concerning rhythm, the use of intervals smaller than a semitone, the predominance of melody, and aesthetic effects of music:

> If a comparison between the ancient music of Greece, which was principally borrowed from the Egyptians, and that of Hindoostan, might be hazarded, it would appear that great similarity exists between the two. The same rhythmical measure, the same subdivision of semitones into minor divisions, the same noisy method of beating time not only with the hand, but also with instruments of percussion; melody without harmony, in its present acceptation; and the similarity of the effects said to have been produced by the music of the two nations.[112]

Willard further names semblances in the building of the scale, such as its division into tetrachords. He then comes to the question of which of the two was developed first and advanced further. Referring to the Indian epics he, like Jones, sides with Indian music:

> If it were inquired whether the nation of Greece or Hindoostan proceeded farther in the cultivation of music, the accounts we have of its state amongst the former, and the living examples at present found in the latter, aided by a review of its flourishing state under the native princes, would decide in favor of Hindoostan. The use of a flute, with holes to produce melodies, was only discovered during

---

[111] Ibid. 4.
[112] Ibid. 33ff.

the latter ages of Greece, as well as the performance on that instrument as a solo; both of which existed in Hindoostan from time immemorial. It was the instrument on which Krishna played.[113]

By comparing Indian music with ancient Greek music Willard strengthens the argument already raised in Jones's essay: Indian music developed before the Greek. Sanskrit India is accordingly included in the rank of civilized societies and, following early Romanticists such as Herder, identified as a possible "root of civilization:"

> Egypt, Greece and Rome are the only ancient countries which the European scholar is taught to reverence as having been civilized and enlightened – all the rest he is to consider as barbarous. India is not generally thought of, as deserving of any approximity in rank; but the acuteness of some has even led them to doubt, whether this country was not in a state of civilization even before the most ancient of those three; nay, whether this was not the parent country – the root of civilization.[114]

Despite the attribution to India as a possible cradle of humankind, Willard, who delivers his readers a hierarchical model of countries regarding their degree of civilization in music, here ascribes India only a middle position. For this he once again mainly assigns responsibility to former Muslim rule – which indirectly opens up the path for the British Orientalists as saviors of Indian arts:

> Every nation, how rude soever, has, we see, its music, and the degree of its refinements is in proportion to the civilization of its professors. She is yet in her cradle with the rude Indians of America, or the "hideous virgins of Congo." With the natives of Hindoostan, she may be said long to have left the puerile state, though perhaps still far from that of puberty, her progress towards maturity having been checked, and her constitution ruined and thrown into decay by

---

[113] Ibid. 34ff.
[114] Ibid. 9ff.

the overwhelming and supercilious power of the Mahomedan government.[115]

In his description of the Indian musical system, Willard further stresses that Indian music, like the ancient Greek, lacks harmony and instead is built on melody which he equalizes with *rāga*.[116] Although this "lack of harmony" is generally identified with a lower level of development, Willard seems to favor melody due to its romantic proximity with nature. Although he writes that "[t]here is no doubt that harmony is a refinement on melody," he continues:[117]

> Although I am myself very fond of harmony, and it cannot but be acknowledged that it is a very sublime stretch of the human mind, the reasoning on harmony will perhaps convince the reader that harmony is more conducive to cover the nakedness, than shew the fertility of genius. Indeed, perhaps all the most beautiful successions of tones which constitute agreeable melody are exhausted, and this is the reason of the poorness of our modern melody, and the abundant use of harmony, which however in a good measure compensates by its novelty. At the same time, we are constrained to allow that harmony is nothing but art, which can never charm equally with nature. "Enthusiastic melody can be produced by an illiterate mind, but tolerable harmony always supposes previous study," – a plain indication that the former is natural, the latter artificial.[118]

Harmony thus seems to be only a poor compensation for a lack of creativity in melody. But it is not only melody or *rāga* which positions Indian musicians closer to nature and to the origin of music, but their use of rhythm, "in which branch it resembles more the rhythm of the Greeks, and other ancient nations, than the measures peculiar to the modern mu-

---

[115] Ibid. 18.
[116] "The general term for melody in Hindoostan is Rag or Raginee." Ibid. 61.
[117] Ibid. 4.
[118] Ibid. 4ff.

sic of Europe."[119] Here Willard once again establishes a parallel between current Oriental and ancient Western musical practice:

> From the certain knowledge of the rhythm of the ancients, and the similarity observed in the practices of the natives of India, Persia, and other Oriental countries, it inclines one to the opinion that the rhythmical measure is the lawful offspring of nature, found in all parts of the world, which existed much prior to the birth of her younger sister, the modern musical measure.[120]

In addition to the use of melody and rhythm, it is also the importance of vocal music in India which Willard takes as a sign for Indian music's ancient origin. As he quotes from Charles Burney's *General History of Music* written at the end of the 18th century: "Dr. Burney says, 'Vocal music is of such high antiquity, that its origin seems to have been coeval with mankind.'"[121] Willard later returns to the issue and goes on to announce the superiority of vocal music:

> Music is either vocal or instrumental. The former is everywhere acknowledged to be superior to the latter. It is not in the power of man to form an artificial instrument so very delicate and beautiful in tone, and possessing all the pliability of a truly good voice.[122]

Willard also touches the questions of the *śrutis*, the microtonal divisions of the Indian scale, whose measurement would in the following become a central point of debate between Indian and Western musicologists working with Indian music. Willard once again establishes a connection with ancient Greek music theory when he compares the Indian *śrutis* with the diesis used in the Greek enharmonic genus:

---

[119] Ibid. 46.
[120] Ibid.
[121] Charles Burney, *General History of Music: from the earliest ages to the present period*, vol.1; quoted in: Ibid. 16.
[122] Ibid. 25ff.

The number of tones is the same as in the modern music of Europe, but the subdivisions are more in the manner of the ancient enharmonic genus of the Greeks. The difference in the subdivision of the tones which characterised the enharmonic, consisted in the notes of the chromatic genus being divided by the diesis or quarter tone.[123]

In his glossary of musical terms preceding the text he likewise does not deliver his readers with an exact measurement of each single *śruti* and instead defines the scale as follows: "Srooti. The chromatic scale of the Hindus, consisting of the sub-divisions of the seven notes of the gamut into twenty-two parts."[124]

The antiquity of Indian music and its close bond with nature also occupies a number of other authors on Indian music, whose writings are brought together in S.M. Tagore's compilation. Most of these writers do, however, mainly refer back to and quote from Sir William Jones's "On the musical modes of the Hindoos" and therefore fail to present their readers with new information. Instead they more or less summarize already existent ideas. The repeated link between Indian and Greek music sometimes also leads to the equation of instruments, such as when William C. Stafford, author of *A History of Music* (1830), refers to the ancient Greek cithara in the context of the description of an Indian string instrument which might be *sārangī*, esrāj or *dilruba*. He writes: "The Hindu *cithara* is furnished with wires, and is played with a bow."[125]

There are, of course, other authors who do not share the fascination displayed by Jones and Willard. In common denunciations of Indian music as monotonous and not progressive enough we find early evidences for negative clichés repeated also in the reviews on Uday Shankar. Colonel P.T. French in his *Catalogue of Indian Musical Instruments* writes:

---

[123] Ibid. 39.
[124] Ibid. Glossary viii.
[125] William C. Stafford, "Oriental Music. The Music of Hindustan or India" in: Tagore, *Hindu Music from Various Authors* 219-228; here 227.

[N]owhere does it appear that the laws of harmony had ever been discovered or invented; and, as a consequence, all Indian music is wanting in this most essential particular. This, and the pedantic divisions into modes, so jealously guarded from infringement, have prevented Hindu music and its science from that improvement and extension which have been attained elsewhere. In this respect music is, like all other sciences of the Hindus, and their philosophy, unprogressive and effete. [...]; but all singing and playing are in unison, and whether trebles, tenors, or basses, which are often joined, and in all instrumental music, the execution is of the same character. It is needless to say that this inevitably produces monotony, and causes Indian music to be generally uninteresting, if not repellant, to European ears.[126]

In spite of his depreciative attitude towards Indian music, the author notes its proximity with ancient Greek music and follows that "it would afford most interesting comparisons with the ancient national music of Europe, which it so much resembles."[127]

The degradation of Indian music as non-progressive and effete seen above has its origin in the writing of Georg Friedrich Wilhelm Hegel. In his *Lectures on the Philosophy of History* (1837), Hegel developed a hierarchical historical model in which the Orient (including India) represents "the childhood of History" whereas Europe stands at its endpoint.[128] The Orient is thus described as childish and backward and identified with despotism and an "unreflected consciousness" unable for progress.[129] India is here directly described as "stationary and fixed" and named the "region of phantasy and sensibility" ruled by imagination and nature.[130] Hegel explicitly refers to India's position outside the realm of world history as being linked with its despotism:

---

[126] Colonel P.T. French, "Catalogue of Indian Musical Instruments," in: Tagore, *Hindu Music from Various Authors* 243-273; here 266ff.

[127] Ibid. 269.

[128] Georg Wilhelm Friedrich Hegel, *The Philosophy of History*, New York: Cosimo 2007: 105.

[129] Ibid. 104.

[130] Ibid. 139; 147.

The spread of Indian culture is prehistorical, for History is limited to that which makes an essential epoch in the development of Spirit. On the whole, the diffusion of Indian culture is only a dumb, deedless expansion; that is, it presents no political action. The people of India have achieved no foreign conquests, but haven been on every occasion vanquished themselves.[131]

Hegel's thought might have been influenced by James Mill's *History of British India* (1818). Mill, although he had never been to India himself, delivers his readers with a massive three-volume work in which he describes Indian culture as rude, backward, despotic and superstitious hereby establishing a number of prejudices to be found later in Hegel.[132]

Whereas in most cases writers on Indian music in the 19th and 20th centuries did not follow Mill's or Hegel's depreciative view of Indian society, it still had its impact on the reception of Indian arts inside and outside India, as seen previously in some of the reviews on Uday Shankar.

As seen above the writings of early British Orientalists on music in the Indian subcontinent focus on an ancient textual Sanskrit or Hindu tradition that was related to Greek classicism. These writings would exercise a strong influence on Indian or especially Hindu nationalist thought, which in the 19th century also entered the spheres of music and dance. One of the main figures in this context was the Bengali S.M. Tagore, editor of the above mentioned compilation, one of whose works will be examined in the following.

1.3.2 S.M. Tagore: "Hindu Music" in the Wake of British Orientalism

The second part of *Hindu Music from Various Authors*, first published in 1882, includes a reprint of an article named "Hindu Music" written by Sourindro Mohun Tagore himself and already published in

---

[131] Ibid. 142.
[132] See Terrence Ball, "James Mill," *Stanford Encyclopedia of Philosophy*, first published November 30, 2005 (http://plato.stanford.edu/entries/james-mill/; last accessed June 21, 2011).

1874 in the *Hindoo Patriot*.[133] The article is mainly a critical reaction to a series of statements and writings on music in India by Charles Baron Clarke, who at that time was a school inspector in Bengal.[134] Influenced by his grandfather Gopi Mohun Tagore, Sourindro had already established an interest in European culture and learning and developed a profound knowledge in Indian music.[135] Tagore, who also worked with and directly supported European researchers on Indian music such as Ellis, follows the text-based approach of the British Orientalists and cites from a number of Sanskrit sources on music.[136] Affirming the importance of Sanskrit he does not translate his Sanskrit quotes into English. He furthermore refers to the writings of Jones and Willard as well as those of a number of European professors of music of his time. Tagore, however, shapes this approach in his own way by claiming a decided Indian, or rather Hindu, point of view.

As Gerry Farrell has already pointed out, the fact that Tagore talks about "Hindu Music" instead of Indian music is not just a coincidence: Hindu music was "Indian music that had returned to the imagined purity of it Sanskrit sources."[137] The concept of Hindu music then reflects the ambiguous milieu in which Indian musicology in the 19th century emerged. It was the British Orientalists' classical text-based approach which became a starting point for the spread of nationalism in the field of the arts. As a Hindu nationalist, Tagore closely aligns Indian arts and music with politics. In his essay he presents himself as a defender of Hindu music's true essence and he even tries to spiritually enlighten his Western readers, especially his addressee Clarke: "We believe he is a searcher after truth, and if he will, in a kindly spirit, accept the light which we, in all humility, offer to him, he may yet find out that priceless

---

[133] According to Gerry Farrell, the *Hindoo Patriot* was "a nineteenth-century Calcutta newspaper which printed a mixture of loyalist and nationalist articles." See Farrell 69.
[134] See Farrell 67.
[135] See Charles Capwell, "Marginality and Musicology in Nineteenth-Century Calcutta: The Case of Sourindro Mohun Tagore," in: Nettl & Bohlman 228-243; here 233.
[136] In their article "Indian Melodies Recorded on the Phonograph," Abraham and Hornbostel mention that, in order to familiarize European scholars with the *śruti*-system, "Tagore, in 1886, sent Ellis a vīnā on which the complete 22-degree scale was fixed by secured frets". Ibid.153, footnote 23.
[137] See Farrell 50ff.

treasure."[138] His ambiguous position was further enhanced by the fact that, despite being a Hindu nationalist, Tagore was very loyal to the British throne and dedicated quite a number of his writings to the Empress or the Prince of Wales.[139]

One of the first aspects Tagore picks out for discussion is the concept of *rāga*. His addressee Clarke apparently equalizes *rāga* with mode, an equation Tagore initially strives to refute in reference to Captain Willard's explanations on the topic. In one of his writings Willard describes *rāga* as a tune while at the same time he states the insufficiencies lying in this translation. He indicates that a *rāga* "is not to be considered exactly in the same situation as a tune is amongst us."[140] Tagore takes these doubts as a starting point for his own remarks and elaborates: "Tune and Rága are thus so distinct from each other that one cannot be used for the other without a confusion of ideas."[141] It is, however, not Tagore's aim to explain to his Western readers what exactly a *rāga* is; for that, he refers them to various treatises in Sanskrit. He instead focuses on the point that this unique and solely Indian concept does not have any equivalent in Western musical terminology. Tagore writes: "The truth is the English language has not a corresponding term for the Rága. [...] The idea which the word Rága conveys has not its counterpart in English."[142] In accordance with his ambivalent position as a Hindu nationalist dedicated to the British monarchy, Tagore, who just stated the impossibility to translate Indian musical concepts into English, soon after defends the necessity to work with approximate terms if one wants to communicate about Indian music at all in English. Strongly influenced by the British approach to Indian or Hindu arts and writing himself in English, he thus welcomes a discussion with the colonial rulers, if only in order to state his position as an Indian or Hindu expert on the topic:

---

[138] Sourindro Mohun Tagore, "Hindu Music," in: Tagore, *Hindu Music from Various Authors* 339-387; here 339.
[139] See Capwell 238.
[140] Tagore, "Hindu Music" 344.
[141] Ibid.
[142] Ibid. 345.

Mr. Clarke finds fault with us for using the term quarter-tone for Srooti. [...] In English there are no corresponding terms for Srooti, Rága, Murchchhaná, Tála and several other words commonly used in Hindu Music, and in employing any one of them in an English composition on music the choice of words conveying an approximate meaning is unavoidable, and in such a case the writer cannot be said to misuse words except by the hypercritical.[143]

Tagore's above-quoted statement on Clarke's criticism of the equation of the Indian *śruti* with a quarter-tone hints at the heated debate between British and Indian musicologists on the nature of the Indian microtones. It is in reference to the *śrutis* and the Indian scale that Tagore takes up a number of topics established by Orientalists such as Jones and Willard. One would be the notion of Indian music's continuous existence since antiquity. Tagore writes: "One who knows to sing can sing both the quarter-tone and the third note without difficulty. It is done every day by practised singers and has been in use amongst us from remote antiquity."[144] He then builds on the relation between music in other Asian or Oriental countries and ancient Greece by calling the *śrutis* "enharmonic tones" – hereby stressing that in Greece, in contrast to the Asian countries, the continuity has been broken:

> [T]he Srooties or enharmonic tones have been used and recognised from time immemorial not only in this country but in Greece, Arabia, China, Persia and several other Asiatic countries. [...] This species was in great vogue among the Greeks by whom it was considered much easier of execution, but it is now lost.[145]

In light of the continuous European upholding of the Greek ideal of art, Tagore's reference to ancient Greek music is surely meant to give the Indian microtones their due respect. Finally, Tagore strongly affronts what he describes as Clarke's "mathematicism," namely Clarke's interest in

---

[143] Ibid. 355.
[144] Ibid. 357.
[145] Ibid. 358.

the mathematical exact identification of each microtonal step in a scale.[146] Citing from Aristoxenus, a few current European professors of music, as well as by naming different sources from Arabia to China and India, he comes to the conclusion that "in all countries [...] the greatest musicians and the most tasteful composers did not pretend to a knowledge of mathematics."[147] Tagore further claims that the Indian scale is more natural than the European "mathematical" one. In reference to a French source he thus indirectly announces Indian music to be of higher value than the current European:

> Hence it is, we contend, that our scale is natural and is well represented by M. Momigny's doctrine which holds that a true scale is derived from nature and requires no mathematical calculations.[148]

Whereas he at once is defying the Western mathematical approach, Tagore at the same time is stressing that Hindu music nevertheless relies on a strong theoretical basis brought about in detail in the existent Sanskrit treatises on music. He explains:

> [W]e will take the liberty to point out that in the book alluded to[149] and in all Sanskrit works on the subject, the theoretical part of music is as fully dwelt upon as in any European treatise, only it is not mystified by obscuring mathematicism. As we have said elsewhere we hold that it is quite possible to build a rational theory of music without the aid of numbers.[150]

---

[146] Ibid. 340.

[147] Ibid. 342.

[148] Ibid. 361. Tagore probably refers to J.J. de Momigny's *Cours complet d'harmonie et de composition, d'après une théorie neuve et général de la musique, basée sur des príncipes incontestables puisés dans la nature, d'accord avec tous les bons ouvrages pratiques anciens et modernes*, Paris 1803.

[149] Tagore here refers to *Sangita Sára* or *The Essence of Music* (1879) written by his teacher Ksetro Mohun.

[150] See Capwell 236; Tagore 360.

In writing this, Tagore partly answers the Western claim for a music theory based on rationality as a distinct foundation of every developed musical culture and also once again repeats the text-based approach to music as executed by the British Orientalists.

At the center of the article stands Sourindro Tagore's discussion of the question of notation. It is in this part where the link between music and Hindu nationalism and identity becomes most apparent. Tagore strongly rejects Clarke's recommendation to introduce Indian musicians to the western system of staff notation. He is instead very determined to further use what he calls "Indian notation," a new system described by his teacher Ksetro Mohun in the aforementioned book *Sangita Sára*. Tagore, who highlights its clear arrangement in contrast to European staff notation, strongly holds the view that each nation should stick to its own original system of musical notation. Tagore states as follows:

> Every nation that has a music of its own has also its own system of notation for writing it. Whether that system be an advanced one or not, it cannot be correctly expressed in the notation of another nation, however improved and scientific it may be. [...] Anglicized as we have become in many respects, we confess we prefer our national system of notation for our national music. The English system of notation, it needs to be observed, is imperfect and insufficient for the purposes of Hindu Music for the simple reason that the genius of Hindu Music is distinct from that of European music.[151]

Writing this, Tagore applies the Western model of historical progress to music, striving to put India at an advanced level. As a strong defendant of notation in Indian music, he had generally taken over the British conviction that Indian music was in a state of decay.[152] Notation, for Tagore, seemed the necessary means for progress, hereby – as Farrell describes it – "fight[ing] the British on their own ground" by "try[ing] to match their music with a Hindu version based on scientific and rational prin-

---

[151] Tagore 366ff.
[152] See Capwell 234.

ciples."[153] Indeed loyal to the British throne, Tagore is eager to avoid any possible misunderstandings:

> To guard against misapprehension, we must say that our object is not to establish the superiority of the Hindu system over the European, but merely to show that our system, as it is, is quite sufficient for all practical purposes, and that the introduction of the European system will not be an improvement.[154]

Tagore finally comes to the question of India's level of civilization, which he solves by subsuming various Asian countries, such as China, Japan and indirectly India, under the keyword "civilized nation:"

> Every civilized nation, that has a music of its own, has also a system of notation adapted to the peculiarities of that music. If we attempt to replace it by the European system of notation, we will be under the necessity of expressing those peculiarities by means of new signs. Take the Chinese music as an illustration. [...] Take again Japan.[155]

Yet Tagore follows the evolutionary model common among European musicologists when he claims that "the different systems of music of different nations are not equally progressive, (and some are not at all progressive)."[156] This helps him to strengthen his point that a shared notational system for all of the world's music, obviously one of Mr. Clarke's intentions, was not possible at that moment in time: "We fear we must defer the prospect of an [sic] universal language of music till the milleneum [sic] arrives."[157]

---

[153] Farrell 67. See also Capwell 236. Capwell here refers to Ksetro Mohun's conclusion on the Greeks' borrowing the idea of notation from India.
[154] Tagore 377.
[155] Ibid. 380.
[156] Ibid. 382.
[157] Ibid.

The examination of Tagore's essay reveals how the author in his writing on music shifts between Indian and Western parameters and approaches. Tagore needs to defend an Indian or rather Hindu musical heritage against British appropriation and misconception and therefore he must resumes threads of discussion dealt with by the British Orientalists. Accordingly, his discussion of music takes place in the framework previously established by western writers. But Tagore extends this framework by closely linking music with a distinct Hindu nationalism. This can be seen in his statement of the impossibility of translating Indian concepts into foreign languages and furthermore in his discussion on notation.

The theme of Indian music and nationalism would to some extent also occupy a British ethnomusicologist in the 20th century: A.H. Fox Strangways. His work, differing in many respects, should nevertheless be regarded in reference to the topics discussed by the British Orientalists.

1.3.3 A.H. Fox Strangways: *The Music of Hindostan*

A. H. Fox Strangways's *The Music of Hindostan* (1914) is one example that shows how the connection between India and ancient Greece in respect to their musical systems and instruments reaches well into musicological writing of the 20th century. Fox Strangways, founder of the journal *Music and Letters*, states in the preface of his monograph:[158] "The study of Indian music is of interest to all who care for song, and of special interest to those who have studied the early stages of song in mediaeval Europe or ancient Greece."[159]He explains his proposition that it is impossible to study melody independent of harmony in European music. And Indian music's lack of harmony opens up the possibility for a better understanding and deeper analysis of European music:

> [H]ere [in Indian music] is melody absolutely untouched by harmony, which has developed through many centuries tendencies which have the force of laws; and the examination of these enables

---

[158] See Zon 198.

[159] Arthur Henry Fox Strangways, *The Music of Hindostan*, Munshiram Manoharlal Publishers: New Delhi 1975 (originally published by Clarendon Press: Oxford 1914): v.

us to some extent to separate the respective contributions of melody and harmony to the final effect in our own music.[160]

Discussing the possibility and necessity of understanding foreign cultures' music, Fox Strangways comes to the conclusion that, for a European, Indian music is essentially as unfamiliar as, for example, European music from the middle ages or early folk-song.[161] This argument is also strengthened by the evolutionary proposition included in the preface of his book, which says that Indian musical practice at present equals mediaeval European music making. One example he uses is in terms of the instruments employed: "India is now, instrumentally, at the same stage as mediaeval Europe, with a great variety of means of supporting the voice but absolutely no sense of orchestration."[162]

One important point of connection between contemporary Indian music and European music from the middle ages he names is the religious element. Starting with the statement that "India is still living the age of Faith," he detects an "extraordinary correspondence in detail both of time and tune with the music of Ecclesiastical Europe [which] justifies the view that a peculiar outlook on the world, such for instance as the specifically religious outlook, does bring as a result a peculiar form of music."[163]

As a member of the *India Society*,[164] Fox Strangways stood in contact with William Rothenstein, Shankar's art teacher at the Royal College of Art in London, and Ananda Kentish Coomaraswamy, whom he mentions as proof reader and donator of photographs and Indian art prints included in the book.[165] Fox Strangways apparently was an admirer of Rabindranath Tagore as he described him as "one who, more than any other, may be said to personify Indian music in its broadest

---

[160] Ibid.
[161] See ibid. 1-3.
[162] Ibid. vi.
[163] Ibid. 6.
[164] The India Society was founded in 1910 by A.K. Coomaraswamy. See Lipsey 53 (see Introduction, footnote 10).
[165] For information on Coomaraswamy see the following subchapter.

sense."[166] Tagore and his music and poetry are furthermore praised in a later part of the book accompanied by transcriptions of some of his songs.[167]

His bibliography and the publications Fox Strangways quotes from and refers to reveal that he was very informed about European texts on Indian music (Britain, Germany, France) as well as Indian texts written in English on the subject. He continually stresses the importance of ancient Indian texts or musical treatises, such as Bharata's *Nātyaśāstra*, and he also demands further adequate English translations to secure a fundamental base for research. This heavily text-based approach puts him closer to the British tradition and the Orientalist approach. Accordingly, Tagore's compilation *Hindu Music from Various Authors* and other works by him as well as references to articles by Sir W. Jones and Captain Willard are included in the bibliography. This text-based approach at the same time differentiates Fox Strangways from the practitioners of comparative musicology, of whose works he is aware and to some extent critical. In the bibliography this is immediately apparent in his reference to the essay "Indian melodies recorded on the phonograph" by Abraham and Hornbostel, which he summarizes as follows: "ignoring Indian theory, treats twenty-eight tunes simply as musical phenomena."[168] Although he criticizes the solely empirical approach of comparative musicology he nevertheless makes regular use of the Cent-system as developed by Ellis, used to explain elements such as the scale in Indian music.[169] Because his main focus, as mentioned above, lies in the comparison of Indian melody and other musical aspects with the ancient Greek and partly European mediaeval musical system, he presents the reader with a wealth of musical transcriptions from Indian and Western music. He thus clearly builds on topics raised before by Jones and Willard, but he also presents a more detailed look at Greek and Indian music theory in order to prove the fundamental connection between both.

Whereas his British predecessors still accentuated the distinctiveness of Indian and European musical cultures, Fox Strangways now

---

[166] Fox Strangways vii.
[167] Ibid. 91-99.
[168] Ibid. 347.
[169] See ibid. 117.

strongly assumes a shared background of both, exemplified by a rather vague impression of "familiarity" European listeners of Indian music experience in the present: "It is this strange familiarity, which we are conscious of in Indian melody, that makes us sure that 'though our language is different and our habits are dissimilar, at the bottom our hearts are one'."[170] He even goes so far as to propose a common ancient origin for Indian and European music based on their shared Aryan background:

> Neither is there any suggestion that Greece borrowed from India, or vice versa; their musical systems, like their languages, were no doubt part of their common Aryan inheritance – with enough likeness and unlikeness to make the comparison convincing.[171]

Fox Strangways here builds on William Jones's discovery of a shared origin of European and Indian languages due to their common Aryan background. The application of a common ancestral Indo-European origin from the level of language to the level of society was, following Romila Thapar, strongly promoted in the work of the German philologist Friedrich Max Müller. As Thapar writes: "Aryan [...], although specifically a label for a language, came to be used for a people and a race as well, the argument being that those who spoke the same language belonged to the same biological race."[172] Max Müller and other comparative philologists, however, differentiated between the northern and the southern Aryans:

> The northern Aryans who are said to have migrated to Europe are described by Max Müller as active and combative and they developed the idea of a nation, while the southern Aryans who migrated to Iran and to India were passive and meditative, concerned with religion and philosophy.[173]

---

[170] Ibid. 3.
[171] Ibid. 122.
[172] Romila Thapar, "The Theory of Aryan Race and India: History and Politics," in: Thapar, *Cultural Pasts* 1108-1140; here 1111ff.
[173] Ibid. 1111.

Fox Strangways follows these and other stereotyped images of Indian society – views also held, for example, by Hegel in his abovementioned
History of Philosophy. This becomes obvious in a number of comments
such as when he describes the Indians as a people without a sense of
history: "His past is like his present and throws little light upon it."[174]
Furthermore, he elaborates on the non-competitive, contemplative, and
first of all spiritually engaged Indian character:

> And it does not interest him to compare one nation with another, or
> to take side in or strike a balance between competing activities. His
> life is in the family rather than the state, in idea rather than fact, in
> the soul rather than the mind. His knowledge is of revelation more
> than of science; his truth contemplative rather than practical.[175]

On the level of music theory he intends to prove the familiarity or shared
Indo-European background by presenting a list of the ancient Greek and
mediaeval ecclesiastical modes with their South Indian (*melakarta*) and
North Indian (*thāt*) equivalents.[176] Going through various musical aspects
such as scale, mode, metre, rhythm, and melody and touching the field of
aesthetics of music, he elaborates on the resemblances between both
systems already outlined in former writings supporting the argument with
detailed examples and the use of terminology. Fox Strangways especially
focuses on the question of analogies between the Indian and Greek scale,
such as in its structure of tetrachords – a point already made by Willard –
, the transition from single tetrachords to the combination of two then encompassing a complete octave (*mūrchana* / *harmoniā* to *rāga* / *tonos*),
the centrality of certain tones in the scales (*amśa* vs. *mesē*), the presentation of certain *rāgas* as equivalents of the three Greek *genera* (chromatic,
diatonic and enharmonic) and the existence of microtones (*śruti* vs.
diesis) in both system.[177] In accordance with the view that research in Indian music can be useful in order to learn more about one's own Euro-

---

[174] Fox Strangways 73.
[175] Ibid. 74.
[176] See ibid. 47.
[177] See ibid. 140ff.; See ibid. 142.; See ibid. 119ff; See ibid. 120; 130.

pean history of music, he deploys his findings on the *śrutis* to hypothes-
ize about and contradict current opinions on the division of the diesis in
ancient Greek music.[178]

In accordance with the Indian-Greek link in music theory, Fox
Strangways, like Jones and Willard, allocates Indian music a place in the
rank of classical fine arts that deserve appropriate recognition. Reversing
common ideas of the primitive and their possible reference to India, he
describes primitivism as a stage of musical development or rather education to be found everywhere in the world at any time in history:

> When primitive man – and he is to be heard in London streets as
> well as in Otahiti or in the glacial epoch – begins to articulate his
> upward whoop or downward wail, he uses his 'musical ear'. It is
> this ear which is in a low state of development when he 'loses his
> key' or 'sings out of tune'.[179]

He also indicates his opinion that the Indians should not be named primitive in respect to their music with the following statement referring to
intervals. He thus places ancient Indian and Greek listening abilities
above contemporary European ones: "If any people hears septimal intervals, the Indians and the Greeks, with the fine ear which practised and the
fine discrimination which recorded the niceties of the *genera* and the
grāmas, would have been among the first to do it."[180]
Like his predecessors, Fox Strangeways identifies Indian music making
as undergoing a process of degeneration. Regardless, he seems to oppose
a forced, artificial return to its origins, but instead wishes music making
to be directly linked to the people's current needs:

> It is all very sad; but there can be only one remedy – to accept the
> conditions and to make music first in spite of them, and afterwards
> on the strength of them. Music which is not built upon the imme-
> diate instincts and needs of the people is no music at all; [...]. It is

---

[178] See ibid. 130.
[179] Ibid. 123.
[180] Ibid. 125.

as far from the truth to say that 'modes' and 'times' must remain in their primitive condition as to say that poetry of the twentieth century must be in Chaucer's English or a Bengali love-song in Vedic Sanskrit.[181]

Just a few sentences later, however, he seems to contradict his own words when he demands that Indian musicians should abandon all European instruments and musical tools already in use among them. This statement leads him into the field of music and nationalism, a topic already mentioned at the beginning of the book in the context of differences between national music cultures in Europe. Concerning India he writes:

> If the rulers of native states realized what a death-blow they were dealing at their own art by supporting or even allowing a brass band, if the clerk in a government office understood the indignity he was putting on a song by buying the gramophone which grinds it out to him after his day's labour, if the Mohammedan 'star' singer knew that the harmonium with which he accompanies himself was ruining his chief asset, his musical ear, and if the girl who learns the pianoforte could see that all the progress she made was sure a step towards her own denationalization as if she crossed the black water and never returned – they would pause before they laid such sacrilegious hands on Saraswatī.[182]

Like the British Orientalists before him, Fox Strangways takes the role of a savior of Indian music trying to lead Indian artists back to their pure – but not necessarily Sanskrit – origins. He thereby strongly sides with the Indian people, propagating a stereotyped yet sympathetic image of its arts, culture and society in the west. His enthusiasm is also evident in a poem written by him praising Uday Shankar.[183]

---

[181] Ibid. 15.
[182] Ibid. 16.
[183] See Khokar, *His Dance, His Life* 91.

In the history of British ethnomusicology Fox Strangways's study surely has to be acknowledged for its step away from "aesthetically delimiting concepts of the linguistic universalism of music in favor of a more culturally individuated methodology."[184] His book, however, builds once again on British Orientalist ideas and musicological topics, while still showing, as Anthony Seeger describes it, a striking "admiration of Indian music," an admiration obviously in part linked to his understanding of a shared Indo-European origin.

1.3.4 A.K. Coomaraswamy: "Indian Music"

Only a few years after Fox Strangways's *The Music of Hindostan*, Ananda K. Coomaraswamy first published his English language compilation of essays entitled *The Dance of Shiva* (1918). The book appears to be an introduction for Western audiences into various areas of Indian arts and culture. In the field of the arts it contains articles on dance and on sculpture as well as an essay entitled "Indian Music." In choosing this title, Coomaraswamy, who in *The Dance of Shiva* also discusses Buddhist art, steps away from the close frame of Hindu arts and sources and the Hindu nationalist tradition connected with it. Due to his major role in the international propagation of a distinctly "Indian" image of Indian arts, a short biography will be included here.

Ananda Kentish Coomaraswamy (1877-1947) was born in Colombo, Ceylon as son of a Sinhalese father, Sir Mutu Coomaraswamy, and a British mother, the former Elizabeth Clay Beeby.[185] His father, who died before his son was two years old, had been a translator of Pāli Buddhist texts and Tamil drama and, in 1861, became a member of the Legislative Council as representative of the Tamil-speaking people of Ceylon. During his extensive stays in Europe he was welcomed and much appreciated by the English higher society and became the first Asian who was accredited for the practice of law in Great Britain. After his father's death in 1879 Ananda grew up in England until he returned to Ceylon in his mid-twenties, in 1903 or 1904, where he stayed until 1907. Originally trained as a geologist, he came into contact with the last phase

---

[184] Zon 198.
[185] See Lipsey 7ff.

of the Arts and Crafts movement in Britain, which flourished under the influence of the ideas of figures such as William Morris and later, at the beginning of the 20th century, by those of the architect Charles Robert Ashbee.[186] Together with John Ruskin, William Morris (1834-1896) was one of the major critics of Victorian industrialism in the 19th century. Along with Ruskin, Morris thought that the Industrial Revolution had led to social alienation. Both regarded the Middle Ages – their architecture, society, and life – as a lost ideal. Morris furthermore saw in India, especially in Indian village life, an example of an ideal anti-materialist society and accepted it as a "viable alternative to the evils of industrialism."[187] In 1908, Ananda K. Coomaraswamy published his first book, *Medieval Sinhalese Art*, with the Morris's Kelmscott Press (which had been reopened with his help). In this text he described the struggle of the traditional crafts in Ceylon and condemned the British government's endeavor to industrialize the region and dismiss its indigenous arts and architecture.[188]

In 1916 Coomaraswamy moved to America and became curator of the Indian section at the Boston Museum of Fine Arts. But although he spent almost all his life in Britain or the United States, Coomaraswamy enters the discussion on Indian music – like his predecessor Tagore before – as an Indian giving his Western readers more authentic insight into Indian arts. His effort apparently proved fruitful as his book was in fact very well received, especially among art connoisseurs.[189] Two of his articles, one of them on dance, would even reach a wider public as they were published in the American society magazine *Vanity Fair*.[190] Up un-

---

[186] See Ibid. 44. See also Guha-Thakurta, *The Making of a New 'Indian' Art* 160 (see Introduction, footnote 6).

[187] Partha Mitter, *Much Maligned Monsters. History of European Reactions to Indian Art*, Oxford: Clarendon Press 1977: 249.

[188] See ibid. 278 and Lipsey 44ff.

[189] Roger Lipsey mentions that already between 1908 and 1910 Coomaraswamy "established himself as a young but considerable authority on Indian art." Lipsey 53.

[190] See Ananda Kentish Coomaraswamy, "The Cave Paintings of Ajanta," *Vanity Fair* (New York), Septermber 1916: 67 and "Oriental Dances in America. And a Word or Two in Explanation of the Nautch," *Vanity Fair* (New York), May 1917: 61. For a detailed examination of Coomaraswamy's article on Oriental dance see Chapter 4.3.2.

til the present his writings remain sources of reference for those interested in Indian art, aesthetics and culture.

As his predecessors Tagore and the British Orientalists had done before, Coomaraswamy starts out his article by stressing the ancient origin of Indian music and refers to the continuous tradition which still links current Indian music practice to its ancient past:

> Music has been a cultivated art in India for at least three thousand years. [...] The art music of the present day is a direct descendant of these ancient schools, whose traditions have been handed down with comment and expansion in the guilds of the hereditary musicians. [...], the musical themes communicated orally from master to disciple are essentially ancient. As in other arts and in life, so here also India presents to us the wonderful spectacle of the still surviving consciousness of the ancient world, with a range of emotional experience rarely accessible to those who are preoccupied with the activities of over-production, and intimidated by the economic insecurity of a social order based on competition.[191]

Strongly influenced by the culture critic of the British Arts and Crafts movement, the introduction into Indian music here is combined with a profound criticism of Western modernity. According to Coomaraswamy, Indian music not only offers a direct link to antiquity, but it still appeals to Europeans and Americans struggling with the conditions of modern life and searching for their origins at the beginning of the 20th century. Indian music apparently also gives access to a depth of feeling people in modernity have lost due to the rules of economic production and the concomitant life conditions in the West. But Coomaraswamy, like Tagore before, can't free himself from a comparison with the West and further writes: "The art music of India [...] corresponds to all that is most classical in the European tradition."[192] He here refers to aristocratic chamber music and accordingly links current Indian music to the Western classical

---

[191] Ananda K. Coomaraswamy, "Indian Music," in: *The Dance of Shiva. Fourteen Indian Essays*, Munshiram Manoharlal Publishers: New Delhi 1982: 102-114; here 102.
[192] Ibid. 103.

past. Indian music is further elevated as an art which, in contrast to its Western counterpart, doesn't allow dilettantism. Thus the artist does not depend on public concerts and "his ability and will to amuse the crowd: [...] The civilizations of Asia do not afford to the inefficient amateur those opportunities of self-expression which are so highly appreciated in Europe and America."[193] Indian music instead relies on pure expert artists and a "model audience" familiar with its technique and aesthetics.[194] The world of Indian music is presented as a closed circle not easily accessible for outsiders.

Following this path, Coomaraswamy, who, as a matter of fact, in his later writings focuses on theoretical aspects of Indian art, stresses musical practice as the only way to really gain insight and thereby further obscures it for his readers. In order for a foreigner to enter into it, he or she has to spiritually and culturally submit him- or herself totally to the Indian teacher and to Indian life:

> Since Indian music is not written, and cannot be learnt from books, except in theory, it will be understood that the only way for a foreigner to learn it must be to establish between himself and his Indian teachers that special relationship of disciple and master which belongs to Indian education in all its phases: he must enter into the inner spirit and must adopt many of the outer conventions of Indian life, and his study must continue until he can improvise the songs under Indian conditions and to the satisfaction of Indian professional listeners. He must possess not only the imagination of an artist, but also a vivid memory and an ear sensitive to microtonal inflections.[195]

Coomaraswamy here clearly indicates that Indian music has its own parameters and standards to be accepted by non-Indians, or, even more: it is hardly accessible or understandable for non-Indians.

---

[193] Ibid.
[194] Ibid.
[195] Ibid. 104.

He then shortly hints at the common opposition between harmony and melody, one topic in the discussion of Indian music having been raised since early on by the British Orientalists. He here shows a slight criticism of the Western system when describing the tempered system as a "compromise" leading to the situation that "the piano is out of tune by hypothesis."[196] Opposing common Western descriptions of the development of harmony as an advancement of purely melodic music, he stresses the advantages of the latter: "A purely melodic art, however, may be no less intensely cultivated, and retains the advantages of pure intonation and modal colouring."[197] His preference for Indian music as one example of a "purely melodic art" is even more directly expressed at a later part of the article. In this part, Coomaraswamy describes modern European music as guided mainly by chords and harmony, which leads to the falsification of the traditional folk-tunes. He writes: "under the conditions of European art, melody no longer exists in its own right, and music is a compromise between melodic freedom and harmonic necessity."[198] He then activates the romantically-inspired views on Indian arts still existent in Fox Strangways's monograph and he pictures how the enjoyment of Indian music for a modern European opens up a path back to its origin, to its purer form, and he also demands a recovery of the senses that have become overstrained under modern conditions:

> To hear the music of India as Indians hear it one must recover the sense of a pure intonation and must forget all implied harmonies. It is just like the effort which we have to make when for the first time, after being accustomed to modern art, we attempt to read the language of early Italian or Chinese painting, where there is expressed with equal economy of means all that intensity of experience which nowadays we are accustomed to understand only through a more involved technique.[199]

---

[196] Ibid.
[197] Ibid.
[198] Ibid. 107.
[199] Ibid.

One might conclude from this that Indian music demands of or allows Western audiences to return to their origins of natural perception, a step which is at the same time obscured as rather impossible. Indian music, in the end, is ranked above Western art – at least above modern western art forms – as we can see in Coomaraswamy's remarks on the concept of *rāga*. He here enters a common field of discussion, especially when he, once again, compares the *rāgas* to the ancient Greek or ecclesiastical modes. He however describes the Indian *rāga* as being "more particularized" due to the fact that it has "certain characteristic progressions, and a chief note to which the singer constantly returns."[200] Accordingly, he uses a comparison common since the British Orientalists as a starting point to elevate the Indian system.

Coomaraswamy ends his essay by stressing the divine character of Indian music. This leads him to his observation that Indian music is first of all impersonal and all-human, an aspect which, in his later writings, becomes a main aspect of his art theory. Coomaraswamy writes: "Indian music is essentially impersonal: it reflects an emotion and an experience which are deeper and wider and older than the emotion or wisdom of any single individual. [...] It is in the deepest sense of the words all-human."[201] He further stresses how the Hindu gods speak through the artists transforming Indian musical practice into "an imitation of the music in heaven:"

> [I]t is then Sarasvati, the goddess of speech and learning, or Narada, whose mission it is to disseminate occult knowledge in the sound of the strings of his vina, or Krishna, whose flute is forever calling us to leave the duties of the world and follow Him – it is these, rather than any human individual, who speak through the singer's voice, and are seen in the movements of the dancer. Or we may say that this is an imitation of the music in heaven.[202]

---

[200] Ibid 105.
[201] Ibid. 111.
[202] Ibid.

Indian music, according to Coomaraswamy, offers a spiritual insight exceeding the narrow personal level generally served by western modern art. It is accordingly presented as a possible solution for western artists striving to surpass modern egoism. His final sentence then even opens up the perspective of a link between all humanity through a common spiritual basis of art when he writes: "the peace of the Abyss which underlies all art is one and the same, whether we find it in Europe or in Asia."[203] Following Tapati Guha-Thakurta, it is his focus on the spiritual in Indian arts which slightly differentiates him from his British predecessors and identifies him with a wave of Orientalist research and writing subsumed under the keyword "New Orientalism."[204] Although Coomaraswamy's occupation with the spiritual will be discussed in more detail at a later point, his important role in stressing the close bond between Indian music and arts and the metaphysical tradition for Western readers in the 20th century should be noted here.[205]

As did the essay of his predecessor Tagore, Coomaraswamy's presentation of Indian music also takes up threads of discussion established in the writings of the British Orientalists. The framework of the Orientalist debate on Indian music with its focus on antiquity, an existent close bond with nature and Indian arts' role in the search for origins is updated and brought to a new level once again. Coomaraswamy hereby doesn't restrict himself solely to the Hindu tradition. Building on Western cultural criticism he elevates Indian arts including music as a possibility to flee modern limitations and return to a supposedly more natural and holistic origin of art. Whereas Tagore already stated the impossibility to translate Indian concepts into foreign languages, Coomaraswamy more decidedly expresses its inaccessibility for, or even indescribability to, outsiders or non-Indians.

Although – or maybe because – Shankar's performances were always accompanied by detailed program texts that give explanations of the music and the dancing, reviews give the impression that for Shankar's audiences Indian music at least partly preserved its aura of inaccessibility due to its ancient, spiritual and therefore exotic character.

---

[203] Ibid. 114.
[204] Guha-Thakurta, *The Making of a New 'Indian' Art* 8.
[205] See Chapter 4.

1.4 "Then Out Came the Musical Instruments." The Presentation of Music in Uday Shankar's Performances

Uday Shankar's performances were, as mentioned before, always accompanied by detailed program notes which included information on the music played as well as essays on Indian music and dance in general. One example can be found in an American *Playbill*-edition from a tour of the company, probably in 1937/38, which contains an article by Vera Milanova named "The Secret of Hindu Music." The title not only perpetuates the inaccessible, inexplicable character of Indian music, but also, through the choice of "Hindu music" instead of "Indian music," coordinates with the group's name as *Uday Shan-Kar and his Hindu Ballet* and directly links its members and the performance with religious aspects. The article starts with information on the concepts of *rāga* and *tāla* and, from there on, in the context of the discussion on rhythm, comes to the then common link between Indian and ancient Greek music as described since the British Orientalists:

> Students of Indian music say that musical time in India is a development from the meters of poetry. I know that in the time of the Greeks there was the same relation between poetry and music. Only today it is not so obvious in our western music. But in India, up to the nineteenth century, there was practically no prose; everything was learned through the medium of verse chanted to regular rules, so that the sense of duration and rhythm – which is the central idea in Indian time - was very high developed.[206]

Through the reference to ancient Greece and the shared close connection between music and poetry, Indian music's antiquity and its position in the realm of classical arts is once again established and linked with Uday Shankar's performances.

---

[206] Vera Milanova, "The Secret of Hindu Music," reprint from *The New York Times*, in: "S.Hurok Presents Uday Shan-Kar and his Hindu Ballet," in: *Playbill* (New York), [season 1937/38a]: n.p.; Dartington Hall Trust Archive.

Similarly, an article entitled "Hindu Music" by Annabel Learned, which is printed in another *Playbill*-edition from the same season in the United States, not only repeats the religious reference, but also claims Indian music's continuous tradition since antiquity when the Indian *rāgas* are described as "melodic modes, preserved and deepened by musicians who have added to their musical truth from century to century and passed them on."[207] Learned, who in her article refers to Coomaraswamy's writings, argues the music's classicism by comparing raga with the ancient Greek modes and draws a parallel between religious Hindu vocal music and Gregorian chant:

> The old Hindu chant, of the type used for the Vedic hymns, is very like our plain-song or Gregorian; even the intervals may be the same. A resonant syllable 'OM' is sometimes heard, which is the sacred syllable for the Hindu Trinity: for Sound that is light, and 'the sum of all language' or being.[208]

Comments such as these in the programs indicate that the group's musical performance derives directly from ancient times as part of a continuous tradition of religious Hindu music in India. The commonly drawn parallel between ancient Greek music, or here Gregorian chant, and Indian music, helps to claim the high artistic as well as spiritual status of the performance. Indian music, as well as the dance, is once again identified with a bygone European artistic or (one might say) religious past and thus find their place in the Western performance world. Art, life and religion are presented as naturally linked with each other. One should further note here the way Solomon Hurok, the company's famous experienced American impresario, prepared the group's arrival for their first tour in the United States in 1932. He here obviously meant to serve images of Indian splendor in order to arouse Western audiences' curiosity for the exotic:

---

[207] Annabel Learned, "Hindu Music," in: "S.Hurok Presents Uday Shan-Kar and His Hindu Ballet," in: *Playbill* (New York), [season 1937/38b]: n.p.; Dartington Hall Trust Archive.
[208] Ibid.

73

We were all dressed up like maharajahs, in very formal attire with sherwanis and turbans, and before we docked the newspaper photographers came with the pilot boat to take our pictures. That was so exciting! It was the idea of Solomon Hurok that we should all be dressed like that. He was our impresario, and the greatest of all time – like a super showman.[209]

Such links with Indian splendor can also be found in another, supposedly biographical article on Uday Shankar printed in another *Playbill* of the 1930s. Under the title "Bronze God," Basanta Koomar Roy describes how Shankar was named after Udaypur, the city of his birth, where his father worked as the Private Secretary of the Maharaja of Jhalawar. He then elaborates on Shankar's early dedication to music and dance as further increased through the artistic life at the royal court:

It so happened that from his earliest childhood Master Uday showed signs of artistic proclivity and precocity. [...] He was exceedingly fond of music; and nothing gave this child of artistic Udaypur more happiness than to dance in ecstasy to the tune of music played by master musicians at his home. The welcome news of the artistic precocity of Master Uday gradually reached the royal ears of the Maharaja; and the royal lover of the arts began to take keen interest in the artistic development of the child of his dear friend and favorite companion. Early in his life Uday learnt to play on different Hindu musical instruments; and took special interest in the dance art of the nautch girls as also in the folk and religious dances of India. He studied the steps of dancing from the great masters of dancing at the Royal court of Jhalawar, and also from the court musicians and dancers of other princes and noblemen of India wherever he went.[210]

---

[209] Shankar, *Raga Mala* 50.
[210] Basanta Koomar Roy, "Bronze God," in: "S.Hurok Presents Uday Shan-Kar and his Hindu Ballet," [season 1937/38a]: n.p.

The company's artistic performance is thus perceived before the background of Shankar's upbringing in the royal court and stresses the artist's total dedication to an original, authentic Indian or explicitly Hindu art of highest esteem.[211]

The authentic and exotic character of the performance was further stressed by placing the musicians, who also wore costumes, with their instruments on stage. Joan L. Erdman affirms this for the early French presentations:

> For Paris, the musicians were seated along the back of the stage in costume so that the players and their instruments became integral to the dance scene and curiosities for the audience. This addition of live musicians in full view added to the exoticism of the performance, which was important in Paris of the 1930s.[212]

Shankar's approach thereby differed fundamentally from that of western Orientalized ballets or operas of his time which were built on elaborate stage designs. In exhibiting a rather pure or minimalistic stage setting, the group stressed the authenticity of its Indian members.

Besides detailed costumes including a lot of color and ornamentation, it was especially – as noted before in the reviews – the range of exotic instruments which visually impressed audiences and critics. In addition to more common classical instruments such as the *vīnā*, *sitar*, or *tablā*, Uday Shankar and Alice Boner had brought from India a variety of folk instruments which were also presented on stage and included in the musical setting of the show. Ravi Shankar, who remembers the group's early years in Paris, mentions how exceptional the range of instruments was:

> Then out came the musical instruments. There were a hundred and fifty varieties, mostly folk ones, but we also had classical instru-

---

[211] According to his biographer Mohan Khokar, Uday Shankar indeed grew up close to the court of the Maharaja Rana Bhawani Singh in Jhalawar. His father Shyam Shankar was Private Secretary to the Maharaja and, in 1922, became Prime Minister of Jhalawar. See Khokar, *His Dance, His Life* 14ff.
[212] Erdman, "Towards Authenticity" 86.

ments: the veena, sitar, sarod, sarangi, sarinda, flutes, shahnai, classical and folk drums, with aboriginal drums from the far North to the far South. Even though I was Indian myself, I had never seen such materials. Not even in a museum have I ever seen such a collection.[213]

The variety of instruments obviously added to the whole visual outlook of the show. Ravi Shankar further describes how Uday advised the musicians to employ the instruments in order to create musical effects supporting the dance presentations:

Uday invented an entire new dimension in both concept and sound by using all sorts of classical, folk, and tribal drums, cymbals, gongs, and little finger cymbals like castanets made of metal or wood, and by devising new ways to play the traditional instruments – playing the *tamboura* with two sticks, for instance. In the beginning, many of us did feel skeptical about Uday's music, but he would sit with us all, giving his suggestions and teaching us and patiently explain the musical effects he was trying to create, making the sound with his voice that he wanted each instrument to produce. A *B-O-O-M* here, a *ktink* there, and a *b-r-r-r-R-R-O-O-O-O-M* on another instrument.[214]

He next stresses how his brother only allowed Indian instruments in his performances and kept away from Western ones, but he notes how Uday was stretching the definition of Indian to other south Asian countries as well:

The aspect of Uday's approach that left the strongest imprint on my mind, even to the present, was his adamant refusal to use even a single Western instrument in his music; he very stringently adhered to his practice of using only those instruments that are traditionally found on the Indian subcontinent. That is, he did not feel it was out

---

[213] Shankar, *Raga Mala* 37.
[214] Shankar, *My Music, My Life* 65 (see Introduction, footnote 5).

of keeping with his principles to use instruments from Java, Bali, or Burma, because the histories of these countries were strongly influenced by the old Hindu culture, and much of their dance and music traditions had been brought in from India in ancient times.[215]

The company's marketing and self-presentation accordingly built on common ideas of Indian music, such as its antiquity comparable to the music of ancient Greece as well as its spiritual character, which had been developed and perpetuated by the British Orientalists. It additionally propagated images of an exotic and splendid Indian artistic past still present in the performance of the company. All these images were linked to the authenticity of Indian music and arts, the presentation's genuine Indianness, which accounted for its novelty and uniqueness.

In one of his last interviews Uday Shankar himself stresses the topic of authenticity and his own precursory role in bringing Indian classical and folk instruments, especially drums, on stage for the first time:

> Of course, I have always used only Indian instruments. Even the violin and harmonium I have not allowed. I have collected hundreds of instruments from all over India. I have eighty kinds of drums alone. Believe me, before I started, no one even touched many of these instruments. I was the first person to bring the use of measured sound for dances on the stage.[216]

---

[215] Ibid.
[216] Khokar, *His Dance, His Life* 168.

2. The Unity of the Arts

2.1 Towards a Re-Unification of the Arts: Uday Shankar's Indian Dances in Germany

When Uday Shankar and his company started their first German tour in the autumn of 1931, the German daily press reacted immediately with positive reviews. News about the enthusiastic reception of the group in other European countries must have already reached the country, as an announcement of their first German-wide performance in Hamburg in the *Hamburger Fremdenblatt* on September 26th, 1931 suggests: "The Indian Ballet Uday Shan-Kar with original Indian Orchestra, received everywhere with rapturous applause, dances this Tuesday, September 29 at the invitation of the Hamburger Bühne in the grand hall of the Curiohaus."[1] As reviews of the tour exemplify, the reception in Germany indeed exceeded that of elsewhere in Europe. This is also confirmed by Ravi Shankar, Uday Shankar's youngest brother, an early member of the troupe and now an internationally well-known sitar player. He named Germany as one of the countries in which the company was especially well-received by audiences: "At that time, in the early Thirties, our troupe had the warmest receptions and greatest successes in two countries – Germany and, most of all, in the United States."[2]

Not only due to the appearance of the group under its original French name *La Compagnie d'Uday Shan-Kar Hindoue Danses et la Musique* – one German translation was "Indische Hindu-Tanzgruppe Uday Shankar und Simkie mit dem Hindu-Orchester" (Hindu dance-troupe Uday Shankar and Simkie with Hindu orchestra) – reviews of Shankar's early performances focused very much on the close link between music and dance exhibited in the company's performances.[3] This had already been stressed by Georges Mussy in *Le Figaro* in a review following the company's initial performance in Paris. In it, he describes the company's performances as "an art in which dance and

---

[1] "Zum Gastspiel des Indischen Balletts" 3 (see Chap.1, footnote 24).
[2] Shankar, *My Music, My Life* 69 (see Introduction, footnote 5).
[3] See program announcement "Württ. Landestheater. Großes Haus" 4 (see Chap.1, footnote 5).

music are also intimately linked."[4] Soon after, in the course of Shankar's first German tour, which led the company between September 1931 and April 1932 through cities such as Hamburg, Stuttgart, Nurnberg, and Berlin, the theme is also repeated by German reviewers.[5] Directly succeeding the group's first German performance in Hamburg, a critic of the *Hamburger Nachrichten* accordingly mentions Shankar's work with: "means of sound and movement, both inseparably linked with each other and in their root one."[6] One day later a reviewer in the *Hamburger Anzeiger* states: "The dances are all indispensably bound to the corresponding music, perhaps the music was even there first."[7] Similarly, another critic praises the "complete fusing of gesture with music" as a wonder.[8]

Yet it was not only the close link between dance and music that fascinated the critics, but also the synthesis of these art forms in their combination with a mythological content. Especially in the German reviews, this became closely identified with the concept of the *Gesamtkunstwerk* or "total work of art" having its roots in Romanticism and further developed by Richard Wagner in his essay "The Art-work of the Future."[9] The dance-drama *Tandava Nrittya* in particular was received in this context, and thus an early German reviewer commented on the presentation as follows:

> The conclusion of the evening built the performance of an archaic dance-drama. That is, with thunder and lightning, with lyric and primeval epic, a representation of the fight between Shiva and the elephant demon Gajasut who threatens the earth. A myth of colos-

---

[4] Mussy n.p. (see Chap.1, footnote 9).

[5] In March and April 1932 Uday Shankar and his company also visited Italy and Czechoslovakia. See "Press Comments," *Roopa-Lekha* (New Delhi), vol.4 no.13, 1934: 26-34.

[6] Mk. n.p. (see Chap.1, footnote 74).

[7] Sdt. n.p. (see Chap.1, footnote 25).

[8] Wilhelm Tidemann, "Zu den Hindu-Tänzen," *Der Kreis. Zeitschrift für künstlerische Kultur* (Hamburg), vol.9 no.10, October 1932: 595-598; here 597.

[9] The translation "total work of art" for German "Gesamtkunstwerk" is taken from Roger Copeland & Marshall Cohen, "III: Dance and the Other Arts," in: R. Copeland & M. Cohen (eds.), *What Is Dance? Readings in Theory and Criticism*, New York: Oxford University Press 1983: 185-191; here 185.

sal degree brought into the cultic form of dance and music. Pre-determined forms of movement, so called "mudras," replace the word; a barely receivable fullness of sound combinations and delightful garment splendor creates the atmosphere of a total work of art; in foreign classical forms the strange vision of ancient religious events materializes.[10]

A look at earlier French reviews shows that already during Uday Shankar's performances in Paris, *Tandava Nrittya*, the final item of the show, had captured the attention of audience and critic alike and was praised and described at length. Termed an "antique ballet," it became a main point of reference for reviewers.[11] In their two-week season in Paris at the Théâtre des Arts from June 4th to June 18th, 1931 the company appeared in a combined program with a presentation of Oscar Wilde's *Salome*. The announcements mention only the "dance drama of archaic character" among all the other items in the program.[12] In Germany a reviewer praised the dance-drama above everything of its genre seen before:

> Tandava Nrittya is the name of an archaic dance-drama, and never has one lived to see a dance drama of such an accomplished and ravishing style in Germany — never such a splendor of dance thoughts, such final completion of idea, such intellectual charm.[13]

Tandava Nrittya told the mythological story of Shiva's fight with the elephant-demon Gajasura in which the god saved Parvati, who, without him knowing, is his incarnated dead wife Sati. Uday Shankar himself danced the part of Shiva while Simkie appeared in the role of Parvati. The part of Gajasura was at first enacted by Uday Shankar's brother Debendra, and

---

[10] Sdt. n.p.

[11] Mussy n.p.

[12] In this case, the Wilde production entailed Georges and Ludmilla Pitoëff and their company; "Spectacles," *L'Oeuvre* (Paris), June 4, 1931: 6.

[13] "Hindu-Tänze," *Berliner Tageblatt und Handels-Zeitung* (Berlin), April 20, 1932, evening edition: n.p.

then at the end of the 1930s by Madhavan.[14] The performance included another female part named Joya, which in the beginning was danced by Kanaklata. From the end of the 1930s Zohra Mumtaz, and then later Zohra Segal, took over this part. The dance-drama presented the spectator with a combination of dance, partly perceived as pantomime, music, a mythological story, and elaborate costumes. It was thus perceived as an example of a unifying approach to the arts and thereby also found its position in the context of modern dance and art at the beginning of the 20th century.

In "Primitivism, Modernism, and Dance Theory," Marshall Cohen states that the theory of modern art mainly concerns itself with two contrasting ideals which can also be referred to the field of dance: the concept of the purity of the medium versus a rather holistic view of the unity of the arts as exemplified by Richard Wagner's concept of the "total work of art."[15] The purist branch of modern aesthetics is regarded as deriving from Gotthold Ephraim Lessing's theoretical treatise *Laocoön: An Essay on the Limits of Painting and Poetry* (1766). In this work, the poet reflected on an ancient Greek sculpture showing the death of Laocoön and his sons, which had been described by Johann Joachim Winckelmann in his treatise *Reflections on the imitation of Greek works in painting and sculpture* (1755).[16] Lessing took this as a starting point to elaborate on the initial inherent differences between poetry and painting due to their essential nature – which he regarded, in the case of poetry, to be temporal whereas he classified painting as a spatial art. Criticizing

---

[14] See D., "Die Hindu-Tanzgruppe im Landestheater. Uday Shan-Kar und Simkie mit einem Hindu-Orchester," *Stuttgarter Neues Tageblatt* (Stuttgart), morning edition, November 21, 1931: 2 and also program "S.Hurok Presents Uday Shan-Kar with Simkie, Kanak-Lata, Debendra, Robindra," in: *S.Hurok Announces: International Dance Festival*, New York Theatre, December 25, 1932 to January 8, 1933: 4-5; Dartington Hall Trust Archive; See "S.Hurok Presents Uday Shan-Kar and his Hindu Ballet" [season1937/38a]: n.p. (see Chap.1, footnote 206) and program "Uday Shankar and His Hindu Ballet and Musicians," Barn Theatre, Dartington Hall, Totnes, Devon, November 15, 1937: n.p.; Dartington Hall Trust Archive.
[15] Marshall Cohen, "Primitivism, Modernism, and Dance Theory," in: Copeland & Cohen 161-187; here 161.
[16] See Norbert Schneider, *Geschichte der Ästhetik von der Aufklärung bis zur Moderne*, Stuttgart: Reclam 2005[4]: 34ff.

painters who based their works on allegorical subjects in order to depict a story, Lessing's purist doctrine can be identified with the idea that "artists must work within the constraints of their own media and not trespass upon the domain of the other arts."[17] At the beginning of the 20th century, however, many artists and dancers followed a somewhat opposing trend towards the reunification of the arts in order to work against the feelings of fragmentation or isolation accompanying modern culture with its growing individuality, urbanity, technical development and consumer capitalism. Their vision was often linked to Wagner's concept of the united work of art which had its roots in German Romanticism.

Following Wolfgang Storch, efforts to establish a total work of art in the German context had from the outset been affiliated with the intention to renew society by way of the arts. As a German answer to the French Revolution, Romantic writers such as Novalis, Hölderlin or the Schlegel brothers looked back at Greek tragedy and its close bind with mythology as a prototype for the transformation of their own present society.[18] Whereas A.W. Schlegel suggested that, in parallel to Greek tragedy's basis on Homer, a new artwork should concentrate on the *Nibelungenlied* (*The Song of the Nibelungs*) as German national myth, his brother Friedrich Schlegel evolved his concept of a progressive universal poetry ("progressive Universalpoesie"). Encompassing all arts and joined with philosophy, poetry was meant to transform all life into a poetic condition. Poets were further urged to study the structures of nature in order to find inspiration for their work.[19] Novalis declared that in poetry the individual could unite with the totality of the universe. In his conception poetry opened up the field for the other arts to enter in order that they all might work together towards one aim: the elevation of humanity above itself.[20]

Around 1800 Friedrich W.J. Schelling proclaimed a re-unification of the arts as ideally exemplified in the Greek drama, which he claimed

---

[17] Roger Copeland, "The Dance Medium," in: Copeland & Cohen 103-111; here 106.
[18] See Wolfgang Storch, "Gesamtkunstwerk," in: K. Barck et al. (eds.), *Ästhetische Grundbegriffe*, vol.2, Stuttgart & Weimar: Metzler 2001: 730-791; here 731.
[19] See ibid. 742ff.
[20] See ibid. 744.

was absent in the present except for its flawed representation in the opera. In his *Philosophy of Art* (1802-03) he wrote:

> I will remark only that the most perfect composition of all the arts, the unification of poesy and music through song, of poesy and painting through dance, both in turn synthesized together, is the most complex theater manifestation, such as was the drama of antiquity. Only a caricature has remained for us: the opera, which in a higher and nobler style both from the side of poesy as well as from that of the other competing arts, might sooner guide as back to the performance of that ancient drama combined with music and song.[21]

Frustrated by the lack of an open, public drama unifying the people of his time through the arts, Schelling detected potential for an inner drama in worship encompassing music, chant, and dance. The vision of a united work of art was thereby associated with the sphere of religion:

> Music, song, dance, as well as all the various types of drama, live only in public life, and form an alliance in such life. Wherever public life disappears, instead of that real, external drama in which, in all its forms, an entire people participates as a political or moral totality, only an inward, ideal drama can unite the people. This ideal drama is the worship service, the only kind of truly public action that has remained for the contemporary age, and even so only in an extremely diminished and reduced form.[22]

This comment of Schelling would later be interpreted by Wagner as an announcement of a united artwork inspired by ancient drama. And at the same time in this comment the foundation of the political and religious moment of the concept was laid.

---

[21] Friedrich W.J. Schelling, *The Philosophy of Art*, ed. and trans. with an introduction by Douglas W. Stott, Minneapolis: University of Minnesota Press 1989: 280.
[22] Ibid.

2.2 Reviving Ancient Greek Tragedy: Wagner, Nietzsche, and the Modern Dance Scene

2.2.1 Richard Wagner's Concept of the United Artwork

Richard Wagner wrote his essay "The Art-Work of the Future" after the breakdown of the revolution of 1848/49 while in exile in Zurich.[23] Referring – such as Schelling and others before him had done – to ancient Greek tragedy, he was seeking a way for the transformation or regeneration of society which he saw to be guided by "the errors, perversities, and unnatural distortions of our modern life."[24] Wagner's strong criticism of modernity also contains a political aspect as he starts off by attacking humanity's current "mere existence, dictated by the maxims of this or that Religion, Nationality, or State."[25] Aiming at the abundance of negative symptoms of modern life, such as fashion, – "the maddest, most unheard of tyranny that has ever issued from man's perversity" or the machine – "the cold and heartless ally of luxury-craving men," he urges man to find orientation once again in nature as a path to free oneself from these external, unnecessary and evil influences of modern life.[26] He writes:

> Man will never be that which he can and should be, until his Life is a true mirror of Nature, a conscious following of the only real Necessity, the *inner natural necessity*, and is no longer held in subjugation to an *outer* artificial counterfeit, – which is thus no necessary, but an *arbitrary* power.[27]

---

[23] See Storch 731; 752ff.
[24] Richard Wagner, "The Art-Work of the Future," in: *The Art-Work of the Future and Other Works*, transl. by William Ashton Ellis, Lincoln & London: University of Nebraska Press 1993:69-213; here 71; reprint from *Richard Wagner's Prose Works*, vol.1, London: Kegan Paul, Trench, Trübner & Co. 1895.
[25] Ibid.
[26] Ibid. 84; 85.
[27] Ibid. 71.

This freed "real Man" is then brought into parallel with "real Art," an art whose "embodiments need be subject only to the laws of Nature, and not to the despotic whims of Mode" and, at the same time, an art that "can only overcome her dependence upon Life through her oneness with the life of free and genuine Men."[28] As the plural already indicates, the real Man is not supposed to oppose modernity on his own, but to build up a community of others as a "vital force" which is the folk (*das Volk*) united by "a common and collective need" which is "the only true Need."[29] It is then the work of art that encompasses the possibilities for the unity of all people as "the brother-kiss that seals this bond, will be the *mutual Art-work of the Future* [...]; for in this Art-work we shall all be *one*, – heralds and supporters of Necessity, knowers of the unconscious, willers of the unwilful, betokeners of Nature, – *blissful men*."[30] This future artwork which will represent all humanity must then contain all different kinds of arts in one:

> The great United Art-work, which must gather up each branch of art to use it as a mean, and in some sense to undo it for the common aim of *all*, for the unconditioned, absolute portrayal of perfect human nature, – this great United Art-work he [the artist] cannot picture as depending on the arbitrary purpose of some human unit, but can only conceive it as the instinctive and associate product of the Manhood of the Future. The instinct that recognises itself as one that can only be satisfied in fellowship, abandons modern fellowship – that conglomerate of self-seeking caprice – and turns to find its satisfaction in solitary fellowship with itself and with the manhood of the Future, – so well as the lonely unit can.[31]

It is the "art of the *Hellenes*," "the great *Folk* itself," on which Wagner is basing his artwork of the future: "let us look far hence to glorious

---

28 Ibid. 71; 72.
29 Ibid. 75.
30 Ibid. 77.
31 Ibid. 88.

Grecian Art, and gather from its inner understanding the outlines for the Art-work of the Future!"[32] However, Wagner regards ancient Greek *musikē* only as a basis from which to develop his current concept. This can be seen by the fact that he describes Hellenic art as being not universal, not human enough. He thereupon develops his idea of a "Religion of the Future," the "Religion of Universal Manhood:"

> Thus have we then to turn *Hellenic* art to *Human* art; to loose from it the stipulations by which it was but an *Hellenic* and not a *Universal* art. [...] – this specific garb of the *Hellenic Religion*, we have to stretch it out until it folds embrace the Religion of the Future, the Religion of *Universal Manhood*, and thus to gain already a presage of the Art-work of the Future. But this bond of union, this *Religion of the Future*, we wretched ones shall never clasp the while we still are *lonely units*, howe'er so many be our numbers who feel the spur towards the Art-work of the Future. The Art-work is the living presentation of Religion; – but religions spring not from the artist's brain; their only origin is from the *Folk*.[33]

George S. Williamson describes how Wagner hereby strongly built on the philosophy of Ludwig Feuerbach. In *The Essence of Christianity* (1841), Feuerbach profoundly criticized Christianity and therein detected the root of modern society's egoism.[34] Making the demand that "any divine entity [...] be abandoned and its predicates transferred back to humanity as a whole," Feuerbach lay the ground for Wagner's new religion of humanity.[35] This would find its ideal expression in the total work of art uniting humanity or the folk by means of a common myth.

Following Wagner, in order to be a "partaker in the unconditioned truth of universal feeling and emotion," Man, the artist, has to use all his

---

[32] Ibid. 89; 90.
[33] Ibid.
[34] George S. Williamson, *The Longing for Myth in Germany. Religion and Aesthetic Culture from Romanticism to Nietzsche*, Chicago & London: The University of Chicago Press 2004: 192ff; 209.
[35] Ibid. 194.

faculties and communicate using the physical gestures of the body, vocal tone and speech.[36] Accordingly, the three branches of art that Wagner describes as "three humanistic (*rein menschlich[e]*) arts," originally and naturally united in the drama, are dance, tone and poetry.[37] He explains:

> The arts of *Dance*, of *Tone*, and *Poetry*: thus call themselves the three primeval sisters whom we see at once entwine their measures wherever the conditions necessary for artistic manifestment have arisen. By their nature they are inseparable without disbanding the stately minuet of Art; for in this dance, which is the very cadence of Art itself, they are so wondrous closely interlaced with one another, of fairest love and inclination, so mutually bound up in each other's life, of body and of spirit: that each of the three partners, unlinked from the united chain and bereft thus of her own life and motion, can only carry on an artificially inbreathed and borrowed life; – not giving forth their sacred ordinances, as in their trinity, but now receiving despotic rules for mechanical movement.[38]

It is, then, the art of dance that Richard Wagner first examines in detail. According to his conception, dance is given a key position in the arts since it is seen as the most realistic one due to its dealing with "the actual living Man; [...] the whole man from heel to crown, such as he shows himself unto the eye."[39] Because "the singing and speaking man must necessarily be a bodily man," it is – in Wagner's understanding – the art of dance, focusing on the entire man's body, which opens up the path for the understanding and emergence of all the other arts.[40] It is, however, in drama that dance, united with the other arts, reaches its fulfillment: "so does Dance withal exalt herself in Drama to her most spiritual expression, that of *Mimicry*. As Mimetic art, she becomes the direct and

---

[36] Wagner, "The Art-Work of the Future" 93.
[37] Ibid. 149.
[38] Ibid. 95.
[39] Ibid. 100.
[40] Ibid.

all-embracing utterance of the inner man."[41] This unity is also due to the rhythmic aspect to which Wagner ascribed a central role in his conception. First stating that by "means of Rhythm does Dance become an art," he in a next step proclaims a natural alignment between the arts of tone and dance by way of rhythm: "Rhythm is the natural, unbreakable bond of union between the arts of Dance and Tone."[42] In a final step it is rhythm, in close alliance with dance, which is capable of bringing together all arts in one united artwork: "the law of Rhythm, begotten from her [the art of dance], is the standard whereby the whole dramatic semblance is brought into agreement ('*Verständigung*')."[43]

It is exactly this description of dance as being able to encompass all the other arts that appealed to modern dancers and dance critics at the beginning of the 20th century. To further understand this, one should also note here that Wagner, when he talked about dance, was not referring to the classical ballet as it existed during his time. On the contrary, the ballerina of his era is described by him as a figure of mere popular and superficial entertainment, mainly a prostitute, not able anymore to represent the reality of mankind. This is especially due to ballet's focus on the lower limbs instead of the whole body:

> all her artistic capability has sunk down from her vertex, through her body, to her feet. Head, neck, trunk and thighs are only present as unbidden guests; whereas her feet have undertaken to show alone what she can do, and merely for the sake of needful balance call on her arms and hands for sisterly support.[44]

For Wagner, who dismisses pantomime as the "most utterly dependent and cripple-like monstrosity," the only present form of dance that he regards as being worth maintaining and elaborating on is the national or folk dance, at least insofar as it is still directly connected with the people

---

[41] Ibid. 104.
[42] Ibid. 101; 103.
[43] Ibid. 104.
[44] Ibid. 106.

and not corrupted by "the world of show."[45] Folk dancing by itself, however, does not seem to represent a rich enough art, as he announces its necessary development and unity with other arts to establish a total work of art:

> Further evolution of the folk-dance towards the richer capabilities of Art is only possible by union with the arts of Tone and Poetry, no longer tyrannised by Dance, but bearing themselves as free agents; for only amid the correlated faculties, and under the stimulation, of these arts can she unfold and broaden out her individual faculties to their fullest compass.[46]

Although Wagner ascribes dance a central position in the conception of his artwork, he nevertheless, in continuation of Schopenhauer, states music's universal potential to unite all other arts in the artwork of the future. This is stated in his chapter on "The Art of Tone," especially in reference to the symphonies of Haydn, Mozart, and Beethoven. Wagner singles out Beethoven's ninth and last symphony which he describes as "the *Apotheosis of Dance* herself; it is Dance in her highest aspect, as it were the loftiest Deed of bodily motion incorporated in an ideal mould of tone."[47] One might understand this sentence as a praise of the art of dance, but Wagner comes to a conclusion which confirms the leading role of music as a universal and synthesizing art form and, at the same time, announces the end of the symphony:

> The Last Symphony of Beethoven is the redemption of Music from out her own peculiar element into the realm of *universal Art*. It is the human Evangel of the art of the Future. Beyond it no forward step is possible; for upon it the perfect Art-work of the Future alone can follow, the *universal Drama* to which Beethoven

---

[45] Ibid. 109; 107.
[46] Ibid. 107ff.
[47] Ibid. 124.

has forged for us the key. *Thus has Music of herself fulfilled what neither of the other severed arts had skill to do.*[48]

Wagner sees the highpoint of the tragedy closely linked to the ancient Greek gods. In contrast to Christianity which is based on "an honourless, useless, and sorrowful existence of mankind on earth" which awaits the "posthumous state of endless comfort and inactive ecstasy," the Greek gods had "created man for a happy and self-conscious life upon this earth."[49] And the enactment of a tragedy was a

> Feast of the God; for here the god spoke clearly and intelligibly forth, and the poet, as his highpriest, stood real and embodied in his art-work, led the measures of the dance, raised the voices to a choir, and in ringing words proclaimed the utterance of godlike wisdom. Such was the Grecian work of art; such their god Apollo, incarnated in actual, living art; such was the Grecian people in its highest truth and beauty.[50]

Wagner, who denounces Christian art as well as modern art, whose "true essence is Industry," presents his readers at the end of "The Art-work of the Future" with the outline of a myth.[51] Introducing his readers to the saga "Wieland the Smith," Wagner opens up the field of the gods and heroes of Germanic mythology which should become the basis of his artistic work.[52] As described in his essay "The Music of the Future" (1860/61) it is through a saga or legend that a whole folk, a whole nation, can grasp itself and communicate this understanding to following genera-

---

[48] Ibid. 126ff.
[49] Richard Wagner, "Art and Revolution," in: *The Art-Work of the Future and Other Works*, transl. by William Ashton Ellis, Lincoln & London: University of Nebraska Press 1993:23-65; here 37; reprint from *Richard Wagner's Prose Works*, vol.1, London: Kegan Paul, Trench, Trübner & Co. 1895.
[50] Ibid. 33.
[51] Ibid. 42.
[52] See Wagner, "The Art-work of the Future" 210.

tions because of the humanistic and thus coherent form inherent in legend:

> The legend, in whatever nation or age it may be placed, has the advantage that it comprehends only the purely *human* portion of this age and nation, and presents this portion in a form peculiar to it, thoroughly concentrated, and therefore easily intelligible.[53]

As for the Grecians it was "the nation itself – in intimate connection with its own history – that stood mirrored in its art-work," similarly Wagner intends to offer the German folk the possibility to view itself in the artwork of the future and celebrate its "free united manhood."[54] Introducing German myth as its artistic content, Wagner saw his music drama "not merely as an aesthetic phenomenon but as the vehicle of a religious experience."[55] He thereby positioned himself in continuation of the Romantic tradition of *Kunstreligion*.[56]

At the beginning of the 20th century, Wagner's united work of art with its basis in Greek tragedy would still inspire numerous artists. This was especially true of early modern dancers. Eclectically combining different ideas and approaches in their newly-developed philosophies, they often built on aspects of Wagner's artistic concept in order to defend and reinforce their own work.

2.2.2 Appropriations in the Early Modern Dance Scene

The conception of Wagner's unified artwork, with its strong insistence on dance as a primary and guiding component, was referring to the ancient Greek origins of European culture in order to develop a new hu-

---

[53] Richard Wagner, "The Music of the Future," in: Edward L. Burlingame (ed. and trans.), *Art Life and Theories of Richard Wagner*, New York: Henry Holt & Company 1904: 132-189; here 170.
[54] Wagner, "Art and Revolution" 52; 58.
[55] Williamson 181.
[56] For further elaborations on myth or mythology, the Romantic *Kunstreligion* and its connection with the reception of Uday Shankar's Indian dances and music see Chapter 4.

manistic artwork for the future that was based in nature. At the same time it both entailed and was fueled by a criticism of classical ballet that dismissed ballet as unable to represent the human being as a whole. Both of these ideas guided the first generation of Western modern dancers. Although modern dance – also known as contemporary dance, new dance, free dance or, in German, *Ausdruckstanz* – generally resists classification, its origins are seen to lie in Germany and the United States at the beginning of the 20th century. Many of the American practitioners, however, celebrated their first successes in Europe.[57] What united dancers of a variety of styles such as Loie Fuller, Ruth St. Denis, Isadora Duncan, Rudolf von Laban and Mary Wigman, was the fact that they all positioned themselves and their movement in contrast to the classical ballet. As Roger Copeland points out, "'originality' in modern dance has always been conceived of as a return to origins, a search for the most natural way of moving."[58] We can find this approach already present in Berlin by 1903, for example, in an essay by the early modern dancer Isadora Duncan:[59] "If we seek the real source of the dance, if we go to nature, we find that the dance of the future is the dance of the past, the dance of eternity, and has been and will always be the same."[60]

The turn towards nature in modern dance was further reinforced by the various reform movements (in German *Lebensreformbewegungen*), which became popular in Europe, especially in Germany and France, around the turn of the century. Working against both feelings of disorientation caused by a growing urbanization and against a trend towards materialism in modern society, reform movements, such as those focused on clothing, nutrition or nudism, aimed at a harmonious link between body and spirit and tried to (re)unite the human being with

---

[57] See Deborah Jowitt, "Modern Dance," in: "Modernism," in: M. Kelly (ed.), *Encyclopedia of Aesthetics*, vol.3, New York & Oxford: Oxford University Press 1998: 259-263; here 259.
[58] Roger Copeland, "The search for origins: Roger Copeland looks at primitivism in modern dance," *Dance Theatre Journal* (London), vol.12 no.1, summer 1996: 8-14; here 10.
[59] See Sabine Huschka, *Moderner Tanz. Konzepte, Stile, Utopien*, Reinbek bei Hamburg: Rowohlt 2002: 110.
[60] Isadora Duncan, "The Dance of the Future" (1902/03), in: Copeland & Cohen 262-264; here 262.

nature and the cosmos. These contemporary trends in cultural critique strongly influenced the modern dance scene, whose artists perceived their movements as being more natural than those of classical ballet.[61]

That Isadora Duncan (1877-1927) had been inspired by Wagner becomes obvious in a short essay she wrote in 1921 entitled "Richard Wagner." She here identified his ideas with a worldwide generation of artists, an artistic epoch, and praises him as "more than an artist: he is the glorious far-seeing prophet, liberator of the art of the future. It is him who will give birth to the new union of the arts, the rebirth of the theatre, tragedy and the dance as one."[62] Following Evelyn Dörr, Duncan "[i]n her article 'Was soll der Tanz sein?' ('What should dance be?') [...] called for a Gesamtkunstwerk – in which dance, poetry, music and architecture would harmonically flow together, to melt together into something whole and unique."[63] With her so-called Greek dances – barefoot dances in a Greek tunic to music by Wagner, Gluck, Schubert and Chopin, partly inspired by reliefs on Greek vases – the American-born artist did not receive a lot of attention in her home country.[64] Instead, from 1899 on, she lived in Europe and performed there with a high level of success.[65] In another of her essays published in the *Theatre Arts Magazine* in 1917/18, she opposes the school of classical ballet with the nature-oriented ancient Greek arts; the former she denounces as sterile, unnatural and even dying, while the latter, she claims, possess the

---

[61] See Diethart Kerbs & Jürgen Reulecke (eds.), *Handbuch der deutschen Reformbewegungen 1880-1933*, Wuppertal: Peter Hammer Verlag 1998. See also Diana Brenscheidt gen. Jost, "Den neuen Menschen tanzen. Tanz und Kulturkritik zu Beginn des 20. Jahrhunderts," in: G. Rebane et al. (eds.), *Humanismus polyphon. Menschlichkeit im Zeitalter der Globalisierung*, Bielefeld: transcript 2009: 55-70.

[62] Isadora Duncan, "Richard Wagner" (1921), in: Copeland & Cohen 266.

[63] Isadora Duncan, "Was soll der Tanz sein," *Die Schönheit* (Berlin), vol. 11 no. 1, April 1913: 34; 37; quoted in and transl. by: Evelyn Dörr, "Wie ein Meteor tauchte sie in Europa auf ..." / "She suddenly appeared in Europe like a meteor ...," in: F.-M. Peter (ed.), *Isadora & Elizabeth Duncan in Deutschland / Isadora & Elizabeth Duncan in Germany*, Köln: Wienand Verlag 2000: 31-49; here 47.

[64] See Dörr, "She suddenly appeared in Europe like a meteor ..." 32.

[65] See Jean Morrison Brown (eds.), *The Vision of Modern Dance. In the Words of Its Creators*, London: Dance Books 1998, 2nd edition: 7.

potential to reach all humanity. She hereby establishes a platform from where to derive her own dances:

> The Greeks in all their painting, sculpture, architecture, literature, dance and tragedy evolved their movements from the movement of nature [...]. This is why the art of the Greeks is not a national or characteristic art, but has been, and will be, the art of all humanity for all time.[66]

The naturalness of ancient Greek (and accordingly Duncan's art) is also acknowledged by Michel Fokine, choreographer of Diaghilev's famous *Ballets Russes*, who described Isadora Duncan's dancing to be founded on "natural movements and on the most natural of all dance-forms – namely, the dancing of the ancient Greeks."[67]

Duncan's focus on the movements of nature as transferred to dance was further rooted in the renaissance of romantic natural philosophy. In the beginning of the 20th century this renaissance was identified with the writings of empiricists and natural scientists such as Wilhelm Wundt, Ernst Haeckel and Ernst Mach: "It operated on the principle that human life represented a part of the cosmic movement of nature, with which the universe builds a morphologically organized entirety."[68] In the field of the arts the unity of man and nature was ideally detected in Greek antiquity: "Classical antiquity was seen as a point of departure since then art supposedly still expressed itself in a 'harmonic-organic form,' as did nature."[69]

Isadora Duncan's interest in natural movement must, however, also be examined in the tradition of François Delsarte (1811-71), a French art-educationalist who during his lifetime was mainly known as a

---

[66] Isadora Duncan, "The Dance," *Theatre Arts Magazine. An Illustrated Quarterly* (New York), vol.2, 1917-1918: 21-22; here 21.
[67] Michel Fokine, "Letter to 'The Times,' July 6th, 1914," in: Copeland & Cohen 257-261; here 258.
[68] Dörr, "She suddenly appeared in Europe like a meteor ..." 39.
[69] Ibid.

Professor of singing and declamation.[70] Already in the 1830s, Delsarte, frustrated by the standardized modes of art instruction at the Conservatory, had developed a new approach to art education encompassing singing, acting, and movement which would have a strong influence on the American as well as the German modern dance scene. His "*Cours d'esthétique appliqué*"[71] or lessons of applied aesthetics were based on a principle of universal trinity – such as the trinity of mind, life, and soul – which he saw at work in God as well as in Man as created according to God's image. Delsarte never wrote down a systematic approach himself, but he had numerous followers and admirers – Wagner obviously also acknowledged his influence.[72] It appears that many of his followers misunderstood Delsarte's original intentions; this is at least claimed by the American modern dancer Ted Shawn in his book on Delsarte named *Every Little Movement* (1963). Shawn quotes from a student of Delsarte, Emily Bishop, who defended his approach against any form of standardization:

> There is no Delsarte walk, no Delsarte standing position, no Delsarte way to sit down, no Delsarte way of doing anything. The only way Delsarte sought is Nature's way. Man can no more *make* natural things than can he *create* truth. He can create unnatural ways and falsehoods; at best he can *discover* Nature's way, and live and express correctly the truth.[73]

Bishop thus identified Delsarte with movement or gesture inspired by nature. For Isadora Duncan the Delsartean approach to movement apparently meant exactly that: movement as derived from nature in contrast to the standardized ballet. Indeed, this is confirmed in Nesta Macdonald's biographical outline of her: "Isadora also learned at some

---

[70] See Ted Shawn, *Every Little Movement. A Book About François Delsarte*, Dance Horizons: New York 1963: 10.

[71] Nancy Lee Chalfa Ruyter, "Delsarte System of Expression," in: S.J. Cohen (ed.), *International Encyclopedia of Dance*, vol.2, New York & Oxford: Oxford University Press 1998: 370-372; here 370.

[72] See Louise Gifford, "Introduction," in: Shawn, *Every Little Movement* 7-9; here 7.

[73] Emily Bishop, *Americanized Delsarte Culture*, 1892; quoted in: ibid 26.

point from a woman familiar with Delsarte's philosophy of free, natural movement."[74] For her, its symbol became the wave, the sign for the constant flow of unity in nature:

> The great and only principle on which I feel myself justified in leaning, is a constant, absolute, and universal unity which runs through all the manifestations of Nature. The waters, the winds, the plants, living creatures, the particles of matter itself obey this controlling rhythm of which the characteristic line is the wave. In nothing does Nature suggest jumps and breaks, there is between all the conditions of life a continuity of flow which the dancer must respect in his art, or else become a mannequin – outside Nature and without true beauty.[75]

Although Michel Fokine neither referred to the ancient Greek drama nor to nature when writing about his own work, like Wagner and later Isadora Duncan had done, he nevertheless reformulated Wagner's concept of a united artwork in a letter published in London in 1914 in *The Times*.[76] In the letter, he proposed a reform of the classical ballet which included "the alliance of dancing with other arts" and thereby stressed the importance of creative freedom in the combination of all artistic aspects in each choreography.[77] He further elaborated as follows:

> The new ballet, refusing to be the slave either of music or of scenic decoration, and recognizing the alliance of the arts only on

---

[74] Nesta Macdonald, "Isadora Re-examined. Lesser known aspects of the great dancer's life. 1877-1900," *Dance Magazine* (New York), vol.51 no.7, July 1977: 50-65; here 50.

[75] Isadora Duncan, "Excerpts from her writings," in: Brown 8-10; here 8.

[76] That the artists of the Ballets Russes were aware of the Wagnerian concept is also con-tested by Alexandre Benois, who designed sets and costumes for the Ballets Russes, and defined ballet as: "A form of theatre spectacle in which all the varied elements must blend into a whole to constitute what Wagner called *Gesamtkünstwerk* [sic]." A. Benois quoted in Robert C. Hansen, *Scenic and Costume Design for the Ballets Russes*, Ann Arbor: UMI Research Press 1985: 14; quoted from: Copeland, "The search for origins" 13.

[77] Fokine 260.

the condition of complete equality, allows a perfect freedom both to the scenic artist and to the musician. [...] It does not impose any specific 'ballet' conditions on the composer or the decorative artist, but gives complete liberty to their creative powers.[78]

Michel Fokine's effort towards a unity of the arts was coordinated with the conception of the *Ballets Russes* by the Russian Serge Diaghilev (1872-1929), the founder and artistic director of the group from 1909 up until his death in 1929. As described by Lynn Garafola, sometime in the 1890s while in Vienna Diaghilev attended a performance of Richard Wagner's opera *Lohengrin*. This event apparently impressed him deeply and resulted in several visits of Diaghilev to Bayreuth. Inspired by the concept of the *Gesamtkunstwerk*, Diaghilev enabled partnerships for the early *Ballets Russes* with composers such as Igor Stravinsky, Claude Debussy, Maurice Ravel, Sergei Prokofiev, and Francis Poulenc as well as painters like Léon Bakst, Pablo Picasso, André Derain, or Henri Matisse.[79] His approach brought together artists from the different art branches and won him the praise of audiences and critics, who thought he had finally realized or even surpassed the Wagnerian concept. Constant Lambert, himself actually a critic of unifying approaches in the arts, wrote in 1936: "Ballet did not reach its Wagnerian stage until the pre-war Diaghilev days."[80] The British critic Adrian Stokes stated: "Where the work of a Gluck or a Wagner is incomplete, the work of Diaghilev is complete."[81] Frank Kermode, quoting the French symbolist Camille Mauclair, later also added: "The Ballets Russes demonstrated the correspondence of the arts so wonderfully that in comparison Wagner's effort was, said Camille Mauclair, 'une gaucherie barbare.'"[82]

---

[78] Ibid.

[79] See Lynn Garafola, "Serge Diaghilev," in: Cohen, *International Encyclopedia of Dance*, vol.2: 406-412; here 406.

[80] Constant Lambert, "Music and Action" (1936), in: Copeland & Cohen 203-210; here 210.

[81] Adrian Stokes, *Russian Ballets*, London: Faber and Faber 1935: 114; quoted in: Cohen, "Primitivism, Modernism, and Dance Theory" 163.

[82] Frank Kermode, "Loïe Fuller And the Dance Before Diaghilev," *Theatre Arts* (New York), September 1962: 6-21; here 8.

The early American modern dancer Ruth St. Denis (1877-1968) likewise bases modern dance on natural, instinctive movement as opposed to the stereotyped movements of classical ballet in her writing. Her link with Delsarte's approach is readily apparent:

> Dancing is the natural rhythmic movements of the body that have long been suppressed or distorted, and the desire to dance would be as natural as to eat, or to run, or swim, if our civilization had not in countless ways and for divers reasons put its ban upon this instinctive and joyous action of the harmonious being.[83]

In an article published in the first edition of the American *Theatre Arts Magazine* in 1916, St. Denis further picks up current ideas on the unity of the arts as exemplified in dance and namely in her own artistic creations. Directly attacking Diaghilev's *Ballets Russes*, in whose productions well-known artists collaborated for the purpose of a united art experience, she stressed the necessity of "one directing, creating genius" for the success of a dance performance.[84] With the help of the "one creator, driven by one inspiration," all aspects of a performance, such as music, costume, scenery, and lighting effects, can be integrated into one united artwork.[85] Ruth St. Denis affirms: "The dance as an art form will succeed best always when there is one creating and directing mind, and all other people are merely the instruments or material which this head uses for working out a unity."[86]

If one combs through the history of modern dance, the concept of a united work of art had already been applied in the context of the reception of modern dancers before Isadora Duncan or the *Ballets Russes*. One dancer to be named here is the American Loie Fuller (1862-1928) – also known by her French stage name Loïe Fuller or La Loïe – who is generally regarded to be one of the forerunners of modern dance.

---

[83] Ruth St. Denis, "The Dance as Life Experience," in: Brown 22-25; here 24ff.
[84] Ruth St. Denis, "The Dance as an Art Form," *Theatre Arts Magazine* (Detroit), vol.1 no.1, November 1916: 75-77; here 76.
[85] Ibid. 77.
[86] Ibid.

Loie Fuller was mainly known for her famous *Serpentine Dance*, a composition for body and silk in which her movements were extended by a long and floating costume made of silk which seemed to radiate and develop a life of its own. Having fought for artistic recognition in the United States, she arrived in Paris in 1892 and began performing at the *Folies-Bergère*. Fascinated by the new possibilities of electricity, she presented her dance in an almost entirely dark theatre on a black stage without any décor. The only illumination was provided by a blaze of light that strengthened the effects of her silk skirt floating around her while she danced.[87] Loie Fuller was immediately praised by the public and named by admirers and critics "*la fée lumineuse* (the luminous fairy)."[88] This appellation would change later on, when she went on experimenting with the use of electric light and color filters, into "[la] Fée de l'Electricité" (the fairy of electricity).[89] Performing in the era of Art Nouveau, during the development of symbolism and the emphatic presentation of technical advancement, such as electricity, she instantly gained the recognition of artists and intellectuals at the Exposition Universelles who saw in her an ideal of a new kind of art. Her play with the abstract presentation of flowers, animals and insects in her dances up until 1905 equaled the use of natural forms, mainly flowers, as patterns of ornamentation in Art Nouveau and also helped signify her dancing as more natural than classical ballet.[90] In her biography (1913), she states that motion by itself is always "faithful to nature" and accordingly claims a new form of bodily expression for dance in harmony with its own nature and nature as a whole: "The human body is ready to express, and it would express if it were at liberty to do so, all sensations just as the body of an animal. [...] I have motion. That means that all the elements

---

[87] See Sally R. Sommer, "Loie Fuller," in: Cohen, *International Encyclopedia of Dance*, vol.3: 90-96; here 90ff.

[88] Ibid. 92.

[89] Gabriele Brandstetter & Brygida Maria Ochaim, *Loïe Fuller. Tanz – Lichtspiel – Art Nouveau*, Freiburg: Verlag Rombach 1989: 86.

[90] This abstract play in her dances is suggested in an number of the titles of her work, including *Violet* (1892), *The Flower* (1893), *La Danse du Lys* (1895) and *Une Pluie de Fleurs* (1898) as well as *La Danse Serpentine* (1891), *The Butterfly* (1892), *Chez les papillons* (1903) and *Flight of the Butterflies* (1905).

of nature may be expressed."[91] One can see Frank Kermode's honoring her in 1962 as "the woman who seemed to be doing almost single-handed what Diaghilev was later to achieve only with the help of great painters, musicians, and dancers" as a reference to her dance's relation to the united work of art.[92] Following Gabriele Brandstetter, Loïe Fuller's dancing as representation of the Romantic dream of synesthesia can indeed be brought in connection with a united artwork.[93] However, it is not connected to the united artwork in the Wagnerian sense, but rather in accordance with the ideas of French symbolism: "a spectacle [...] which defies all definition [...] Art, nameless, radiant [...] a homogeneous and complete place [...] indefinable, absolute [...] a fire above dogmas."[94]

Another name to be mentioned in the context of the total work of art is Mary Wigman (1886-1973). As a pioneer of German *Ausdrucktanz*, she was strongly influenced by the Hungary-born Rudolf von Laban, inventor of a notational system of dance named Labanotation.[95] A closer look at her work, however, shows that Wigman in the beginning pursued a rather aesthetically purist path. Following the aim of "the final equation and equal ranking of dance with the other absolute arts," Wigman developed a form of absolute dance which made only sparing use of music, rhythm, costume, and scenery.[96] An enthusiastic German reviewer accordingly praised her strict focus on "the moving bodies in space" instead of decorative costume and scenery. John Martin's reference to her in the context of the unity of the arts then belongs to a later phase in her career and was written at the time of her three extended tours in the United States in the 1930/31, 1931/32, and 1932/33 seasons. From the late 1920s on Wigman followed the "vision of a new form of theater based on dance," which she attempted to realize in *Totenmal* presented at the Third

---

[91] Loïe Fuller, "Light and the Dance," in: Brown 13-19; here 18.
[92] Kermode, "Loïe Fuller And the Dance Before Diaghilev," 8.
[93] See Gabriele Brandstetter, "Loïe Fuller – Symbol des 'Art Nouveau'," in: Brandstetter & Ochaim 106.
[94] Frank Kermode, "Poet and Dancers before Diaghilev" (1958-61), in: Copeland & Cohen 145-160; here 146.
[95] See Ann Hutchinson Guest, "Labanotation," in: Cohen, *International Encyclopedia of Dance*, vol.4: 95-98.
[96] Mary Wigman, "Tänzerische Wege und Ziele," *Die Neue Rundschau*, vol.2, Berlin & Leipzig: S. Fischer Verlag 1923: 1021-1024; here 1024.

Dancers' Congress in Munich in 1930.[97] This new form of dance theater also included so-called "movement choirs," originally a concept of Laban which brought together large groups of nonprofessional dancers in a dance activity. Her realignment of dance and theater brought Wigman close to ideas in the field of the total work of art.

In Rudolf von Laban's work one thus also finds mention of a concept of synesthesia in the arts. In *Die Welt des Tänzers* (1920) Laban defines the total work of art as a perfect unity of the aesthetic, the constructive-intellectual, and the religious form of art.[98] These three art forms he sees ideally combined in dance:

> The dance artwork as integrating peak: The integrated artwork, in which the aesthetic and the constructive element are visible representatives of the religious, is the moving art of form: the dance. The concept of dance, the dance, is "the being" par excellence. No other art has brought together all motives of expression and effect in such an evident and pure manner without one of them exclusively prevailing. Dance is the vivid expression of the relativity of world affairs, it is thus of finite and infinite meaning at the same time.[99]

Laban's conception accordingly melts aesthetics with religion, this time culminating in the dance work. Dance gains metaphysical importance, becomes an expression of being exemplifying the whole cosmos. This also puts him in the context of the ideas of the various reform movements at the beginning of the 20th century, with which he came in close contact during the summer of 1912 in Monte Verità at the Lago Maggiore, meeting place of various reform branches at that time.[100]

---

[97] Susan A. Manning, "Mary Wigman," in: Cohen, *International Encyclopedia of Dance*, vol.6: 389-396; here 393.
[98] See Rudolf von Laban, *Die Welt des Tänzers. Fünf Gedankenreigen*, Stuttgart: Verlag von Walter Seifert 1920: 239.
[99] Ibid.
[100] See Valerie Preston-Dunlop: "Rudolf Laban," in: Cohen, *International Encyclopedia of Dance*, vol.4: 89-95; here 89

Though having its roots in Romanticism, ideas of a total work of art, ideally uniting the different artistic branches, reach the early modern dance scene mainly through Wagner. While early modern dancers at the beginning of the 20th century only eclectically rely on Wagner's writings, main aspects such as the search for orientation in antiquity, the link between art, mythology and religion, the arts' close bond with nature and even the concept's political impulse towards a renewal of society find their way into modern dancers' individual philosophies and are reformulated in close connection with the critique of contemporary culture. It would be audiences' and artists' interest in a unity of the arts which would partly build the background for the enthusiastic reception of Uday Shankar's Indian dances, especially of his dance drama *Tandava Nrittya*, as will be examined below.

While Wagner's importance for the arts in the 20th century is here acknowledged, there is, however, one other author to be considered in continuation of the discussion on a united artwork. With his writings on ancient Greek tragedy as based in mythology and his description of the Apolline and Dionysiac principles, Friedrich Nietzsche not only resumes and complements Wagner's discussion, but also – partly due to his reception in the context of the criticism of modern culture – strongly inspired modern dancers and art critics up into the 20th century. As will be seen further on, Nietzsche's ideas thereby also found their way into the reception of Uday Shankar.

2.2.3 Friedrich Nietzsche: Dance and the Dionysiac Principle

In his first book, *The Birth of Tragedy from the Spirit of Music* (1870-71), Friedrich Nietzsche presents his ideas about an ideal wedding of Apolline and Dionysiac principles in ancient pre-Socratic Greek tragedy, which he saw possibly reenacted in Richard Wagner's works. Nietzsche here first differentiates "between the Apolline art of the image-maker or sculptor (*Bildner*) and the imageless art of music, which is that of Dionysos."[101] He then goes on to describe how they were originally united in the attic tragedy:

---

[101] Friedrich Nietzsche, "The Birth of Tragedy," in: F. Nietzsche, *The Birth of Tragedy and Other Writings*, edited by R. Geuss & R. Speirs, translated by R. Speirs,

These two very different drives (*Triebe*) exist side by side, mostly in open conflict, stimulating and provoking (*reizen*) one another to give birth to ever-new, more vigorous offspring in whom they perpetuate the conflict inherent in the opposition between them, an opposition only apparently bridged by the common term 'art' – until eventually, by a metaphysical miracle of the Hellenic 'Will', they appear paired and, in this pairing, finally engender a work of art which is Dionysiac and Apolline in equal measure: Attic tragedy.[102]

It is then the sun god Apollo who, "as the god of all image-making energies," is identified with dream, prophecy, and "the lovely semblance produced by the inner world of fantasy" which he is calmly preserving against everyday reality.[103] Referring back to a concept of Schopenhauer from *The World as Will and Representation* (1819) Nietzsche compares Apollo to the human being captivated in the "veil of maya" and accordingly identifies him with the "*principium individuationis*" or the principle of individuation, the belief in a stable individuality which is by itself built on a dream-like state.[104] When this stability with its clear boundaries is suddenly shaken or even collapses, one gets, following Nietzsche, an impression of the Dionysiac principle, a state most closely comparable with intoxication. This state of events is positively described as "blissful ecstasy which arises from the innermost ground of man, indeed of nature itself," which then leads to a unity of all human beings as well as to a reunification with nature.[105] Ultimately this process leads to the state of the "mysterious primordial unity (*das Ur-Eine*)."[106] This

---

Cambridge: Cambridge University Press 1999: 14. According to American academic convention, a more common translation seems to be "Dionysian" and "Appolinian" instead of "Dionysiac" and "Appoline." See Friedrich Nietzsche, "The Birth of Tragedy," in: W. Kaufmann, *Basic Writings of Nietzsche*, New York: The Modern Library 2000: 1-144.

[102] Nietzsche, "The Birth of Tragedy," translated by R. Speirs 14.

[103] Ibid. 16.

[104] Ibid. 16ff.

[105] Ibid. 17.

[106] Ibid. 18.

ultimate union is described thus: "Not only is the bond between human beings renewed by the magic of the Dionysiac, but nature, alienated, inimical, or subjugated, celebrates once more her festival of reconciliation with her lost son, humankind."[107] It is in this moment, in connection with the Dionysiac principle, that Nietzsche mentions dance: "Singing and dancing, man expresses his sense of belonging to a higher community; he has forgotten how to walk and talk and is on the brink of flying and dancing, up and away into the air above."[108]

Nietzsche positions music in the centre of his elaborations on ancient tragedy, and dance – where mentioned – only receives attention as inspired by music or as one part of a unity of all arts linked with nature, such as in the figure of the satyr as "a copy of nature and its strongest impulses, indeed a symbol of them, and at the same time the proclaimer of her wisdom and art; musician, poet, dancer, seer of spirits, all in one person."[109] The primacy of music also becomes obvious in his reflections on Dionysiac in contrast to Apolline music:

> The music of Apollo was Doric architectonics in sound, but only in the kind of hinted-at tones characteristic of the cithara. It keeps at a distance, as something un-Apolline, the very element which defines the character of Dionysiac music (and thus of music generally): the power of its sound to shake us to our very foundations, the unified stream of melody and the quite incomparable world of harmony.[110]

It is in Nietzsche's description of the cultic Dionysiac dithyramb that dance, in its close alliance with nature, comes to the forefront:

> In the Dionysiac dithyramb man is stimulated to the highest intensification of his symbolic powers; something that he has never felt before urgently demands to be expressed: the destruction of the

---

[107] Ibid.
[108] Ibid.
[109] Ibid. 45.
[110] Ibid. 21.

veil of maya, one-ness as the genius of humankind, indeed of nature itself. The essence of nature is bent on expressing itself; a new world of symbols is required, firstly the symbolism of the entire body, not just of the mouth, the face, the word, but the full gesture of dance with its rhythmical movement of every limb. Then there is a sudden, tempestuous growth in music's other symbolic powers, in rhythm, dynamics, and harmony.[111]

It is this announcement of a new symbolism of movement encompassing the whole body and the "full gesture of dance with its rhythmical movement of every limb," that opened up the possibility for modern dancers, who opposed the catalogue of ballet movement focusing on the lower limbs as artificial, to further build on Nietzsche in their dance philosophies. Besides, following Nietzsche, dance was understood to unite humanity, allow a return to nature, and lead society back to its supposed cultic or mythic origins. Nietzsche's thought could thus be incorporated by cultural critics at the beginning of the 20th century and from there be absorbed by the modern dance scene. But Nietzsche, following Wagner and Schopenhauer, confirmed music as the Dionysiac origin of all arts. Similar to Wagner he presented the folk-song as a last remnant leading towards the unification of the two principles in which melody emerges before the word: "Thus *melody is the primary and general element* [...] In the naive estimation of the people it is also by far the more important and essential element. Melody gives birth to poetry, and does so over and over again, in ever new ways; this is what the strophic form of the folk song is trying to tell us."[112] Due to "music's world-symbolism," music represents the "original contradiction and original pain at the heart of the primordial unity and thus symbolizes a sphere which lies above and beyond all appearance."[113]

Similar to Wagner, Nietzsche establishes a close connection between myth and tragedy and states that myth, which "needs to be felt keenly as a unique example of something universal and true which gazes

---

[111] Ibid.
[112] Ibid. 33ff.
[113] Ibid. 36.

out into infinity," finds "its most profound content and most expressive form" in tragedy.[114] It is not the word, but music, which can fulfill this task: "for it is so easy to forget that what the word-poet failed to achieve, namely the highest spiritualization and idealization of myth, he could accomplish successfully at any moment as a creative musician."[115] Following Schopenhauer's understanding of music as the "language of the Will," it is from music that myth can reemerge in order to reconnect modern people with the Dionysiac principle: "music is able to give birth to *myth*, i.e. to the most significant example, and in particular to *tragic* myth, myth which speaks of Dionysiac knowledge in symbol."[116] But, following Nietzsche, myth can only develop its full impact if the Apolline and Dionysiac principles are merged or balanced in the audience's perception. It is the Apolline aspect in tragedy which, by ways of what Nietzsche describes as "Apolline illusion," leads one away from the universal in order to identify once again with the individual and his or her suffering as embodied on stage.[117] By means of the Apolline aspect of individuation the audience is saved from Dionysiac totality and can overcome its vulnerability and tendency towards orgiastic self-destruction.[118] In the end it is, however, the Dionysian principle which – according to Nietzsche – wins over and "closes with a sound which could never issue from the realm of Apolline art. Thereby Apolline deception is revealed for what it is: a persistent veiling, for the duration of the tragedy, of the true Dionysiac effect."[119] This leads Nietzsche to a conclusion regarding myth which once again shows the close interconnectedness of the two principles: "The tragic myth can only be understood as the transformation of Dionysiac wisdom into images by means of Apolline artistry."[120]

In a later paragraph Nietzsche comes to the importance of myth for contemporary modern culture and refers to current endeavors in the

---

[114] Ibid. 83; 54.
[115] Ibid. 81.
[116] Ibid. 79.
[117] Ibid. 102.
[118] See ibid.
[119] Ibid. 103.
[120] Ibid. 105.

German music scene – meaning Wagner – to reactivate mythology. Through a common myth, audience members will experience themselves as part of a larger whole inspired by nature: "Without myth, however, all cultures lose their healthy, creative, natural energy; only a horizon surrounded by myths encloses and unifies a cultural movement."[121] Modern culture, following Nietzsche, obviously lacks myth and continuity regarding its common roots and accordingly happens to be in a state of crisis:

> Now mythless man stands there, surrounded by every past there has ever been, eternally hungry, scraping and digging in a search for roots, even if he has to dig for them in the most distant antiquities. The enormous historical need of dissatisfied modern culture, the accumulation of countless other cultures, the consuming desire for knowledge – what does all this point to, if not to the loss of myth, the loss of a mythical home, a mythical, maternal womb?[122]

Nietzsche here not only denounces the methods of classical philology – he himself was trained as a classical philologist – and anthropology of his time. His writing further shows a severe criticism of modern society and its focus on knowledge and consequently functioned as a predecessor of the cultural criticism of *Lebensphilosophie* (philosophy of life) at the turn of the century.[123] Contemporary modern culture is here attacked under the name of Socratic or Alexandrian culture and characterized by "theoretical man, equipped with the highest powers of understanding and working in the service of science."[124] This highly rational contemporary culture was ideally exemplified in "the culture of the opera" as preceding

---

[121] Ibid. 108.
[122] Ibid. 109.
[123] See also Jason Gaiger, "Lebensphilosophie," *Routledge Encyclopedia of Philosophy* (http://www.texttribe.com/routledge/L/Lebensphilosophie.html; last accessed June 21, 2011).
[124] Nietzsche, "The Birth of Tragedy" 86.

Wagner.[125] Eclectically building their dance philosophies on various sources, early modern dancers such as Isadora Duncan or Ted Shawn surely turned to Nietzsche, especially because they were attracted to his thoughts on the Dionysiac aspect as being linked with antiquity, myth, and the (dancing) body promising a new approach to life.[126] His conception of a unity of the two opposing principles in the Attic tragedy and its reactivation in his time, such as he foresaw it in Wagner's work, connects him with the tradition of a total work of art. Through Wagner as well as through Nietzsche, the ideal of a united artwork would reach the dance scene at the beginning of the 20th century and thereby would also influence the reception of Uday Shankar and his company of dancers and musicians.

2.3 The Dance-Drama *Tandava Nrittya*: Indian *Nātya* as a United Artwork

Uday Shankar's performances were generally accompanied by written notes on each item of the show. In the case of *Tandava Nrittya* the programs mostly contained a description of the mythological story presented. In a British program subtitled as "a dance-drama of archaic character," this description would be regularly repeated in the reviews of *Tandava Nrittya*.[127] In numerous American and British *Playbill*-editions

---

[125] Ibid. 89. Nietzsche further contrasts Socratic culture with artistic or Hellenic and tragic or Buddhist culture, the latter also equalized with Indian culture. See ibid. 85. Tragic culture's "most important feature lies in putting wisdom in place of science as the highest goal. This wisdom is not deceived by the seductive distractions of the sciences; instead it turns its unmoved gaze on the total image of the world, and in this image it seeks to embrace eternal suffering with sympathetic feelings of love, acknowledging that suffering to be its own." Ibid. 87ff.

[126] See Natalia Stüdemann, *Dionysos in Sparta. Isadora Duncan in Russland. Eine Geschichte von Tanz und Körper*, Bielefeld: transcript 2008. See also Ted Shawn's reference to Nietzsche in his article "Gods Who Dance. 'Now There Danceth a God in Me ......' Nietzsche," undated, unknown source: n.p.; Deutsches Tanzarchiv Köln.

[127] "Uday Shankar and His Hindu Ballet and Musicians" n.p. Whereas "Tandava" refers to Shiva's vigorous male dance, "Nrittya" appears to be a mixture of *Nrtta*, defined by Coomaraswamy as mere "rhythmic movement without a theme and therefore without 'flavour'," and *Nrtya*, described as those dances "which set forth in narrative fashion the activities of the Gods and Titans." See Matthew Harp Allen, "Rewriting the Script for

109

and programs from the 1930s the story of the piece is presented in a text whose details are nearly identical from program to program. This text shares a preponderance of similarities in both words and content with an earlier outline written in German, supposedly by Alice Boner, as the main program text was also written by her:

> The drama opens with the chorus lauding Shiva and his divine wife, Sati. Shiva is the God of Creation and Destruction. His dance creates and destroys the universe. Sati, who symbolizes conjugal fidelity, dies of the grief she suffered when her own father mortally offended Shiva. Shiva, in deep affliction, retires into solitude and falls into a state of meditation, so that all creation is at a standstill.
>
> But Sati, through her profound devotion, succeeds in being reborn and returns as Parvati, who symbolizes the Earth, and as such she desires that creation continue. Every day she approaches Shiva and tries to rouse him. Meanwhile, the earth has been threatened by Gajasura, the elephant-demon. One day, encountering Parvati and seeing her young and beautiful, he decides to abduct her. He displays his strength and power before her. Parvati, frightened, repulses him, but when he is about to carry her off by force, she throws herself to the feet of Shiva, imploring his aid. Shiva awakes and the Earth trembles as he challenges Gajasura. With divine weapons they fight; they hurl at each other the five elements, the winds, the lightning, the forces of the Earth, the Atmosphere and the Sky. Shiva employs even the serpents of his arms which, in the air, seem to transform themselves into a mortal wind. Parvati, who also represents the Reservoir of Energy, stands valiantly by, reinforcing her divine mate. Shiva kills Gajasura and, stripping the hide off the demon, dances an ecstatic dance of triumph with Parvati. Then he dances the world and its move-

---

South Indian Dance," *The Drama Review* (Cambridge, Mass.), vol.41 no.3, Fall 1997: 63-100; here 80; Ananda K. Coomaraswamy, *The Mirror of Gesture. Being the Abhinaya Darpana of Nandikeśvara*, New Delhi: Munshiram Manoharlal 2003[6]: 7; 9. On Shiva's *tāndava* dance see also Coomaraswamy, "The Dance of Shiva," in: *The Dance of Shiva* 83-95; here 84ff (see Chap.1, footnote 191).

ment, and he dances his admiration for Parvati. But having delivered the Earth of its evil forces, he shows his determination to return to his meditation and to his thoughts of Sati. Parvati, desolate, begins her penance that she may find eternal grace in the eyes of Shiva.[128]

By basing the dance-drama on the story of Shiva, Parvati, and Gajasura and by presenting a detailed story outline in the programs, the reception of *Tandava Nrittya* is from the beginning strongly linked to mythology. The dance drama centers on the god Shiva who is described by Alice Boner as the unifier of the arts: "He is the master of Sangit, of the threefold art of drama, music and dance, which forms an inseparable whole in India."[129] Shankar's focus on Shiva apparently was influenced by Ananda Kentish Coomaraswamy. In his biography on Uday Shankar, Mohan Khokar tells how during the dancer's tour with Anna Pavlova the scholar gave Shankar a copy of his translation of the *Abhinaya Darpana*, an Indian treatise on dance by the author Nandikeśvara.[130] This book entitled *The Mirror of Gesture* prominently contains a picture of a Shiva statue.[131] In his introduction to the translation Coomaraswamy explains the mythological origin of Indian drama as described in the first chapter of Bharata's *Nātyaśāstra*, a treatise on Sanskrit drama and theater which was composed between 100 B.C. and 100 A.D.[132] Accordingly the god Brahma created drama out of the four already existent Vedas:

---

[128] "Uday Shankar and His Hindu Ballet and Musicians" n.p.; see also "S.Hurok Presents Uday Shan-Kar and his Hindu Ballet," in: *Playbill* (New York), [season 1937/38b]: n.p.

[129] Alice Boner, "Der Indische Tanz," in: "Gastspiel der Brahmanischen Inder (Hindus) mit Uday Shan-Kar" n.p. (see Chap.1, footnote 6). Also published in: *Der Kreis. Zeitschrift für Künstlerische Kultur* (Hamburg), vol.8, 1931: 524-526.

[130] See Khokar, *His Dance, His Life* 42 (see Introduction, footnote 8).

[131] See Coomaraswamy, *The Mirror of Gesture* plate I.

[132] See Lars-Christian Koch, *Zur Bedeutung der Rasa-Lehre für die zeitgenössische nord-indische Kunstmusik. Mit einem Vergleich mit der Affektenlehre des 17.und 18. Jahr-hunderts*, Bonn: Holos Verlag 1995: 6.

"Let me make a Fifth Veda, to be called Nātya (Drama), combined with epic story, tending to virtue, wealth, (pleasure and
spiritual freedom), yielding fame – a concise instruction setting
forth all the events of the world about to be, containing the significance of every Scripture, and forwarding every art." Thus, recalling all the Vedas, the Blessed Brahmā framed the Nātya Veda
from the several parts of the Four Vedas, as desired. From the Rg
Veda he drew forth the words, from the Sāma Veda the singing,
from the Yajur Veda gesture, and from the Atharva Veda the flavour.[133]

By quoting from this source, Coomaraswamy stresses the compound character of the Indian *nātya* which would bring it close to the idea of a *Gesamtkunstwerk*. This corresponds with its original holistic conception as a
representation of the whole world including its good and bad sides. Further, following Coomaraswamy who again quotes from the *Nātyaśāstra*,
this is strongly exhibited through dance:

I made this play as following the movement of the world (*loka-
rt'-anukaranam*), whether in work or play, profit, peace, laughter,
battle, lust, or slaughter [...]. Drama is that which accords with
the order (*sva-bhāva*) of the world, with its weal and woe, and it
consists in movements of the body and other arts of expression
(abhinaya). The theatre is such as to afford a means of entertainment in the world, and a place of audience for the Vedas, for philosophy, for history, and other matters.[134]

Coomaraswamy further explicates the holistic approach of Indian art and
states that *nātya* signifies both dancing and acting. He here critically opposes the Indian theater, which reflects the totality of life, with its
Western counterpart:

---

[133] Coomaraswamy, *The Mirror of Gesture* 2.
[134] Ibid. 2ff.

It should be noted throughout that the words *Nātya*, etc., imply both acting and dancing; we have used the word 'dance' in our translation only for want of any English word combining the ideas of dancing and acting. The reader will go far astray if he understands by dancing anything but rhythmic shewing. Indian acting is a poetic art, an interpretation of life, while modern European acting, apart from any question of the words, is prose, or imitation.[135]

While not in *The Mirror of Gesture*, yet in an earlier article named "Oriental Dances in America" published in *Vanity Fair* in 1917, Coomaraswamy had already linked the concept of *nātya* with ancient Greek *musikē* when he wrote: "Indian culture – like that of the old Greeks – employs a single name for the common art of acting and dancing; and this word *Natya*, in its Indian vernacular form, becomes *Nautch*."[136] In an article on Uday Shankar's dancing from 1937 he repeats this comparison by establishing a shared Greek and Indian aesthetic position: "Alike from the Indian and the ancient Greek point of view the drama effects a *katharsis* or purgation."[137] Cross-references between Indian and Greek art and mythology and the question of which originated first had been of some concern among British Orientalists and early Romantic writers since the 18th century. By the time of the first performances of Uday Shankar's company of dancers and musicians, however, specialists in the field had already challenged the thesis of a derivation of one from the other. In the English translation of the *Nātyaśāstra* by Manomohan Ghosh (1950), the translator claims: "As early as 1890 Sylvain Lévi noticed that Indian Nātya differed from the Greek drama from which the Westerners derived their early conception of the art."[138]

---

[135] Ibid. 5.

[136] Coomaraswamy, "Oriental Dances in America" 61 (see Chap.1, footnote 190).

[137] Ananda Kentish Coomaraswamy, "Uday Shankar's Indian Dancing," *Magazine of Art* (New York), vol.30 no.10, 1937: 611-612, 645; here 612. For further examination of this article see the Conclusion.

[138] Manomohan Ghosh, *The Natyaśāstra. A Treatise on Hindu Dramaturgy and Histrionics. Ascribed to Bharata-Muni*, Calcutta: The Royal Asiatic Society of Bengal 1950:XLII.

In 1929, concerning a supposed link between Indian and Greek myths, Helmuth von Glasenapp also doubted the dependency of one from the other. Yet he supported their comparison in reference to their importance in world literature and claimed that only very few peoples had produced such enormous ancient works which, concerning their position or status in the history of intellectual life, should be regarded as equally important.[139]

As the reviews of Uday Shankar's performances reveal, the Indian-Greek reference – although partly criticized by experts – was still alive in popular newspaper criticism. Accordingly a German reviewer writing for the daily newspaper *Hamburger Nachrichten*, also referring to Nietzsche's figure of the Dionysus, is convinced that *Tandava Nrittya* is more of ritualistic than of solely artistic significance:

> This was just as much a theater play as it had been for the Greeks; whoever has seen Shiva's dance of triumph following the demon's death knows that Dionysus once was there in person.[140]

It is, then, the spiritual unity as felt through dance which connects the Indian dance-drama with its Greek counterpart and, accordingly, allows a return to the origins of European culture:

> [I]t was this embodiment of the gods which forced on us the image of Greek cult, which builds the foundation of our own occidental history; the image of Dionysus, which never had unfolded as vividly before our mental eye as it was displayed here before our bodily eye.[141]

Also, influenced by Wagner's and Nietzsche's writings, other German critics refer to the close link between art and the spiritual when the performance is described as born out of religious tragedy: "An evening of

---

[139] See Helmuth von Glasenapp, *Die Literaturen Indiens von ihren Anfängen bis zur Gegenwart*, Wildpark-Potsdam: Akademische Verlagsgesellschaft Athenaion 1929: 81.
[140] Mk. n.p.
[141] Ibid.

primordial music and dance, which emerged out of the spirit of religious tragedy."[142]

On the level of artistic means, the dance-drama obviously brought together dance and music, as a description in an edition of the American *Playbill* magazine suggests: "Religious music accompanied by the drums and all other instruments and song."[143] Dance and music were received as closely intertwined and furthermore built on a strong percussion section of the ensemble consisting mainly of a variety of drums. In this way the presentation of *Tandava Nrittya* seemed to fulfill Wagner's conception of a natural alignment of the different arts by means of rhythm as he had outlined it in his "Art-Work of the Future:" "Rhythm is the natural, unbreakable bond of union between the arts of Dance and Tone."[144] And following Wagner's concept of the primacy of music (derived from Schopenhauer and repeated by Nietzsche), some critics even state that it is the music that guides the dancing in Uday Shankar's performances: "It is the dancer who gets lost in the music, not vice versa."[145] Another German reviewer notices the "inner connection between these dancers and musicians."[146] For Wilhelm Tidemann, writing for the Hamburg-based journal *Der Kreis*, the Indian dancers have reached or even surpassed the ideal formulated by Wagner and Nietzsche:

> Only with this level of discipline the art of the body achieves the dual miracle: the return to nature and the complete fusion of gesture with music, [...]. Thus from the other side of the hemisphere a compositional idea emerges which not only equals or completes the entire occidental artistic work but basically surpasses it.[147]

---

[142] F.K., "Kultur der Gegenwart: Bühne und Musik: Der Gott und die Bajadere. (Tanz-abend der Brahmanen-Gruppe Udaj-Schan-Kars im Weinberger Stadttheater)," *Prager Presse* (Prague), March 24, 1932: 8.
[143] "S.Hurok Presents Uday Shan-Kar and His Hindu Ballet," [season 1937/38a]: n.p.
[144] Wagner, "The Art-Work of the Future" 103.
[145] v.M., "Indische Tänze. Uday Shan-Karr [sic], Simkie und ihr indisches Orchester," *Hamburgischer Correspondent* (Hamburg), morning edition, October 10, 1931: 6.
[146] D. 2.
[147] Tidemann 597.

Also the American dance critic John Martin, staff critic of the *New York Times* between 1927 and 1962, acknowledges how Uday Shankar reached an ideal in his successful performances that strongly guided the modern dance scene of the 1930s in Europe (mainly Germany), and in the United States:[148]

> Musically the accompaniments are remarkably satisfying. They are inseparable in mood and design from the dances and seem to have attained the ideal toward which Wigman and the Germans as well as a large number of contemporary American dancers, are striving.[149]

In comparison with Wagner's original conception of the *Gesamtkunstwerk*, however, *Tandava Nrittya* might have been understood as lacking speech or, following Wagner, the word as strongly linked to the "art of tone" (*Tonkunst*). Indeed, his praise of the last movement of Beethoven's ninth symphony reveals as much. Marshall Cohen, though, refers to an assumption often expressed by primitivists as well as some symbolists who claim that "dance's non-verbal language of gesture can express meanings and ideas with greater force, precision and economy than is possible for abstract 'verbal' language."[150] This same argument reappears in the German and American programs of Uday Shankar in which the Indian *mudras* or symbolic gestures are described as replacing speech: "Die Worte sind durch Mudras (symbolische Gesten) ersetzt, die die Gefühle und Ideen ausdrücken. / The 'Mudras' (smybolic gestures) are used, instead of words, to express the ideas and emotions."[151] This is subsequently repeated by reviewers who describe the *mudras* as "ancient gestures which stand for words" or by those who state that: "Each gesture (*mudras*) not only signifies a sentiment, a thought, but often even a single

---

[148] See "The Four Pioneers: Introduction," in: Brown 43-47; here 45.
[149] John Martin, "The Dance: Art of India. Its Culture Is Interpreted by Shan-Kar and His Group of Hindu Performers," *The New York Times* (New York), September 4, 1932: n.p.
[150] Cohen, "Primitivism, Modernism, and Dance Theory" 163.
[151] "Gastspiel der Brahmanischen Inder (Hindus) mit Uday Shan-Kar" n.p. / "Uday Shankar and His Hindu Ballet and Musicians" n.p.

word."[152] In addition, another German reviewer writing for the news-paper *Germania* presents his readers with details on ancient Indian theatre while acknowledging the performance's unity of gesture, music, and mythological content in which the words are represented indirectly via gesture:

> The Indian theater follows an ancient tradition from Vedic times. [...] It is bound by a perfect unity of music, word, song, and dance. Out of this abundant wealth we only saw the dance, individual dances, and a dance-drama of archaic character, and listened to the music. Each gesture is in concordance, which is prescribed by an old tradition, with the words and the music. Thereby an entirely unique aesthetic value emerges right before our very eyes.[153]

One final aspect of the Indian performance with which reviewers and audiences apparently identified the concept of a united artwork was the use of magnificent dress. At least from the time of the *Ballets Russes*, audiences had been used to the integration of elaborate costumes in dance performances. As we can see in the German reviews, costumes played an integral part in the current understanding of a total work of art and audiences therefore appreciated the colorful dresses and ornaments of Uday Shankar's dancers. This is, for example, proven by a comment of a German reviewer, already quoted at the beginning of the chapter: "a barely receivable fullness of combinations of sound and delightful garment splendor creates the atmosphere of a total work of art."[154] The use of costumes furthermore seemed to underline the authentic character of the presentation. Indeed, the *Nāṭyaśāstra* contains a chapter on the use of costume and make-up in Indian theatre.[155] Helmuth von Glasenapp,

---

[152] René Daumal, "Dance Chronicle: Uday Shan-Kar and the Hindu Dance," translated by Vera Milanova, *Hound & Horn* (Cambridge), vol.4 no.2, January-March 1933:288-292; here 292; Szamba, "Tanzbriefe: Paris," April 1931: 14 (see Chap.1, footnote 79).
[153] Dr. Paul Adams, "Indisches Theater. Theater des Westens," *Germania. Zeitung für das deutsche Volk* (Berlin), April 21, 1932: n.p.
[154] Sdt. n.p.
[155] See Ghosh LXIff.

117

writing on Indian drama in 1929, furthermore refers to the minimalism of scenery compared to the importance of costume for actors or dancers, a conception which Uday Shankar apparently repeated in his performances.[156]

The examination of the reviews following the company's performances as well as the closer look at their accompanying programs lends credence to the thesis that German and, to a lesser extent, American audiences perceived the Indian presentation in the context of ideas of a united artwork. *Tandava Nrittya* united dance or pantomime, music, and costume in order to enact a mythological content. This was geared especially for German spectators. It apparently fulfilled an ideal prevalent in the context of German Romanticism which had by the beginning of the 20th century also reached the American art scene. For their critics, the dance and music presentations of Shankar's company hereby directly led back to an ancient past, to the origin of art itself. As the German author Max von Boehn had written in his book *Der Tanz* (1925) in his chapter on "Der Tanz der Naturvölker" (Dance of the Indigenous Peoples): "on the earliest level of their exertion, when dance and music were still one."[157] For some reviewers the unity between dance and music – or one might say the whole concept of a united artwork – was thus associated with a state of primitivism, a reference which also entered the reception of Uday Shankar.

2.4 Uday Shankar, Modern Dance, and Notions of Primitivism

After the company's first performance in Germany, a critic writing for the *Hamburger Nachrichten* described how the Indian presentation fundamentally differed from Western artistic dance due to its basis in a holistic worldview identified with primitive society:

---

[156] See Glasenapp, *Die Literaturen Indiens von ihren Anfängen bis zur Gegenwart* 184. In his remarks on Indian drama Glasenapp also quotes from *The Mirror of Gesture* confirming the spread of Coomaraswamy's writings in Germany; see ibid. 187. See the photograph of Shankar and his company on the cover of this book.
[157] Max von Boehn, *Der Tanz*, Berlin: Wegweiser-Verlag 1925: 10.

This dance has nothing in common with that of the occident. After the arts were displaced and became independent in the 18th century, the dance of the occident went its own way up until the century's end: to virtuosity and the cult of "personality." It was exactly the real personalities which intended to finally bring dance back to its conceptual foundation; the dancing of Laban and Mary Wigman once again strove towards that foundation from which emerges the dance of the people of India as well as all primitive people: the closed world view identified with a state of consciousness which we have to call (following Ernst Cassirer) the mythical consciousness.[158]

Some reviewers apparently perceived Uday Shankar's Indian dance and music presentations as linked with a state of primitivism in the arts. The performances thus stood for a holistic approach uniting life and the arts which Western artists and audiences longed for as it promised a direct access to the supposed origin of all arts.

Following a definition of Frances S. Connelly, primitivism refers to the temporal dimension as it is identified with an idealized past in ways that it "always involves a going back, a return to, a recovery of some early state of being that is perceived to be simpler or more vital or more innocent; for primitivism always has at its core a sense of loss."[159] As it tries to escape the inevitable progress of time in modern European culture it presents itself as a "search for origins."[160] Temporality corresponds to timelessness and an unchanging nature, which means in effect, that "the 'primitive' is necessarily in opposition to all that does change or develop, namely the 'civilized.'"[161]

At the beginning of the 20th century notions of primitivism were present in the field of modern dance, but these notions were not confined merely to an idealized look at the past, such as in the search for the origin of

---

[158] Mk. n.p.
[159] Frances S. Connelly, "Primitivism," in: Kelly, vol.4: 88-92; here 88.
[160] Ibid.
[161] Mark Antliff & Patricia Leighten, "Primitive," in: R.S. Nelson & R. Shiff, *Critical Terms For Art History*, Chicago & London: The University of Chicago Press, 2003^2:217-233; here 217.

movement in nature, but they also involved, to a large extent, ideas of primitive unity. Yet dancers and critics not only thought of a unifying artistic concept such as Wagner's united artwork. It was the art of dance by itself which was identified with primitive unity and hereby allowed a way out of modern society's condition of fragmentation and individualism.

In "The Search for Origins," Roger Copeland examines both the current criticism as well as aesthetic approaches of modern dancers (since Isadora Duncan) to trace ideas that utilize "the primitive as an idealised antidote for all of the discontents of contemporary urban civilization."[162] Copeland here refers back to an article written in 1961 by Frank Kermode, who spotted elements of primitivism in writings on dance since the end of the 19th century. According to Kermode, from the end of the 19th century dance has been regarded as an art form primordial enough to overcome the Cartesian separation of body and mind:

> The peculiar prestige of dancing over the past seventy or eighty years has, I think, much to do with the notion that it somehow represents art in an undissociated and unspecialized form – a notion made explicit by Yeats and hinted at by Valéry. The notion is essentially primitivist; it depends upon the assumption that mind and body, form and matter, image and discourse have undergone a process of dissociation, which it is the business of art momentarily to mend. Consequently dancing is credited with a sacred priority over the other arts [...].[163]

Kermode describes how there was among early modern dancers and dance critics who followed Wagner's concept of dance no disagreement from the fundamental principle that dance is the most primitive, non-discursive art, offering a pre-scientific image of life, an intuitive truth. Thus it is the emblem of the Romantic image. Dance belongs to a period

---

[162] Copeland, "The search for origins" 8.
[163] Kermode, "Poet and Dancer Before Diaghilev" 146.

before the self and the world were divided, and so achieves naturally that "original unity."[164]

As Marshall Cohen points out, Wagner's ideal of the *Gesamtkunstwerk* has been and continues to be been brought together regularly with some form of primitivism in ways that make it seem to function as both a means to restore a unity of experience and as an idea characteristic of primitive art.[165] Not only did Wagner demand an artwork of the future and thus combine all different arts to a holistic unity for which he found inspiration in the past and in German mythology and folk song. He furthermore allocated a prime position to dance because it refers to "the actual living Man; [...] the whole man from heel to crown, such as he shows himself unto the eye."[166] Based on Wagner, dance could be claimed to be the most primitive or original of all arts that represent the whole human being. Frank Kermode mentions how these ideas were at the same time strengthened by the efforts of anthropologists and folklorists to find the origin of the art in all kinds of ritual dance.[167] He also refers to *The Dance of Life* (1923) by Havelock Ellis in which the author assigns dance its origin in times even before humanity and describes it as a "primitive expression alike of religion and love:"

> Dancing and building are the two primary and essential arts. The art of dancing stands at the source of all the arts that express themselves first in the human person. The art of building, or architecture, is the beginning of all the arts that lie outside the person; and in the end they unite. [...] their origin is far earlier than man himself; and dancing came first.[168]

---

[164] Ibid. 147ff.

[165] See Cohen, "Primitivism, Modernism, and Dance Theory" 161. Cohen at the same time denounces this "undifferentiated unity of the primitive world" as "itself a myth – a modern one" which only gains importance in the realm of Western aesthetics. Ibid. 164.

[166] Wagner, "The Art-work of the Future" 100.

[167] See Kermode, "Poet and Dancer Before Diaghilev" 146.

[168] Havelock Ellis, *The Dance of Life*, New York: The Modern Library 1923/1929: 35; Ibid.

One can also spot approaches similar to that of Havelock Ellis and Richard Wagner in the writings of early modern dancers. Loie Fuller, for example, claimed that dancing emerged in the earliest times of human history and demanded an investigation into its origins for the presence and future:

> To rediscover the primitive form of the dance, transformed into a thousand shapes that have only a very distant relationship to it, we shall have to go back to the early history of the race. We then get a notion (of) what the origin of the dance must have been and what has made it what it is to-day.[169]

Ruth St. Denis perceived dancing as a primitive art form and expression of life which, if one discovered its roots, could help modern culture to overcome the separation between body and spirit: "Let us, therefore, regard the dance fundamentally as a Life Experience, as the primitive and ultimate means of expression and communication."[170] Isadora Duncan, in her search for the primordial source of human movement, not only looked at Greek antiquity, but also conjured up a "childhood" or "animal state" of life, ideas commonly identified with primitive society: "She was 'of the opinion, that if one wanted to rediscover dance as free movement and art, one had to go back in history to the Greeks and in life to childhood and to an animal state.'"[171]

The Ballets Russes as well were, due to their Slavic background, generally perceived as linked with primitivism. Their unifying approach proved itself very successful with audiences as well as critics. Camille Mauclair, for example, described Richard Wagner's effort as *une gaucherie barbare*.[172] This approach was, as Roger Copeland elaborates

---

[169] Fuller 16.

[170] Ruth St. Denis, "The Dance as Life Experience" (1924/25), in: Brown 22-25; here 23.

[171] Karl Federn, "Introduction," in: I. Duncan, *Der Tanz der Zukunft. Eine Vorlesung*, Jena 1929²; quoted in: Dörr "She suddenly appeared in Europe like a meteor ..." 43.

[172] Kermode, "Poet and Dancer Before Diaghilev" 145.

on in reference to reviews and intellectual comments of the time, understood as part of their primitive holistic worldview:

> To the Parisian intellectuals like Mauclair, the Russians weren't Europeans. They were Slavs (which is to say, 'primitives'). Lacking Western ego or personal individuation, they had (according to the myth of primitivism) not yet fallen from collective grace into the evils of competitive individualism. And consequently they were thought better suited to 'seamless' collaborations than their Western counterparts.[173]

Ellis's concept of dance as the most original and primitive art form was still prevalent in the 1950s and apparent when the critic Eric Bently praised the American modern dancer Martha Graham for having surpassed Wagner's as well as Nietzsche's theoretical conceptions by ways of dance's direct access to the depth of life:

> The pantomimic theater depicts life, holds the mirror up to nature. The ecstatic theater affirms life and celebrates nature – by awakening in us the vital, natural forces. The one shows life as it has become – what we call psychology and sociology. The other is concerned with life still unlived, unindividuated, primordial, life unfiltered, still in the wellspring. This other theater has been forgotten. Or if not forgotten, remembered only by theorists like Nietzsche or by creative artists like Wagner and O'Neill, who for different reasons never succeeded in reviving it. None of these men was primitive enough, had direct enough access to the depths. Martha Graham has the edge over them in that dance is of itself more primitive than literature or opera.[174]

In the early 20th century context of the modern dance scene, dance itself came to be identified with primitivism, with the origin of the arts from

---

[173] Copeland, "The search for origins" 13.
[174] Eric Bentley, "Martha Graham's Journey" (1952), in: Copeland & Cohen 197-202; here 197ff.

nature and a holistic approach to life. Combined with rhythmical aspects, primitivism in the field of dance further evoked a connection with ritual and cult. Dance allowed a return to an idealized past, to a time before the separation of body and spirit. The supposed natural, original character of movement in modern dance was thus opposed to the artificiality of the classical ballet. As Frances S. Connelly notes: "the 'primitive' existed in a dialectical relationship with the classical tradition."[175] The understanding of what is primitive changed after the second half of the 18th century: in the beginnings the primitive mainly consisted of archaic Greek and Gothic images whereas by the 20th century it was comprised of living African, Native American, and Oceanic art.[176]

The research by British Orientalists on the ancient Indian Sanskrit tradition inaugurated by Sir William Jones had evoked an image of India as part of the world's classical civilizations. Inspired by the work of the British officials and by early travel writings, Romantic writers developed the thesis that India was the cradle of all humankind. Yet, as Gerry Farrell has already pointed out, in contrast to other classical civilizations of the past, such as Greece or Rome, India was a living culture.[177] Presuming that a fundamentally undisturbed, continuous tradition of art, philosophy and religion existed in India up until the 20th century, Indian culture was perceived as allowing direct access to antiquity in the present or, in negative terms (such as with Hegel), as being unprogressive.[178] Parallel with the examination of its classicality, the supposed unchanging nature of Indian culture then additionally led to the identification of India's arts and its people with the primitive.

As mentioned at the beginning of the chapter, Uday Shankar's performance was perceived in some of the reviews as exemplifying a primitive world view. Furthermore, following the early Romanticists view of India's prime importance in the origin of humanity, critics described how the Indian presentation opened up the way to the origin of all arts and mankind, to a utopian past. This is confirmed by an author writing for a Hungarian paper: "The performance of Shan-Kar and his

---

[175] Connelly 91.
[176] See ibid. 89.
[177] See Farrell 18 (see Chap.1, footnote 90).
[178] See here also Chapter 1.3.

company gave us the impression of seeing for an instant the lost paradise."[179] This utopian past is further described as a mythological one, marked by notions of timelessness, as the following quote shows: "dances such as the big 'Tandava Nrittya' whose origin disappears in the night of times."[180] Similarly, a German newspaper critic positions the dance-drama *Tandava Nrittya* somewhere at the beginnings of Indian culture by stating: "apparently the piece which dates back the most to Indian primordial times."[181] One American reviewer more directly connects the performance with primitivism and mankind's origin: "Uday Shan-Kar, who learned his art in the cradle of life, language and religion, reveals primitive mankind's first thoughts and hopes by his dances."[182] In accordance with Connelly's definition of primitivism which detects at its basis a sense of loss, a longing towards a more simple state of being, a German reviewer combines his admiration of the Indian performance with a slight criticism of Western modern society when he makes use of the opposition between "the primitive" and "the civilized" and characterizes Uday Shankar's presentation as "untouched by our [...] fashionable civilization art."[183] In the same culturally critical fashion a French reviewer contrasts the Indian performance with the "barbarism" of Occidental art: "It is while listening to a work like *Tandava Nrittya* that we understand that there is something barbaric in Western civilization."[184] Compared to its Western opposite, Indian dance is understood as being based in nature and myth:

[179] *Pester* (Budapest); quoted in: Khokar, *His Dance, His Life* 57.
[180] "Zum Gastspiel des Indischen Balletts" 3.
[181] H.W., "Württembergisches Landestheater. Gastspiel der indischen Hindu-Tanzgruppe. Stuttgart. 21. Nov.," *Schwäbischer Merkur* (Stuttgart), November 22, 1931: 6.
[182] Leo Rabbette, *Boston Sunday Post* (Boston), March 19, 1933; quoted in: Joan L. Erdman, "Blurred Boundaries: Androgyny and Gender in the Dance of Uday Shankar," in: *Border Crossings: Dance and Boundaries in Society, Politics, Gender, Education and Technology*, Proceedings Society of Dance History Scholars, Toronto, 10-14 May 1995: 117-124; here 121.
[183] R.P., *Münchner Neueste Nachrichten* (Munich), July 18, 1932: n.p.
[184] Vuillermoz n.p. (see Chap.1, footnote 8).

The dance also lives according to the laws of nature. It not only lives in accord with them, it lives solely on them and fulfills them in magic embodiment. [...] it is nature, which dances; the master of nature leads the round dance and the entire moving world answers him through dance. There answer wind and wave, plant and animal, humans and gods.[185]

The Indian performance is once again perceived as surpassing the sphere of mere art. Following a French reviewer in *Le Miroir du Monde*, the presentation in its combination of dance, music, and myth corresponds with the artists' supposed holistic worldview:

> But shows like this do not live on the strength of their aesthetic beauty alone, though that be one of their purest expressions. So many different elements enter into its composition which makes it obvious that the echoes, lights and thought of an entire world, an entire soul, an entire metaphysical system are projected into a performance which could appear to the less observing a simple, though powerfully picturesque display of folk-lore.[186]

The French writer and poet René Daumal paints an exceptionally enthusiastic, dreamlike picture of the performance. His description, translated by his wife Vera Milanova, in which he makes us of classical mythology's image of the golden age, exemplifies the longing towards an idealized more beautiful, honest, and spiritual past. He sees this past brought to life again in the performance of Uday Shankar and his company:

> The beauty of these musicians and dancers, of their instruments, of their attitude of sustained attention, of continual reality, as well as of the accurate and yet most real harmony of their costumes, the truth of all that, the complete absence of scenery; that marching, sonorous splendor, that dance which moves, and that

---

[185] Mk. n.p.
[186] *Le Miroir du Monde* (Paris); quoted in: Khokar, *His Dance, His Life* 56.

moving music which exactly fills the duration signifying eternal immobility; all the marvel, I still believe, sometime to have dreamed it only, as one dreams of an ancient country of wiser and more beautiful people, a golden age.[187]

Comments, such as the above one by Daumal, reveal the shifting classification of the Indian performance between the primitive and the classical. Regardless, they are reflective of the enthusiasm of Western audiences who saw in Shankar's performance an answer to the felt loss and longing towards unity that was apparently lacking in modern society. For modern dancers, art critics and informed audiences, especially in Germany, Shankar obviously achieved and outperformed the ideal of a total work of art pursued since Romanticism and once again revived at the turn of the century

---

[187] Daumal 292.

3. Movement and the Body

3.1 Towards a Definition of Oriental Dance

Various reviews dating back to Uday Shankar's first European and American tour at beginning of the 1930s show that the troupe was received as coming from the Orient, as being Oriental. In Europe, Wilhelm Tidemann announced in *Der Kreis*: "And now these Orientals are coming."[1] In the United States writers such as Mary Watkins from the *New York City Herald* summarized Shankar's performance as follows: "He has brought the Orient to us."[2] Indeed, as Joan Erdman outlines in one of her articles on Uday Shankar, although each country already had its own idea of the Orient due to colonial extensions and linguistic discourses, India was generally perceived as part of it and therefore India must be examined here in reference to the debate on Orientalism.[3]

Orientalism is a Western phenomenon which not only gained importance in the field of dance, where it developed its own distinct outlook as so-called Oriental dance, but which also swept over a large number of arts and popular entertainments. In her article in the *International Encyclopedia of Dance* Trudy Scott defines Orientalism as a European and American phenomenon, an "adaptation or affection in Western art of what are assumed to be the customs, traits, or habits of expression characteristic of the people of the Near East and Asia."[4] Scott further stresses how in the field of dance or performance Orientalism has always strongly been based in exoticism: "Applied to performance, Orientalism denotes

---

[1] Tidemann 597 (see Chap.2, footnote 8).

[2] Mary F. Watkins, "Uday Shan-Kar and troupe offer Program of ancient rituals at New Yorker," *New York City Herald* (New York), December 27, 1932:n.p.; printed in: "Press Comments" 35-36; here 35 (see Chap.2, footnote 5).

[3] See Joan L. Erdman, "Dance Discourses. Rethinking the History of the 'Oriental Dance'," in: Gay Morris (ed.), *Moving Words: Re-Writing Dance*, London: Routledge 1996: 288-305; here 289.

[4] Trudy Scott, "Orientalism," in: Cohen, *International Encyclopedia of Dance*, vol.5: 44-47; here 44 (see Chap.2, footnote 71).

the use or the perception of Oriental elements in a performance (whether authentic, imitative, or derivative) as primarily exotic."[5]

Whereas French, British, and German philological interest in the Orient had already begun at the end of the 18th century and strongly included India,[6] the highpoint of Orientalism in the field of the arts is generally seen – parallel to the increased political involvement of Europe in the Middle East and Asia – to lie in the 19th century, as part of the Romantic movement in poetry, literature, painting, music, theater, and dance.[7] The list of examples from the various arts is extensive. There are the paintings of French 19th-century artists such as Jean-Léon Gérôme or Eugène Delacroix,[8] Théodore Chassériau and Eugène Fromentin,[9] literary works such as, for example, Goethe's *West-östlicher Divan*, Victor Hugo's *Les Orientales*, Gérard de Nerval's *Voyage en Orient*, Samuel Taylor Coleridge's *Kubla Khan*,[10] Karl May's *Orientzyklus*,[11] and orientalized Romantic ballets such as Nikolai Rimsky-Korsakov's *Schéhérazade*, Marius Pepita's *La Bayadère*,[12] Léo Delibes' comic opera *Lakmé*[13] and Giuseppe Verdi's *Aida*.[14] Further, one should not forget the

---

[5] Ibid.

[6] See, concerning India, the Latin translations by Abraham Anquetil-Duperron of the Persian *Zend-Avesta* (1771) and the Sanskrit *Upanishads* in France, the English translations of the *Bhagavad-Gita* (1785) by Charles Wilkins and *Śakuntalā* (1789) by Sir William Jones and Georg Forster's German rendition of *Śakuntalā* (1790) made from Jones's English version of the drama. See Germana 1ff (see Chap.1, footnote 63).

[7] See Scott 44.

[8] See Linda Nochlin, "The Imaginary Orient," in: L. Nochlin, *The Politics of Vision. Essays on Nineteenth-Century Art and Society*, London: Thames and Hudson 1991: 33-59.

[9] See Scott 44.

[10] See Hans-Günther Schwarz, *Der Orient und die Ästhetik der Moderne*, München: Iudicium 2003: 22ff.

[11] See Nina Berman, *Orientalismus, Kolonialismus und Moderne. Zum Bild des Orients in der deutschsprachigen Kultur um 1900*, Stuttgart: M&P 1997: 41ff.

[12] See Scott 45.

[13] See John M. MacKenzie, *Orientalism. History, theory and the arts*, Manchester & New York: Manchester University Press 1995: 151.

[14] See ibid. 155. See also Edward Said, *Musical Elaborations*, New York: Columbia University Press 1991: 65.

impact of oriental symbolism on popular visual arts, such as clothing, jewellery, building decoration, furniture and ornaments.[15]

It is with this background and in this context that the genre of Oriental dance emerged in Europe and the United States at the turn of the century. It ran parallel to and often coincided with the new developing field of modern dance.

3.1.1. Oriental Dance: A Western Genre

At the beginning of the 20th century Western dancers invented and performed dances described by themselves, their critics, and their audiences as exotic or specifically oriental. Joan Erdman delivers a definition of Oriental dance which bases it in its Western perspective, the Western perception of what the Orient might be:

> "Oriental Dance" was an occidental invention. Not created to steal initiative from the Orient, "oriental dance" was initially a term used by Europeans and Americans to describe innovative and balletic dances which were eastern in theme, content, mood, costume, musical accompaniment, inspiration, or intent.[16]

While Oriental dance is described by Erdman as an independent genre, she states that it nevertheless was "characterized by ambiguous boundaries, an inconsistent record, and an anecdotal discourse."[17] Following Erdman's definition, the genre "Oriental dance" initially referred to works by Western dancers which were, in accordance with the above criteria, in one or the other way associated with the East. At the beginning of the 20th century numerous western popular, ballet, and modern dancers performed in this context. The presentation of Indian dance themes (in the widest sense), which were also perceived as part of Oriental dance, was not novel at this time and became popular in Europe

---

[15] See Scott 44. See also MacKenzie, "Orientalism and architecture" and "Orientalism and design," in: MacKenzie 71-137.
[16] Erdman,"Dance Discourses" 288.
[17] Ibid. 291.

at least since Mata Hari (1876-1917). Born in the Netherlands as Margaretha Geertruida Zelle she got married to Captain Campbell MacLeod in 1895 with whom she lived in Java and Sumatra. Back in Europe the couple separated and she started to perform "Indian" dance. Under the name Mata Hari ("Eye of the Day") she had her first public performance at the Musée Guimet, a museum of Asian art, in Paris on March 13, 1905.[18] About the same time the Canadian dancer Maud Allan (1873-1956) developed her controversial dance piece *The Vision of Salome* (1906) which, after her debut in London in 1908 at the Palace Theatre, brought her tremendous success and encouraged a number of imitators and a "Salomania."[19] Already at the Paris Exposition Universelle of 1900 the American dancer Loïe Fuller (1862-1928) had performed Salome's *Dance of the Seven Veils* in a pavilion which Henri Sauvage had built her. With a musical setting by Florent Schmitt based on Oscar Wilde's play *Salome* of 1893, the dance, according to Çelik and Kinney, was "another variation on 'Islamic' dancing."[20] John MacKenzie further adds how Loïe Fuller's performance, due to her floating dress and enhanced by the music's "erotic and highly-coloured setting," was "representing physical liberation from the constrains of the Victorian period."[21] Following Trudy Scott, Loïe Fuller as well as other pioneers of

---

[18] See Gabriele Brandstetter, *Tanz-Lektüren. Körperbilder und Raumfiguren der Avantgarde*, Frankfurt am Main: Fischer Taschenbuch Verlag 1995: 85ff.
[19] See the article "Maud Allan" on the website of the Dance Collection Danse, Toronto, Canada (http://www.dcd.ca/pih/maudallan.html; last accessed June 21, 2011). See also Amy Koritz, "Dancing the Orient for England. Maud Allan's 'The Vision of Salome'," in: Jane C. Desmond (ed.), *Meaning in Motion. New Cultural Studies of Dance*, Durham: Duke University Press 1997: 133-152. Thinking of the so-called Salomania and its reference to Oriental dance, it is also interesting to note that in Paris starting June 3, 1931 and continuing at least up until June 14, Uday Shankar and his company performed in a combined program at the Theatre des Arts in which Shankar's "Danses Hindoues" followed a presentation of Oscar Wilde's "Salome" by Georges and Ludmilla Pitoëff. See Edmond Sée, "Première au Theatre des Arts. Salomé d'Oscar Wilde. Danses Hindoues," *L'Œuvre* (Paris), June 6, 1931: 6.
[20] Zeynep Çelik & Leila Kinney, "Ethnography and Exhibitionism at the Expositions Universelles," *Assemblage. A Critical Journal of Architecture and Design Culture* (Cambridge, Mass.), vol. 13, 1990: 35-59; here 58 and see MacKenzie 161ff.
[21] MacKenzie 162.

modern dance in America "were a part of the culmination of the Orientalist movement in dance."[22]

The inspiration for oriental and – in the context of this thesis – specifically Indian theme dance at the beginning of the 20th century in many cases originated in the exhibition of dancers and musicians from eastern countries at World Fairs and Colonial Expositions such as the Great Exhibition in London (1851) or the Universal Expositions in Paris (1878, 1889, 1900). During the early years of his career Uday Shankar would also perform in this context, at venues such as the Empire Exhibition at Wembley in 1924 and, together with his whole troupe, in a show named "Le Monde Colonial qui chante et qui danse" in November 1931 at the Colonial Exposition in Paris.[23]

In 1903 the Luna Park amusement center at Coney Island in the United States opened its gates. In the next year, following the example of the international expositions in Paris as well as the Columbian Exposition in Chicago (1893), it included an exhibit named "The Streets of Delhi" which left a strong imprint on the American dancer Ruth St. Denis (1879-1968). Having founded her career on the American vaudeville stage and having been familiar with the ideas of the Theosophical Society and Christian Science sect (due to her mother's influence), St. Denis, originally named Ruth Dennis, gained a good deal of success with a number of oriental theme dances throughout her career. These include her Indian dances *Radha* (1905/06), *Nautch* (1919) or *Dance of the Black and Gold Sari* (1923).[24] St. Denis, who had read Ananda Coomaraswamy's *Buddha and the Gospel of Buddhism* written in 1916, was to some extent appreciated by the Indian aesthetician.[25] In an article published in *Vanity Fair* in 1917, Coomaraswamy shortly hints at the American dancer as the one who "has reproduced the atmosphere of Indian life and feeling with

---

[22] Scott 45.

[23] See Khokar, *His Dance, His Life* 41 (see Introduction, footnote 8) and "A l'Exposition Coloniale," *L'Oeuvre* (Paris), November 7, 1931: 6.

[24] See Allen 85ff (see Chap.2, footnote 127).

[25] See Ruth St. Denis, *An Unifinished Life: An Autobiography*, New York: Harper & Brothers 1939: 285ff; quoted in: Christena L. Schlundt, "Into the mystic with Miss Ruth," *Dance Perspectives* (New York), no. 46, summer 1971: 1-54; here 45.

marvelous sensibility."[26] According to Trudy Scott, "St. Denis attempted to lend an air of authenticity by studying Hindu and Buddhist philosophy, researching visual source material, and using Asian performers in her company."[27] Although St. Denis obviously taught Oriental dance at the Denishawn School in California, Scott describes her style, even after her travels to Asia, as in line with "the Orientalist tradition of combining stereotypes, using her increased awareness of authentic detail."[28] John Schikowski, a contemporary witness and writer on dance, gives a short description of St. Denis's Indian performance, and he stresses her focus on atmosphere and setting:

> In her dance performances Ruth St. Denis seeks to conjure up the splendor, the flavor, the radiance and blossom, the entire atmosphere of the tropical Orient. Amid a rich scene of palm trees, temples, and Hindus she appears as an enthroned idol, a snake charmer, etc. By means of slow smooth steps and sways, raging whirls, and by the monotone accompaniment of strange instruments she presented reproductions of Indian dances.[29]

St. Denis's later husband Ted Shawn (1891-1972), with whom she founded a troupe called the Denishawn Dancers, also shows a keen interest in Coomaraswamy's writings. During a tour of the Denishawn Dancers in Asia in spring 1926, Shawn invented a dance piece called *Cosmic Dance of Shiva* in which he danced five cosmic stages, namely "the creation, preservation, destruction, reincarnation, and the ultimate salvation of the universe."[30] The exact same order can also be found in Coomaraswamy's description of Shiva's five activities in dance as

---

[26] Coomaraswamy, "Oriental Dances in America" 61 (see Chap.1, footnote 190). On the preceding page a photograph of Ruth St. Denis is included as part of the article subtitled: "Ruth St. Denis. In One of Her Matchless Indian Dances, Showing Something of the Spirit of the Nautch". Ibid. 60.
[27] Scott 46.
[28] Ibid.
[29] John Schikowski, *Geschichte des Tanzes*, Berlin: Büchergilde Gutenberg 1926: 136.
[30] Ted Shawn (with Gray Poole), *One Thousand and One Night Stands*, New York: Da Capo 1979 (1960): 197ff.

included in *The Dance of Shiva*.[31] This tour further led the troupe to Calcutta where they had a performance at the Empire Theatre which was attended by Rabindranath Tagore. After the performance the poet appeared backstage and even asked St. Denis if she would teach at his Visva Bharati University, an offer she denied, but which led to a joint recital in New York in 1930.[32] In contrast to her husband, who conducted research and talked to scholars and a swami for the preparation of his Shiva choreography, Ruth St. Denis never intended to present authentic Indian or Oriental dance. Instead, she sought to convey a certain mood, as she later stated in her autobiography: "[...] but at no time, then or in the future, have I been sufficiently the scholar or sufficiently interested to imitate or try to reproduce any Oriental ritual or actual dance – the mood to me is all, and inevitably manifests its own pattern."[33] As Matthew Harp Allen concludes, through the Indian works of St. Denis and Shawn "an awareness of Indian dance (however drastically mediated) was awakened in audiences throughout the United States and Europe and in the minds of young aspirants creating the new field of modern dance."[34]

Although Coomaraswamy, as his article in *Vanity Fair* shows, obviously appreciated Ruth St. Denis's dancing, he nevertheless had a preference for another so-called Indian dancer: "it is only Roshanara, associated with Ratan Devī, who has presented this season on the New York stage for the first time in America, what can rightly be called an authentic Nautch."[35] Following Olive Holmes, Roshanara was the daughter of a British government official who had lived in India for some time. In 1910 she toured together with Anna Pavlova.[36] Ratan Devī, originally Alice Richardson, was Coomaraswamy's second wife and a former mu-

---

[31] See Coomaraswamy, "The Dance of Shiva" 87 (see Chap.1, footnote 191). In "Gods Who Dance" Shawn states that "Harvell [sic] and Coomaraswamy, Gangoly and Krishna Sastri all agree that the Cosmic Dance is made up of five movements", ibid. n.p. (see Chap.2, footnote 126).
[32] See Suzanne Shelton, *Divine Dancer: A Biography of Ruth St. Denis*, New York: Doubleday 1981: 198; quoted in: Allen 88.
[33] St. Denis, *An Unifinished Life* 56ff; quoted in: Allen 90.
[34] Allen 91.
[35] Coomaraswamy, "Oriental Dances in America" 61.
[36] See Olive Holmes (ed.), *Motion Arrested. Dance Reviews of H.T. Parker*, Middletown: Wesleyan University Press 1982: 257.

sic student of Cecil Sharp in London. They went together to India where she took lessons in Indian song and learned to accompany her performances with an Indian *tānpūrā*.[37] Coomaraswamy gave introductions to her performances and these can be found in a review on "Ratan Devi's Indian Songs," published two years earlier in the London *Times*.[38] As press announcements and reviews in the London *Times* and the *New York Times* show, the public was aware of the performers' English background.[39] According to a review in the *New York Times* recalling Ratan Devi, the American-born Ragini Devi alias Esther Luella Sherman started touring the United States only a few years later and then subsequently India and parts of Europe with her Indian dances and songs.[40] Another example is the half Indian Nyota Inyoka, who appeared on European stages at the beginning of the 1930s obviously presenting Indian or Hindu dances.[41] We then also find references to the American dancer La Meri, originally Russell Meriwether Hughes, who showed an interest in all kinds of "ethnic" dancing, which included a high amount of Indian

---

[37] See Lipsey 91ff (see Introduction, footnote 10).

[38] See "Ratan Devi's Indian Songs," *The Times* (London), November 27, 1915: 11.

[39] See "Indian Dances at the Tivoli," *The Times* (London), September 30, 1913: n.p.; "Roshanara Dances at Palace," *The New York Times* (New York), January 6, 1914: n.p.; "Aid France's Fine Arts. Roshanara and Ratan Devi in Dances and Songs of India," *The New York Times* (New York), March 17, 1917: n.p. and "Adolf Bolm Gives His Exotic Dances. [...] Roshanara and Ratan Devi in East India Nautch [...]," *The New York Times* (New York), August 21, 1917: n.p.

[40] See Marianne Nürnberger, *Tanz/Ritual: Integrität und das Fremde*, Habil., April 2010: 239 (http://homepage.univie.ac.at/marianne.nuernberger/Nuernb_Habil.pdf; last accessed June 21, 2011). See "Ragini Devi Sings and Dances," *The New York Times* (New York), April 29, 1922: n.p.; "Concert to Aid Indian Poor of East London," *The Times* (London), October 25, 1938: n.p. and O.C. Gangoly, "Classical Indian Dancing. Ragini Devi's Interpretation," Reprint from *Amrita Bazar Patrika* (Kolkata), September 23, 1934: n.p.; Dartington Hall Trust Archive. See also photo, with subtitle, in "People [...]," *The Illustrated Weekly of India* (Bombay), September 17, 1933: 38ff; here 38.

[41] See Jacqueline Robinson, *Modern Dance in France. An Adventure 1920-1970*, Amsterdam: Harwood Academic Publishers 1997: 91. See also the following reviews: "Arts Theatre Club," *The Times* (London), October 8, 1930: n.p.; Eduard Szamba, "Tanzbriefe. Paris," *Der Tanz* (Berlin), vol. 6 no. 2, Februar 1933: 8-10; here 9; "Nyota-Inyoka et l'enchantement de son ballet Indou," *Archives Internationales de la Danse* (Paris), no. 1, January 15, 1934: 43.

dance.[42] In 1941 La Meri even published a book under the title *The Gesture Language of the Hindu Dance* with a foreword written by Ananda K. Coomaraswamy.[43]

In the 1930s, parallel to Uday Shankar's first tour in Europe and the United States, one can still find references to performances by lesser known European oriental dancers in the press, such as by the Dutch dancer Dini von Essen who obviously spent some time in the Dutch East Indies. Von Essen presented modern dance by incorporating so-called Indian dance elements in the Netherlands and Germany.[44] One can also find similar references to the German dancer Stella d'Oriente alias Erika Britz.[45]

Another dancer who made the genre of Oriental dance popular for wider audiences even earlier was the Russian ballerina Anna Pavlova (1881-1931). She danced the leading role in highly orientalist works such as Marius Pepita's Indian-themed ballet *La Bayadère* and appeared in 1909 with Serge Diaghilev's Ballets Russes known for their popular ballets based on oriental themes. These included ballets based on themes from India (e.g. *Le Dieu Bleu*), Egypt (*Cléopâtre*), Russian folklore (e.g. *Thamar, Sadko*) as well as *Schéhérazade* based on the Arabian tales of *A Thousand and One Nights* mixed with ballets based on biblical stories (e.g. *Salomé*).[46]

After a trip to India in 1922/23 during which she, like Ted Shawn and Ruth St. Denis, rather unsuccessfully tried to see Indian dancing but witnessed a Hindu wedding, Pavlova became interested in creating dances based on authentic Indian movements. In London she was intro-

---

[42] See Judy Farrar Burns, "La Meri," in: Cohen, *International Encyclopedia of Dance*, vol. 4: 354-355 and Henriette Bassoe, "Flights Beyond the Horizon with La Meri," *The American Dancer* (Los Angeles), April 1941: 11; 32.

[43] See La Meri, *The Gesture Language of the Hindu Dance*, New York: Benjamin Blom 1941.

[44] See hw., "Tanzabend Dini von Essen," *Schwäbischer Merkur* (Stuttgart), November 21, 1931: 5.

[45] See M. Waker, "Internationaler Tanz-Wettbewerb und Volkstanz-Treffen Wien 1934. 27. Mai bis 16. Juni 1934," *Der Tanz* (Berlin), vol. 7 no. 7, July 1934: 6.

[46] See Jean-Michel Nectoux, "*Schéhérazade* – Musik und Tanz," in: C. Jeschke et al (eds.), *Spiegelungen. Die Ballets Russes und die Künste*, Berlin: Verlag Vorwerk 1997: 105-112; here 107.

duced to the young Indian art student Uday Shankar, whom she asked to choreograph two dance pieces, *A Hindu Wedding* and *Rhada-Krishna* (both 1923). It was Anna Pavlova who eventually encouraged Uday Shankar as well as Rukmini Devi and Ram Gopal to return to their Indian tradition to develop or rather revive a dance form that would be genuinely Indian.[47]

In contrast to Ruth St. Denis, for example, who took inspiration from Oriental themes or ideas for her exotic dances, artists such as Ted Shawn or Anna Pavlova intended to create Oriental or Indian dance based on authentic sources. Others even studied the exotic dance or music culture they represented in its home country, such as Ratan Devī, who took music lessons in India. This dual nature of Oriental dances and the changes occurring since the 19th-century is described by Inge Boer:

> Tracing the history of the Oriental components in Western taste, one finds a continuing fascination with non-European others, foregrounding their exoticism. Exoticism and representations of the Oriental other had both phantasmic overtones and aims to reflect a reality. In comparison to the eighteenth century, more men and women travelled to the Orient in the nineteenth and twentieth centuries.[48]

Looking at Mata Hari, Pavlova, the Ballets Russes, Ruth St. Denis, or other Western performers of Oriental dances, their focus – although interested in or inspired by Oriental dance movements – was still more marked by Orientalized themes, figure stereotypes, costumes, settings and decor. With the emergence of dancers from so-called Oriental countries at world fairs, expositions, and in the western dance scene, a new understanding of Oriental dance and its movements did evolve.

---

[47] See Gowri Ramnarayan, "Rukmini Devi: A Quest For Beauty. A Profile (Part I)," in: *Sruti* (Madras), June 1984, vol. 8: 17-29, here 29; See Ram Gopal, "Pavlova and the Indian dance," in: A.H. Franks (ed.), *Pavlova. A Biography*, New York: Da Capo Press 1979: 98-110.

[48] Inge Boer, "Orientalism," in: Kelly, vol.3: 406-408; here 406 (see Chap.2, footnote 57).

3.1.2 A New Level of Authenticity: Oriental Dancers on Western Stages

By the time Uday Shankar and his company started to perform in Europe and the United States, western audiences and writers on dance had already developed a closer idea of what Oriental dancing might be due to their familiarity with dance presentations at the European and American expositions and world fairs as well as through Western Orientalized performances. In accordance with the general understanding of "the Orient as a highly eroticized space," the public formed the impression of Eastern dance movement as first of all of an erotically suggestive nature.[49]

At the Chicago World's Fair of 1893 Algerian and Egyptian women performed a *danse du ventre* (belly dance) which led to widespread protest by churches and the National Association of Dancing Masters.[50] This, of course, only resulted in an enhancement of their popularity so that "the 'shocking' and 'indescribable' movements were promptly imitated in dance halls, vaudeville, and burlesque houses by a number of 'Little Egypt' dancers doing their version of the 'hootchy-kootchy'."[51] The name "Little Egypt" here originally referred to a dancer supposedly from Armenian or Greek origin, who performed her version of belly dance at the Chicago World's Fair of 1893.[52] In Paris, at least since the Exposition Universelle of 1889, "belly dances formed the core attraction"[53] in respect to their coverage in exhibition accounts and the increasing elaboration of choreography. The number of daily spectators in 1889, for example, reached an average of two thousand.[54] Following Çelik and Kinney it was, of course, "anything but pure belly dance that

---

[49] Ibid. 407.
[50] See Scott 45.
[51] Ibid.
[52] See John Martin, "The Dance. Its March from Decadence To a Modern 'Golden Age'," *The New York Times Magazine* (New York), December 12, 1937: 10-11, 30; here 11.
[53] Çelik & Kinney 39.
[54] See Anouar Louca, *Voyageurs et écrivains égyptiens en France aux XIXe siècle*, Paris: Didier 1970: 193ff; quoted in: Çelik & Kinney 39.

was presented as an Islamic ethnic form at the universal expositions, where, moreover, its performative aspects were refashioned for the benefit of Parisian audiences."[55] From the late 19th century on belly dancing also reached the field of Western popular dancing, such as with "La Belle Fathma" alias Rachel Bent-Eny, an Algerian of Jewish origin, who not only performed at the 1889 exhibition, but also at theaters on the Champs Elysées.[56] By 1900 erotic belly dance performances were common attractions in the small theatres at Chicago and Paris.[57] Çelik and Kinney conclude: "The belly dance survived on different soil by aligning with a part of the entertainment industry that capitalized upon and domesticated eccentricity."[58]

The success of Western dancers such as Mata Hari, who was only "superficially acquainted with East Indian dances," but more importantly "willing to appear virtually nude in public," surely spread the image of Oriental dance as primarily encompassing sexually connoted movements.[59] Even before that the Paris Exposition Universelle of 1889 had encouraged the "Moorish dance" of the French dancer La Goulue alias Louise Weber who performed at the famous Moulin Rouge.[60] On a distinct popular level, the label Oriental dance also became associated with more spectacular movements, such as that of Paris in 1900 when "Egyptian *almées* were described as balancing candles and glasses on their head and chests" as well as objects that were understood as typically Islamic, such as the narghile.[61] Another example is the *Princess Rajah Dance* presented at the St. Louis World's Fair in 1904, in which a supposedly Oriental dancer – besides her apparently objectionable movements – picked up a chair with her teeth and spun it around with increasing speed.[62]

---

[55] Çelik & Kinney 40.
[56] See ibid. 43.
[57] See Greenhalgh 103 (see Chap.1, footnote 17).
[58] Ibid.
[59]"Mata Hari," in: *Encyclopedia Britannica* (http://www.britannica.com/EBchecked /topic/368879/Mata-Hari; last accessed June 21, 2011).
[60] See Çelik & Kinney 50ff.
[61] Scott 45; See Çelik & Kinney 54.
[62] See Astrid Böger, "The Princess Rajah Dance and the Popular Fascination with Middle Eastern Culture at the St. Louis World's Fair," in: Heike Schaeffer (ed.),

Apart from spectacular dance performances of this kind, the World Fairs and *expositions universelles* claimed to be sites of ethnographic and educative appeal. Yet the distinction between ethnography and popular spectacle apparently became confused. As Zeynep Çelik and Leila Kinney explain: "the ethnographic displays rested upon their theatrical presentation, in which documentation intermingled with certain kinds of entertainment deemed culturally authentic."[63] Already the Paris Exposition Universelle of 1889 presented singers, musicians and also dancers from Africa, the Middle East and Asia in the guise of a "traditional ethnic spectacle."[64] According to John MacKenzie, one of the main successes – at least among musicians and composers of the time – was a performance of "Javanese dancing to the accompaniment of performers upon the gamelan."[65] The Javanese dancing girls apparently also appeared at the Exposition Universelle in Paris in 1900.[66] MacKenzie further mentions a group of Cambodian dancers appearing in Paris in 1906 creating a huge success, as well as another group of Balinese dancers and gamelan at the Paris Colonial Exposition of 1931.[67] These dancers would later have an immense influence on Antonin Artaud and his "theatre of cruelty."[68] From the Paris Exposition Universelle of 1889 onward and in accordance with the rise of anthropology, exotic countries and their inhabitants were on display. In what Greenhalgh describes as "human showcases," "people from all over the world were brought to sites in order to be seen by others for their gratification and education" and presented in

---

America and the Orient, Heidelberg: Universitätsverlag Winter 2006: 203-216. Çelik & Kinney describe that dances with chairs were "reminiscent of the notorious quadrille of the Louis XIII chair, which in 1886 had become the 'signature dance' of Aristide Bruant's Le Mirliton." Çelik & Kinney 54.

[63] Çelik & Kinney 39.

[64] MacKenzie 157.

[65] Ibid.

[66] See the written account on the Exposition Universelle by Paul Morand, quoted in: Greenhalgh 84ff.

[67] See MacKenzie 198; 201. See also "L'exposition. Les danses de Bali à Vincennes," *Je suis partout* (Paris), no. 30, June 20, 1931: 10 and André Levinson, "Les Danseurs de Bali," *Candide* (Paris), no. 385, July 30, 1931: 10.

[68] See Brinkmann 117 (see Chap.1, footnote 19).

ways of "a more or less authentic tableau-vivant fashion."[69] Numerous Asian or Oriental dance performances, often combined with demonstrations of religious rituals, were thereby transplanted into the Western context and apparently satisfied Western exotic strivings.[70] Çelik and Kinney conclude: "Exoticism is dependent upon trade and transportation. In practice, it requires a transplantation of some sort, one that can simultaneously preserve the peculiarity of the foreign object and insert it into a new environment."[71] This alignment, however, leads to the paradox that the exotic loses its authenticity – as described from the perspective of semiotics by Jonathan Culler: "The paradox, the dilemma of authenticity, is that to be experienced as authentic it is mediated, a sign of itself and hence not authentic in the sense of unspoiled."[72]

Yet it was the presentation of dance from so-called Oriental countries at the world fairs as well as the interest in and the depiction of Oriental themes by Western dancers which opened the door for dancers from the East to appear on Western art stages. Already by being Oriental, or in the context of this work, Indian, they were seen as bringing a new level of authenticity to dance which changed audiences' and critics' perception of former western oriental dancers and oriental dance in general.

Reviews show that at the beginning of the 1930s not only Uday Shankar, but also other so-called Oriental dancers appeared on European and American stages. In dance and art magazines as well as newspapers from the 1930s on quite a number of performances by dancers from various Eastern countries are mentioned and reviewed. In addition to Uday Shankar, there are references to a number of other dancers, such as the Indian dancer Menaka,[73] originally Leila Sokhey, from Bombay, who be-

---

[69] Greenhalgh 82.

[70] See ibid. 83.

[71] Çelik & Kinney 42.

[72] Jonathan Culler, "Semiotic of Tourism," *American Journal of Semiotics* (Pensacola), vol.1, 1981: 137; quoted in: Carlos Rincón, "Exotisch / Exotismus," in: Barck, vol.2, 2001: 338-366; here 351ff (see Chap.2, footnote 18).

[73] See for example André Levinson, "La Danse: Mirages d'Orient," *Candide* (Paris), November 13, 1930: 15; "Informations Internationales. France," *Archives Internationales de la Danse* (Paris), no.1, January 15, 1933: 37 and Eduard Szamba, "Tanzbriefe. Paris," *Der Tanz* (Berlin), vol.6 no.1, January 1933: 12.

came a dancer in the North Indian style of Kathak; Indra Ramosay;[74] a lesser known dancer called Ishvani Goolbano, who obviously performed a mixture of Hindu, Cingalese and Cambodian dances,[75] and, towards the end of the 1930s, Ram Gopal.[76] There are further references to Indonesian dancers from Java and Bali that were earlier often announced as Indian due to the designation of these places as part of the Dutch East Indies. These include Raden Mas Jodjana,[77] who often performed together with his student Roemahlaiselan;[78] Mas Madjadjawa[79] and Devi Dja;[80] the Burmese dancer Hasoutra.[81] Further, a number of Japanese performers are referred to, including Michio Itow, also named Ito, who already performed several years before Uday Shankar, but in the 1930s still appeared in Hollywood Bowl concerts;[82] Toshiko Umemoto;[83] Yeichi Nimura;[84] Misao und Takaya Egutschi;[85] Joshio Aoyama;[86] M. Toshi

---

[74] See Eduard Szamba, 'Tanzberichte. Paris', *Der Tanz* (Berlin), vol.6 no.4, April 1933: 15 and Eduard Szamba, "Paris," *Der Tanz* (Berlin), vol.7 no.1, January 1934: 8.

[75] See "Indian Dances at the Ballet Club. Miss Ishvani Goolbano," *The Times* (London), December 27, 1933: 6.

[76] See for example John Martin, "The Dance: Ballet Union; Massine and de Basil Companies Merged—Programs of the Week," *New York Times* (New York), April 24, 1938: 8; Dorathi Bock Pierre, "Dance Events Reviewed. California. Ram Gopal," *The American Dancer* (Los Angeles), May 1938: 46 and Dorathi Bock Pierre, "Ram Gopal. Young Hindu Dancer," *The American Dancer* (Los Angeles), July 1938: 25-26.

[77] See André Levinson, "Javanese Dancing. The Spirit and The Form," *Theatre Arts Monthly* (London), vol.14, December 1930: 1056-1065; here 1064.

[78] See J. Lewitan, "Der erste internationale Solotanz-Wettbewerb. Warschau (9.-16. Juni 1933)," *Der Tanz* (Berlin), vol.6 no.7, July 1933: 8 and A.G., "Tanzberichte Berlin," *Der Tanz* (Berlin), vol.8 no.3, March 1935: 4.

[79] See Levinson, "Javanese Dancing" especially 1057-1058 and 1063ff.

[80] See, for example, "Old Ladies from Bali," *Time* (New York), November 6, 1939 (http://www.time.com/time/magazine/article/0,9171,762762,00.html; last accessed June 21, 2011) and Dorathi Bock Pierre, "Dance Events Reviewed: Bali and Java Dancers with Devi Dja," *The American Dancer* (Los Angeles), March 1940: 37.

[81] See J. Lewitan, "Tanzberichte. Berlin," *Der Tanz* (Berlin), vol.6 no.3, March 1933: 5.

[82] See "Give Japanese 'Noh' Dance. Michio Itow in Novelty 'Tamura' at Neighbourhood Playhouse," *The New York Times* (New York), January 9, 1921: 2 and Scott 46.

[83] See Szamba, "Paris," January 1934: 8 and J. Lewitan "The Month in Berlin," *The Dancing Times* (London), vol. 23, 1932: 257-259; here 258.

[84] See for example Szamba, "Tanzbriefe. Paris," January 1933: 11; "Arts Theatre Club," *The Times* (London), November 13, 1934: n.p. and Marion Schillo, "Dance Events

Komori[87] and Kenji Hinoki.[88] As the following subchapter will show, one might even include La Argentina, performer of Spanish dance, in the genre.[89]

The increasing European interest in dancers from Asian or Oriental countries is also attested by the number of "conférences-démonstrations" (lecture-performances) at the Archive International de la Danse in Paris since 1934. Examples include the performance in March 1935 put on by a Mr. Rao who presented "the traditional method of Hindu folk dancing accompanied by Hindu musicians," and Persian dancing by Medjiid and Mahidé Rezvani in the same month.[90] And Nyota Inyoka is the very first to appear at the A.I.D. in a lecture-performance, whose data in unknown, on "traditional Indian dance."[91] In the course of the 1930s and 1940s one also finds a rather large number of articles in dance and art magazines generally describing and trying to explain dances of the Orient or Asia. In 1937 alone the Los Angeles-based journal *The American Dancer* includes at least four articles on the topic.[92] The subject of Oriental dance also reached monographic writings such as the dance histories of the time. An earlier German example is

---

Reviewed. Critiques and News from the East, Mid-West and West. Chicago," *The American Dancer* (Los Angeles), May 1937: 27.

[85] See Elli Müller-Rau, "Tanzberichte. Misao und Takaya Egutschi. Bach-Saal, 26. Oktober 1933," *Der Tanz* (Berlin), vol.6 no.12, December 1933: 10.

[86] See Joseph Krüll, "Tanzberichte Wien," *Der Tanz* (Berlin), vol.8 no.1, January 1935: 13.

[87] See "Informations Internationales. France" 37.

[88] See "Kenji Hinoki," *The American Dancer* (Los Angeles), January 1937: 20, 26.

[89] See the examination of André Levinson's article "The Spirit of the Spanish Dance" in Chapter 3.1.3.

[90] See "Übersicht der von den A.I.D. organisierten Wortveranstaltungen ('conférences-démonstrations') und anderer wichtiger Programmpunkte 1934-1950," organized by Marion Bastien & Franz Anton Cramer, in: Baxmann 154-160; here 154 (see Chap.1, footnote 13).

[91] See ibid.

[92] See Edna Emroch, "Dance of the Orient," *The American Dancer* (Los Angeles), January 1937: 24, 26; Edna Emroch, "The Noh Dance of Japan," *The American Dancer* (Los Angeles), March 1937: 16, 40; Harriet Huntington, "The Balinese Live For Art. Dancers On a Magic Island," *The American Dancer* (Los Angeles), June 1937: 22-23, 62; Ragini Devi, "Living Traditions of the Hindu Dance," *The American Dancer* (Los Angeles), June 1941: 14, 32.

John Schikowski's *Geschichte des Tanzes* (1926) whose author, influenced by the evolutionary approaches of culture history, seeks to present an all-embracing history of dance from its beginnings to the present. Having a look at the book's table of contents, the chapter simply entitled "Orientalische Tänze" (Oriental Dances) is positioned at the end of the chronological order. Starting off with descriptions on the dances of the "Urvölker" (indigenous peoples) and "antiken Kulturvölker" (ancient civilizations) of Greece and Rome, the author elaborates on the role of dance in the German middle ages and the subsequent modern era, further passing over European (national) dances. The chapter on Oriental dance stands immediately before his descriptions on classical ballet and modern dance in the 20th century. From this thematic order one can conclude that the author apparently distinguishes between Oriental dances and primitive ones. Schikowski even explains the interest of his time in Oriental dance by posing a link between Western modern, especially German, dance and certain dance forms of the Orient:

> The modern development which art dance went through (particularly in Germany), drew attention and interest to certain forms of dance which are alive in the Orient and which meet with the latest occidental fashions.[93]

Schikowski here obviously refers to Rudolf von Laban and, even more explicitly, Laban's former student Mary Wigman. Due to the fact that he praises how Wigman led modern dance to the "peak of perfection", his following comment must aim at the two practicioneers: "Only the last phase of development of modern art dance has brought occidental man close to the marvels of oriental dance, and slowly we begin to penetrate into its deep and dark secrets."[94] It is then due to the exponents of German *Ausdruckstanz* that Oriental dancing is further explored and received in the West. Schikowski though leaves it to his readers to identify those wonders and secrets of Oriental dance. He nevertheless gives a few hints, such as when he describes the importance of rhythm, an element he de-

---

[93] Schikowski 99.
[94] Ibid. 141; 136.

tects in primitive dance. Although earlier examined apart from each other, primitive and Oriental dancing here overlap once again. Referring to Laban, Schikowski observes:

> Here, for the first time in the history of dance, the art of rhythmical movement is captured in its entire magnitude and depth. What the primitive peoples exercised unsuspectingly, what was admittedly awake in ancient classical dance, but emerged highly impaired, what was finally entirely buried by the ballet, shines in the theory of Laban as a pure, purposeful, established doctrine.[95]

Another hint might be his reference to the prominent use of movements of arms and hands in the dances of Mary Wigman.[96] It is, however, even more possible that Schikowski bases the link with Oriental dancing in a certain inner attitude, a holistic worldview commonly identified with the primitive. In the words of Laban: "All being is movement, all actions are dance."[97]

In the course of his chapter Schikowski further differentiates between Near Eastern dance – which he describes as due to the Muslim religious background almost non-existent – and Asian dance. Whereas he regards most of the Asian dances presented on European stages as "so much arranged according to the liking of occidental audiences, that one does not get an idea of the essence of Oriental dance," he still names one apparently more authentic example, a Javanese Tandak-ensemble having performed in Germany in the Berliner Künstlerhaus the preceeding winter organized by the Deutsch-Niederländische Gesellschaft. This is the only reference to a performance he seems to have witnessed in person. Schikowski stresses the indigenous background of the dancers and the performance's ethnographic value due to its primitive though high cultural ("Überkultur") background. In reference to Javanese dancing's thematic occupation mainly with mythology he refers to its high degree of stylization – leading him to the description as a "frozen art." He further

---

[95] Ibid. 140
[96] See ibid. 142ff.
[97] Laban in ibid. 139.

distinguishes Javanese from European dance forms by the predominant use of arms and hands, its expressively calm but ornamental character and the fluency of the movements causing only slow and soft changes between contraction and release:

> Three native Javaneses, two male and one female dancer, performed the dances dressed in rich costumes. What we saw was not only ethnographically instructive, but also artistically striking: wonderfully appealing suggestive movements from the joints of the shoulders, the elbows and particularly the fingers; a ballet of arms and hands. Each dance was a dramatic tableau which illustrated a scene from the epics of the gods, saints or heroes. There was nevertheless no touch of pantomime, but all was of a perfectly elaborated abstract design. A form of Asian rococo art, product of a primitive "Überkultur", an artistic exercise bound by tight rules, maybe even already ossified. Fundamentally different from European dance. Nothing that excites, nothing that whips up, no exultation and no lamentation. No verves, but all rises and subsides in waves of contraction and release in very subtle, hardly noticeable variations.[98]

Schikowski further explores the field of Asian dancing and hereby bases his observations in European travel writings, such as when he quotes a lengthy passage from *Heute in Indien* (1924) by Colin Roß. Roß here comments on a performance of Javanese temple dance which he witnessed in Bali. The Javanese dancing girl's presentation, enthusiastically denoted as "the composition of a religious-mystic-erotic artwork," is then strongly opposed to common Oriental street dancing, "the coarse erotic demonstrations by which girls or boys entertain the locals as well as strangers in the dance halls of major oriental cities."[99] The temple dance performance accordingly completes the erotic connotation of the dance because of its link with the religious sphere; it thereby elevated to an acceptable level for Western audiences. Quoting from Sven Hedin's travel

---

[98] Ibid. 100.
[99] Quoted in ibid. 102.

report *An der Schwelle Innerasiens* (1923), he goes into detail about the erotic dance presentations by Persian, Afghan, Tajik and Uzbek girls and boys in the city of Samarkand in Uzbekistan, thereby serving the popular image of Oriental dance.[100]

Schikowski, however, ends his chapter on Oriental dancing with a reference to India. He therefore relies on Hermann Graf Keyserling's observations on Indian Nautch dances from his *Travel Diary of a Philosopher* (1919). Keyserling here describes the endless and apparently formless character of Indian dances marked by soft, floating and ephemeral movements.[101] Schikowski uses this quote as an occasion to talk about the absent-mindedness and dreaminess of the Oriental mind with its link to non-competitiveness as he sees it reflected in dance. These descriptions once again strongly remind of Hegel's concept of Indian culture as mainly guided by fantasy, sensibility, and imagination such as elaborated on in his *Lectures on the Philosophy of History*:[102]

> These dances reflect the Oriental soul, which does not want to be aroused, to be spurred to a higher validation of its powers, but instead wants to reassured, comforted, lulled into obliviousness. They appear like the quiet, gentle sound of the sea, are the floating in dreams. Nirvana-Dances.[103]

Schikowski apparently regards India as part of the Orient, as the observations in his chapter on Oriental dance confirm. He here repeats the image of Oriental dance movement as entailing an erotically suggestive nature, yet this image is further separated from Asian and specifically Indian dance and complemented by the erotic-spiritual dance of the temple dancing girl bridging the two spheres. One though has to mention that by then the here-adopted motif of the temple dancer already had its own history in Western artistic representations of the Orient. John MacKenzie not only gives the example of Johann Wolfgang von Goethe's poem *Der*

---

[100] See ibid. 102-104.
[101] See ibid. 105.
[102] See Hegel 139; 147 (see Chap.1, footnote 128).
[103] Schikowski 105.

Gott und die Bajadere (1798), but also refers to the opera *Les Bayadères* (1810) by the French composer Charles Catel and the Russian ballet version entitled *La Bayadère* (1877) by Ludwig Minkus.[104] Regarding the question of movement, Schikowski, who takes recourse to earlier travel reports, mentions the focus on movements of the upper body in Oriental or, more specifically, Asian dancing which is further understood to be marked by a high degree of stylization with movements executed at a slow pace.

The description of Asian dancing as slow, calm and dominated by upper body movements already appears in earlier writings. One example is found in the *History of the Indian Archipelago* (1820) by the British Orientalist scholar John Crawfurd.[105] Writing on Javanese music and dance at the beginning of the 19th century, he stresses the serious character and the use of the whole body, especially arms and fingers, in Asian dance – in contrast to a focus on the legs in Western ballet dancing:

> Whatever be the occasion in which dancing is exhibited, it is always grave, stately and slow, never gay nor animated. As in all Asiatic dancing, it is not the legs but the body, and especially the arms, down to the very fingers, that are employed. Dexterity, agility or liveliness, are never attempted.[106]

Crawfurd though explains the rather slow movements in Asian or Javanese dance in reference to the climate and further depreciates it by mentioning the problems Western spectators might have when attending a performance:

---

[104] See MacKenzie 192ff.

[105] See Gareth Knapman, "Race, Empire and Liberalism: Interpreting John Crawfurd's History of the Indian Archipelago," paper for the 17th Biennial Conference of the Asian Studies Association of Australia in Melbourne, July 1-3, 2008 (http://arts.monash.edu.au/mai/asaa/garethknapman.pdf; last accessed June 21, 2011).

[106] John Crawfurd, "Music and Dancing," in: *History of the Indian Archipelago*, vol.1 (1820); excerpt in Tagore, *Hindu Music from Various Authors* 297-312; here 304 (see Chap.1, footnote 93).

To the gravity and solemnity which belong to the inhabitants of a warm climate, any display of agility would appear as indecorous, as their stately and sluggish minuet dancing appears insupportably tiresome to our more volatile and lively tempers.[107]

The description and classification of Oriental dance movement still concerns and is elaborated on by dance experts, dancers and critics in the 20th century. Dance movements from East and West are hereby strongly opposed as can be seen in André Levinson's reflection on Spanish dance ideally exemplifying the confrontation of the styles of the Orient and the Occident.

3.1.3 André Levinson: Dance Movements East and West

One writer who is known for his systematization of Eastern and Western dance elements is André Levinson (originally named Andrei Yakovlevich Levinson). Born in St. Petersburg in 1887 and the son of a physician, by 1917 he was part of the young intellectual elite in Russia. Levinson was major defendant of classical ballet and its symbolism and an idealist opposing realism who, following Acocella and Garafola, believed dance to be "a revelation of spiritual truth."[108] He published writings on dance all throughout his life. In the wake of the Russian Revolution he left Russia in 1921 together with his wife and daughter and settled in Paris.[109]

In his article "The Spirit of the Spanish Dance" (1925) Levinson develops a definition of Oriental dance according to its choreographic elements. Here Oriental dance is defined in direct opposition to Occidental dance, claiming an incoherency of both styles. In order to establish these two opposing categories, Levinson builds on the history of dance in Spain, especially Andalusia, the place where the confrontation between

---

[107] Ibid.
[108] "Introduction," in: Joan Acocella & Lynn Garafola (eds.), *André Levinson on Dance. Writings from Paris in the Twenties*, Hanover & London: Wesleyan University Press 1991: 1-26; here 11.
[109] See ibid.: 2ff.

oriental and occidental culture led to a "centuries-long conflict between Moslem and Christian[,] which has had a profound influence on all of the Spanish art, and particularly on the dance."[110]

Beginning with ancient Spanish dancing whose former but by-gone magnificence Levinson regrets, the author names various historic and present dance forms in the region. He shortly hints at the "gypsy dances," still maintaining their "definite and picturesque qualities," and the "wild taut savagery of the *bailes de flamenco*," and then comes to the role of dance at the court in Madrid where indigenous Spanish elements, such as the national *fandango*, were mixed with foreign ones, such as the French minuet.[111] In the wake of Romanticism, Spanish dance reached the rest of Europe and by the middle of the 19th century it had entered the ballet of the opera and from there influenced the ballets of Petipas, Fokine and Diaghileff.[112] Levinson then mentions a number of outstanding Spanish artists whose work as "a true art of stage dancing for a time held the scene in Spain" including Dolores Serral, Pepita de Oliva, Lola Montes and Lola de Valencia.[113] Levinson asks the reader: "What were these magnificent dancers? Were they merely Spanish Gypsies of Albaicin gotten up as they are today for the purpose of beguiling foreigners?"[114] He negates their popular profile and identifies them as ballet dancers, members of the opera of Madrid, which accomplished a successful mixture of current styles and theoretical approaches of the time as well as Spain's own diverse cultural heritage:

> The opera of Madrid had assimilated the choreographic experience of the other Latin countries, the theories of Paris and Milan, and for a time was able to adapt all of this to the Spanish fashion, drawing upon their own rich inheritance of Castilian

---

[110] André Levinson, "The Spirit of the Spanish Dance," *Theatre Arts Monthly* (New York), vol.9 no.5, May 1925: 307-320; here 311.
[111] Ibid. 307; Ibid; See ibid. 308.
[112] See ibid. 308ff.
[113] Ibid. 309.
[114] Ibid. 310.

pomp and Andalusian rhythm, as well as the Oriental sinuosity of the Moors.[115]

One here gets a first impression of how the author defines Oriental dance – as signified by sinuous movements. It further shows that, according to Levinson, Spanish opera dance originally consisted of a blending of Oriental and Occidental dance elements. He, however, directly follows: "But now the ballet of Madrid exists no more."[116] Levinson ascribes the "death" of the art to the dance "eventually turning its back entirely on its popular and ancestral origin to restrict itself to Italian virtuosity."[117] The Spanish dance became corrupted and lost its former magnificence, apparently because it negated its Oriental elements and attached itself too much to the Western language of dance.

That Spain and its arts do indeed differ from the rest of Western Europe is also expressed in a subtitle to a painting printed in the article which shows men and women dancing together. Levinson writes: "Group dancing has always had a particularly important place in the Spaniards' social life, extending even to their religious observances."[118] He then hints at the comparatively primitive state of Spanish society by quoting Havelock Ellis: "The supreme religious importance of dancing among primitive peoples is pointed out in *The Dance of Life* by Havelock Ellis, who adds that 'it is in Spain, where dancing is a deeper and more passionate impulse than elsewhere in Europe, that religious dancing took firmer root and flourished longest.'"[119] While this quote first of all reflects the contemporary image of Spain as European exotic or primitive other, one might wonder if that image is derived from the perception of Spain's historical connection with the Orient.

It is one single artist, the dancer La Argentina, whom Levinson names as being able to reconnect current Spanish dancing with its ancient

---

[115] Ibid.
[116] Ibid.
[117] Ibid.
[118] Ibid. 312.
[119] Ibid.

past.[120] La Argentina, originally named Antonia Mercé (1888-1936), was born in Buenos Aires. Influenced by her Andalusian father and her Castilian mother, both of whom were professional dancers, she took ballet classes. At some point during her career she decided to concentrate on Spanish or Andalusian native dancing and obviously blended them with her ballet technique.[121]

According to Levinson, her style is described as mainly Andalusian since it represents a mix of Oriental or Moorish elements with Occidental, which is here Castilian. He writes: "This is a style that organizes and completely realizes the plastic elements of the Andalusian improvisation, which modifies the ardors of Moorish fancy by the discipline of Castilian decorum."[122] As Levinson explains, this cultural mix of dance elements is not a harmonious one, but instead it has been continuously marked by a conflict between Orient and Occident, even as the country itself has been:

> What then are the essential dynamic and plastic characteristics of the Spanish dance – the actual origins of its peculiar style? It seems clear that the splendours and the miseries, the glory and the decadence of the Spanish dance have been determined by the uninterrupted duel between the East and the West, which is characteristic of the country itself. The burning ardors of the Moor have been grafted upon the austere race of Castile. An exceptionally violent and sensual nature is held to the rules of an unusually strict society. Andalusia has remained, as far as the dance is concerned, an eternal battle field.[123]

Here Levinson once more identifies the Oriental nature with strong emotions, with extreme violence and sensuality, and, accordingly, it cannot go together with the severe and strict character of the Castilian society.

---

[120] See ibid. 313.
[121] See Holmes 223.
[122] Levinson, "The Spirit of the Spanish Dance" 313.
[123] Ibid. 313ff.

This leads to a deep conflict that is at once strongly reflected in dance, but nonetheless unsolvable.

The oppositional character of Oriental and Occidental dance is further stressed in Levinson's description of its choreographic elements, which above all reveals his solidarity with western classical ballet:

> the movement of Oriental dance is concentric – the knees bent in, the arms embracing the body, everything converging to the centre – while the movement of the dance of Western Europe (the most perfect expression of which is to be found in the traditional classic dance) is just the opposite – the body of the dancer being extended, the arms and legs turned outward, the entire being dilated to its extreme capacity. The European dancer, be she a ballerina or a peasant, moves about freely, she leaps in the air and glides and runs, while the Oriental dancer turns in upon herself, lives upon herself, like a statue, turning upon a pedestal. She crouches and stretches. She is a plastic form, coherent but changing. The back hollows, the abdomen swells and sinks. The almost fluid muscles ripple under the glossy skin of the arms, whose sinuous curves ondulate in an internal rhythm.[124]

Oriental dance is here further defined as statuesque and rhythmic, marked by curved and rather slow movements which are all directed towards the center. Levinson then applies these categories to the Spanish or Andalusian dance and to Argentina, in contrast to the classical ballet dancer, and further develops them. He describes how every position in classical ballet, every "pose of classic equilibrium" can be best demonstrated by "straight lines that cut the vertical at different angles. The decorative curves play about this rectilinear frame. The arms are held parallel to the legs or else in balanced opposition to them."[125] In contrast to the straight lines of Western dance, Andalusian dance – as apparently all Oriental dance – is marked by curved lines, "like the line followed by the stone

---

[124] Ibid. 314.
[125] Ibid.

cutters of the Alhambra or of the painters of Ajanta."[126] It is the Western ballet dancer who extends outward in his or her turns while the Oriental dancer turns inwards:

> In a pirouette the leg of the classic dancer describes a periphery around a central point – she radiates outward – while Argentina in making a turn follows the line of a continuous spiral – like a capital S. That capital S is the image and emblem of oriental beauty and is depicted quite as lovingly in the Persian miniature as in the Japanese wood carving.[127]

The Spanish dancer Argentina is identified as an Oriental dancer based on these characteristics. The outline of curves is not only represented in her body movements, but also strengthened and varied by other details, such as the movements of the wrists, the eyebrows, the lashes and different glances.[128]

Finally, Levinson opposes the costumes of these two schools. Whereas the Western dancer commonly chooses a dress that leaves her arms and shoulders uncovered and allows the legs to move freely, the Spanish dancer – similar to the "ghawazi or Egyptian street dancer" – likes to cover herself, wears a scarf over her neck and in this way "accentuates the mystery of her body."[129] André Levinson here repeats the popular cliché and identifies oriental dance with sexuality and the erotic, in strict contrast to the Western ballet:

> In this connection it should be remarked in passing that what one might almost term the semi-nudity of the classic dancer is purely functional, serving to facilitate the mechanism of her art. Hence its complete absence of sexual significance. What the oriental withholds from view, on the other hand, no less than the folds of the shawl draping the figure of the Spanish dancer and held up by

---

[126] Ibid. 319.
[127] Ibid.
[128] See ibid.
[129] Ibid.; Ibid. 320.

the shoulder or by the crooked elbow, are replete with erotic suggestion.[130]

Levinson ends his article by once again referring to the difficulties the ballet schools confronted when trying to unite Oriental or Andalusian and Occidental (here Italian) dance in one natural, harmonious dance form. He claims that the "ballet masters of Madrid went so much too far in their attempts to achieve a mechanical and violent synthesis of these two styles of choreographic expression" and laments that "the Andalusian curves broke under the school master's ferrule."[131] According to André Levinson, this breaking of the curves led to the current "decadence of the Spanish dance with a few isolated artists [primarily Argentina] as the sole remaining stars in an extinguished firmament."[132]

In his article Levinson delivers his readers with what appears to be the first in-depth analysis of dance movements East and West. Writing as an advocate of Western classical ballet, he builds his approach on the thesis that Oriental and Occidental dance differ fundamentally from each other and cannot be reconciled. Following Levinson, this becomes especially apparent in the Spanish or Andalusian dance where both schools, due to historical circumstances, ideally confront each other. Yet it remains questionable as to how far the supposed irreconcilability of these two styles applies to modern dance whose practitioners often developed their dance movements inspired by the movements of dancers from the so-called Orient. These doubts are confirmed by the comment such as that made by the American art critic and impresario Lincoln Kirstein writing in *Playbill* in the 1970s. Kirstein here claims the profound effect Oriental movement and philosophy had on the approaches of modern dancers. Yet he utilizes André Levinson's systematization of Oriental dance as centrifugal versus Western dance as centripetal as his starting point. This pair of opposites is then compared to modern dance versus the classical ballet:

---

[130] Ibid.
[131] Ibid.
[132] Ibid.

A prime distinction exists between occidental and oriental dancing: open against closed, centripedal against centrifugal; kinetic against (dominantly) static; fast against slow. This is over-simplification, but a like parallel might be set for ballet against 'modern': aerial versus terrestrial. From Denishawn down to today, the orient, both in movement and morality, strongly influenced 'modern-dance.'[133]

3.2. From Oriental to Asian Dance

3.2.1 The Genre of Asian Dance: Levinson and Others

In dance writings from the beginning of the 20th century, Indian dance is commonly subsumed under the rubric of Oriental dancing. Yet already in John Schikowski's *Geschichte des Tanzes* published in 1926 one could identify a trend towards further differentiation, when Schikowksi – though still under the heading Oriental dance – distinguishes a few exemplary Asian dance performances from other more common Oriental styles due to their religious impetus. Several years after his examination on Oriental and Occidental dance movement Levinson wrote an article on Javanese dancing that used the example of Spanish dance. Published in 1930 in *Theatre Arts Monthly*, he here initiates the distinction of Asian dance from the general field of Oriental arts.

Whereas Asian dance is still presented as a very vague category encompassing a huge field of varying dance forms "spreading from Africa into Europe," Levinson shows an awareness of its diversity while acknowledging a specific uniformity when he mentions "its infinite variety of expressions having a certain semblance of unity."[134] Levinson expresses a keen interest in differentiating and defining "the original character of each of these dialects of the language of form, the details and not the generalities, the points in which various modes of

---

[133] Lincoln Kirstein, "Classical Ballet: Aria of the Aerial," *Playbill* (New York), May 1976; in: Copeland & Cohen 238-243; here 240ff (see Chap.2, footnote 9).
[134] André Levinson, "Javanese Dancing" 1056 ; Ibid.

dance differ from, instead of resembling, each other."[135] Yet in the end he is less concerned with questions of geography and instead he intends to focus on "the features of a living dance" which he, in this case, detects in Java.[136] While he describes Javanese dancing as a "prolongation and a modification of Hindu, Buddhist, or Shiva-istic art," he is convinced that religious statues or reliefs alone cannot express dance's character appropriately.[137] He explains: "But the key to Javanese dancing is not in sculptured monuments, in the composition of reliefs, and the attitudes of statues."[138] To further prove this he elaborates on the importance of the shadow-play Wayang-Kulek in Java that historically precedes many sculptured reliefs.

Levinson soon after returns to the link between Javanese dance and statues and hereby states the oppositional character of Javanese dance movements to its counterpart in the Occident:

> At the outset we find ourselves at the antipodes of every Occidental notion of the dance. In Europe, whether in the theatre or in the fields, the dancer, trained or untutored, glides, leaps, whirls, and displaces air. The Javanese dance knows neither extension nor elevation; it is pre-eminently *static*; it is a figure walk, punctuated with stops, or – better yet – a succession of rests linked by transitions, a sequence of equilibriums. The gestures and displacements of the body are so many phases in the metamorphosis of a statue. There is no soaring in space, no urge, but a measured unfolding and travelling of the gesture in a tempo that is always slow – *adagio*.[139]

According to Levinson, Javanese dancing is marked by slow, rather static movements creating a constant equilibrium in direct contact with the ground. The identification of the dance with "the metamorphosis of a

---

[135] Ibid.
[136] Ibid.
[137] Ibid. 1059.
[138] Ibid. 1060.
[139] Ibid. 1061.

statue" clearly reminds the reader of Levinson's definition of Oriental dance as statuesque in his former article "The Spirit of the Spanish Dance," wherein he describes it as "a plastic form, coherent but changing."[140] Javanese or Asian dancing apparently remains a subcategory of Oriental dance. But there are differences to be detected, as Levinson neither refers to the spiral movements of Oriental dance compared with the capital S (according to him "the image and emblem of oriental beauty"), nor to the sinuous arm movements before identified by him with Oriental dance.[141]

Whereas Javanese court dancing is compared with French ballet due to its "aesthetic of deliberation, the attribute of everything noble,"[142] Levinson mentions the fact that the dancers mainly make use of the bare flat foot, a characteristic he also finds in "Egyptian statues. [...] The knees are constantly crossed, inflected in a half-bend and turned out, so that we see the ankles and feet in profile."[143] Starting from these positions of the legs the upper body and the arms develop their varying and elaborate movements: "[W]hile the base of the moving statue travels or pauses, the torso and the arms execute about the vertical pivot a wide play of curves, twisting, and contortions."[144] Levinson then describes a position which he claims to find in various Oriental cultures past and present, the "lotus position" identified with Buddha, "common to the idols of Borobudur, the Egyptian scribes of the old Empire, and the humblest cobbler of present-day Cairo."[145]

In a next step Levinson announces the importance of stylized gestures of the head, the arms and the hands in Javanese dancing, "formulae which conform strictly to ancestral tradition and intangible conventions."[146] Further, he draws a parallel between these and ancient Greek hand and finger movements. While he is convinced that these gestures have their origin in Buddhist sculptures, he laments the fact that

---

[140] Levinson, "The Spirit of the Spanish Dance" 314.
[141] Ibid. 319; See ibid. 314.
[142] Levinson, "Javanese Dancing" 1061.
[143] Ibid.
[144] Ibid. 1062.
[145] Ibid.
[146] Ibid.

for modern Javanese people they have "become mere *forms*. Their ideal content has vanished; their plastic prestige persists. They have become beautiful gestures, ornaments or *fioritura* phrases. [...] From a mystic experience they have become an aesthetic fact."[147] Levinson accordingly not only draws the common parallel between ancient Greek and Asian arts, a comparison regularly made use of by British Orientalists and Romanticists regarding Indian art, but he refers these cultures to the canon of classical nations. He further repeats the common cliché of the contemporary decadence of the arts in these countries. This opens the door for Western agents to come to their rescue, since it is understood that the real Asian dance still lays concealed deep within the traditions of these countries, such as in their ancient religious sculptures.

Javanese dancing accordingly now lacks its former mystic or spiritual quality, its religious rootedness – the main criterion of all Oriental, especially Indian, art. According to Levinson, Javanese dancing has become secular and therefore lost its original idealistic purpose:

> The soul of India "moves through a forest of symbols". For the Oriental all reality is only an illusion of the senses, Mahayama, or an illusion to some metaphysical entity, a reference to the Great Beyond. The soul of Java, on the contrary, delights in its earthy paradise. That is why its *sacred* dance had become *secular*.[148]

For Levinson, a defender of classical arts and an idealist who opposes realism and describes the current dancing in Java as "*royal* pastime," this development obviously means a degradation of the art form. However, it apparently did not affect the formal aspects of the art which still adhere to the "conventions of an ancient art."[149]

Indian religious arts here become the ideal with which Javanese dancing is compared. Although Levinson still regularly uses the categories Oriental and Asian interchangeably, it is especially Asian dancing as

---

[147] Ibid. 1063.
[148] Ibid.
[149] Ibid. 1065.

mainly based in slow, statuesque, stylized movements of the upper body which is elevated as a classical art, an art of ancient origin.

Levinson's occupation with Oriental or Asian dancing, its movement, and theme apparently stirred the wider discussion on oriental dance. One example is an article by Edna Emroch printed in the Los Angeles based dance magazine *The American Dancer* in January 1937. Under the title "Dance of the Orient," the author here focuses on various Asian dance styles including ones from India, Ceylon, Japan, China, Java, and the Philippines. Her focus is made clear from the very beginning in her subtitle, "A general survey of the philosophy and the art of the dance in the East," as well as in her introductory description of the Orient as "subdued by a sacred atmosphere."[150] Though Emroch hints at the still common link between Eastern dancing and its erotic nature, other namely "philosophical" aspects gain prime importance in her essay: "Since, however, the dance in the East is primarily a philosophical expression rather than a 'danse du ventre,' I shall delve into its spiritual and aesthetic qualities."[151] For the coming general overview she then mainly relies on writings by the American modern dancers Ted Shawn and Ruth St. Denis.

Concerning movement in Asian dance, Emroch describes the use of expressive details, such as movements of the eyes and the hands, all guided by rhythm: "All through the East we find professional dancers lending expression to their dance by using every part of their body. As the eyes express emotion, the hands and feet simultaneously indicate rhythm."[152] She then comes to the classification of Oriental dancing as more or less stationary and uninterested in wide jumps and turns as are common in Western classical ballet. Levinson had called this the "outward radiation" of the ballet dancer. Oriental dance is instead qualified as mainly consisting of movements of the upper body conducted from a centralized fixed position: "Movement, in the dance of the Orientalist, is mainly from the waist upwards, and as the body 'revolves around its own axis' one or both legs remain stationary."[153] The statuesque character is

---

[150] Emroch, "Dance of the Orient" 24.
[151] Ibid.
[152] Ibid.
[153] Ibid.

further stressed by the help of an anonymous quote referring to Eastern dancing as a "succession of beautiful postures," a description which parallels Levinson's reference to the "many phases in the metamorphosis of a statue" as found in Javanese dancing.[154]

In another of Emroch's articles from the same year she examines "The Noh Dance of Japan" in the context of oriental art, when she describes it as a "mystical poetic dance-drama full of the reality of life and the somberness of all things oriental."[155] Emroch here repeats her approach to Oriental dance exhibited in her former article and focuses on its stylized gestures rooted in an ancient spiritual tradition. She accordingly detects the essence of the Noh to lie "in the beauty of its gestural representation of a philosophy molded by tradition and enriched by a sacred background" and claims as its dominant theme the "harmony of mind and body."[156] She further stresses the ancient origin of the art form's movements whose perfection lies "in the exact interpretation and imitation of the postures of hundreds of years ago."[157]

In Curt Sachs's *World History of the Dance* (1933) the author ascribes Indian dance a prime position in Asia. Sachs who, as the title already suggests, intends to encompass the dance of the whole world from its origin until the present, here follows the evolutionist approach of German *Kulturkreislehre* and accordingly starts off from animal dances.[158] In his chapter entitled "The Evolution to the Spectacular Dance and the Oriental Civilizations," Curt Sachs refers to dancing in Egypt, India and Japan. He describes Indian dance in the context of "gesture dance" ("Gebärdentanz"); India becomes the example of all Asian dance cultures which generally tend towards abstraction, imagination and stylization. Sachs explains this choice with the fact that the gesture dance emerged in India: "The superb art of the gesture dance originated in India thousands of years ago and from there penetrated to the East in the eighth century A.D. at the latest."[159] In a Romantic fashion it is India which is here once

---

[154] Ibid. 26; Levinson, "Javanese Dancing" 1061.
[155] Emroch, "The Noh Dance of Japan" 16.
[156] Ibid.
[157] Ibid.
[158] See Chapter 1.2 of this book.
[159] Sachs, *World History of the Dance* 232ff (see Chap.1, footnote 46).

again referred to as a place of origin. He further stresses dance's stylized character based in an ancient tradition written down long ago:

> India has in its own way forced this art into a rigid system of set rules: the *Nātya Śāstra* of Bhárata – written about the fifth century A.D., but based on traditions considerably older – and, somewhat more briefly, the *Abhinaya Darpana*, the 'mirror of gestures' of Nandikéśvara, are its greatest manuals. These works establish a language of gesture in which the entire representational field of the dramatic dance, according to the theme and emotion expressed, is assigned, down to the last detail, to the various parts of the body.[160]

While Sachs admiringly names a number of exemplary Indian gestures or *mudras*, he nevertheless mentions how their conventionalization poses a problem when it meets with the liberty and individualism of Western art: "We cannot help but see in it an abstractness, a hardening into convention, which is hopelessly removed from our ideals of free and personal art."[161]

As a review on a performance of dances from India printed in *The American Dancer* in 1936 also shows, Oriental dance had by then mainly become associated with sinuous dance movements which in turn were identified with erotic themes. Indian dance, however, is less and less thought of in this context. The erotic connotation here further shifts towards a connection between dance and spirituality. Following a concert at the Los Angeles based Dance Theatre by Sumita and Lilivati Devi presenting "Sacred Temple and Seasonal Dances of India," the reviewer observes:

> [T]hese dances were untouched by any suggestion of the theatrical, or any of the sinuous movements which have become associated in our minds with all Oriental dancing. These dances gave not the slightest hint of such movement. They were esthetic, inter-

---

[160] Ibid. 233.
[161] Ibid.234.

163

pretive dances used in their seasonal and religious rituals, very spiritual in quality, lofty in interpretive ideal and completely separated from any earthly or physical suggestiveness.[162]

Asian including Indian dance is thus exceedingly described as of spiritual importance and thereby differentiated from oriental dance as the latter is identified with theatricality, spectacle, and eroticism.

While still carried out under the more general label of Oriental dance, Levinson's examination of Javanese dancing and its movements reveals a growing interest in Asian dance traditions. His as well as other examples attest a shift and a further differentiation in the genre of Oriental dance in the first half of the 20th century. The popular image of eroticized sinuous Oriental dance movements is increasingly replaced by a new focus on the stylized movements of the dance and theater traditions of various Asian countries (prominently India). Western dancers and writers on dance here detect what they then identify as the real, authentic Oriental, or rather Asian dance, namely movements of spiritual impetus rooted in a tradition continually preserved since antiquity. These religious dance forms are described as being in danger, but regarded worth being revived in the present as a possible source of inspiration for Western modern dancers in search for the origins of their art. This intention also explains the growing number of discussions of Oriental dance in Western dance and art journals. It is here interesting to note that in the following years we will also find articles by dancers from Oriental countries themselves giving insights into the expressive qualities and the spiritual heritage of their dance cultures. One example is Ragini Devi's article on "Living Traditions of the Hindu Dance" published in the dance magazine *The American Dancer* in 1941.[163]

In accordance with the Romantic fascination with India, its arts, and its philosophies – a fascination that gets carried on into the 20th century – Indian dance in particular becomes a prime example for the dances of the

---

[162] Dorathi Bock Pierre, "Dance Events Reviewed. Critiques and News from the East, Mid-West and West: California: The Dance Theatre, May 17, Gould Studios, L.A.," *The American Dancer* (Los Angeles), July 1936: 31.
[163] Devi 14, 32.

East. A closer examination of the reception of Uday Shankar in terms of the reviewers' descriptions of Indian dance movements will follow this trend and reveal a further differentiation between Asian and Oriental dance. It will also reveal the emergence of a distinct understanding of the movements and themes of Indian dancing as supported by the company's self-presentation.

3.2.2 Uday Shankar: Presenting Indian Dance Movements in the West

Reviews dating from the early 1930s, the time when Uday Shankar and his company appeared for the first time in Europe and the United States, reveal that the audiences and critics were greatly interested in the way the dancers and Uday Shankar (as the leader of the group) were moving. Their movements apparently still differed a great deal from what Western spectators were used to viewing in ballets or modern dance performances. Whereas the Indian dancers were associated with Oriental dancing, many elements of movement observed in the reviews remind of Levinson's description of Javanese or Asian dance. Reviewers increasingly identify specific Indian movement elements and themes in the performance.

Critics commenting on the dance movements in the presentations of Uday Shankar and his group classified Indian dance primarily as part of the wider field of Asian dances. The movement elements hereby detected parallel or confirm those described by Levinson in his examination of Javanese dancing. One example would be the already-established link between dance and ancient sculpture. Accordingly, in one of the first French reviews published following Shankar's debut performance in Paris, Georges Mussy praises "the plastic beauty and the sculptural attitudes of Uday Shan-Kar."[164] A reviewer from the Swiss *Tages Anzeiger* also takes up the link between Shankar's dance and antique sculpture: "Often the oldest Indian sculptures seemed to spring into life."[165] A German critic writing for the *Hamburger Anzeiger* similarly detects the source of Uday Shankar's dances in "thousands-of-years old Indian

---

[164] Mussy n.p. (see Chap.1, footnote 9).
[165] *Tages Anzeiger* (Zurich), undated; quoted in: Khokar, *His Dance, His Life* 57.

165

sculptures;" though he describes the movements as rather primitive, "almost primitively simple" due to an identified lack of toe dance and ballet leaps.[166] He continues:

> these are without exception stepped dances; steps with the ball of the foot and short jumps serve the purpose to let ring rattles fastened to the ankles clang; spinning figures prevail, seldom leads a strong effect to runs and a few swinging turns.[167]

Having characterized Indian dance once again as concentric and inward-turning, the same reviewer mentions the distinctive movements of the upper body. He further identifies a typical war dance pose as a common feature of all Eastern or Oriental dancing:

> The characteristic gesture arises from a well-executed timed mobility of the hips and shoulders; the hands and arms, predominantly raised out of the elbow, are often conducted in parallel twining movements; occasionally the head makes a strange sidelong movement. One also sees the characteristic war-dance pose of the East: with the legs spread bouncing and the knees bent.[168]

Another critic, Franc Scheuer, further classifies the Indian performance in the general context of Asian or Oriental dance. Writing from Paris for the British *Dancing Times*, he describes Uday Shankar's use of certain fixed dance positions as centers for a number of smaller movements, especially of the arms and shoulders, as a typical sign of all Asiatic dancing:

> Arms and shoulders, the most traditional exponents of Asiatic dancing, together with heel and ankle (these terrestrial means!), play an important role in the choreography of Uday Shan-Kar, and are used by him almost exclusively to invoke or portray the

---

[166] Sdt. n.p. (see Chap.1, footnote 25).
[167] Ibid.
[168] Ibid.

divinities of his native land. Indra, Krishna, Radha, all the major and minor Gods of the Hindu pantheon, are symbolized about a slightly changing centre of gravity in a manner, which, to the Occidental eye, might easily appear static and monotonous.[169]

The apparently monotonous outlook of the dancers (for Western audiences) is also mentioned by a German critic who declares a total lack of facial expressions: "Dances without any mimicry, at most the dancer Uday Shankar plays with the lower lip or the brows."[170] The same reviewer however goes on positively acknowledging the wealth of expressive possibilities within this monotony: "Dances of monotonous movement, mostly from the arms, always from the ankles, often from the shoulders, sideways from the hips – but inside this monotony [there is] an inexhaustible richness of expression."[171] Similarly Raoul Brunel, writing for the Parisian magazine *L'Oeuvre*, mentions the predominant use of the hands and upper body before the legs and assures the reader of their expressiveness: "The gestures of the hands and the contortions of the trunk therein take more space than the steps and the language of the feet. They are nevertheless eloquently expressive."[172]

Mary F. Watkins from the *New York City Herald* regards the predominance of hand and arm movements as well as the play of the facial muscles as an element typical of all Oriental dance: "The Oriental does not believe that the only thing to dance with are the feet; he favors, if anything, hands and arms, but his torso is almost equally pliant and eloquent as are eyes, eyebrows, lips."[173] She then cannot stop herself from comparing Uday Shankar's play of hands with flying birds and therefore, once again, presupposes a closeness between the Oriental (or the Indian)

---

[169] Scheuer 15 (see Chap.1, footnote 15).

[170] Hi., "Hindu-Tänze," *Berliner Tageblatt und Handels-Zeitung* (Berlin), April 20, 1932, evening edition: n.p.

[171] Ibid.

[172] Brunel 5 (see Chap.1, footnote 67).

[173] Watkins, "Uday Shan-Kar and troupe offer Program of ancient rituals at New Yorker," 36.

and nature when she writes: "Shan-Kar's hands are miracles of fluency, as supple, strong, and delicate as the flight of birds."[174]

A German reviewer from the *Fränkische Tagespost* in Nürnberg also acknowledges the Indian dancers' mastery of movement, mainly of the upper body, which he in many cases regards to be motivated by appearances in nature; he nevertheless seems to regret the lack of jumps:

> Sure enough, gymnastic jumps are seldom performed by the men, never by the women. Almost everything happens slowly, as pacing or walking. Instead the torso is employed, up into the tips of the finger, up to a rhythmic glance, for dancing expression. [...] The heads in their strangely jerking matchless movements remind of the display dances of erotic birds. Rhythmically rolling or poking movements of the shoulder, the body and the hips complete the technical skills. The impressive posture of rest is also an effectively utilized artistry.[175]

The same reviewer further identifies sinuous, serpent-like arm movements in the Indian performance and hereby evokes the common cliché of Oriental dance: "With vibrating and fluttering fingers the arms move like darting, coiling snakes."[176] This is further repeated in a review printed in the Zurich *Tages Anzeiger* that praises the "soft and serpent-like play of the arms, hands and fingers" of the dancers.[177] Also, American reviewers focus on winding movements as a hallmark of the dance presentation: "The whole performance is remarkable for its sensuous and undulating movement. Bodies and hands flow from one getsure [sic] into another in curves that never end. Arms, wrists and fingers, so perfect in their ease and interesting postures, carry a wealth of expression."[178]

---

[174] Ibid.

[175] Brunck n.p. (see Chap.1, footnote 78).

[176] Ibid.

[177] *Tages Anzeiger* (Zurich), undated; quoted in: Khokar, *His Dance, His Life* 57.

[178] S.A., "The Dance – International Dance Festival Opens at New Yorker Theater – Shan-Kar makes American Debut," *New York City Post* (New York), December 27, 1932: n.p.; printed in: "Press Comments" 40-41; here 40.

Oscar Thompson, fascinated by Uday Shankar's perfect command of his body, finally evokes the exotic image of the Indian snake charmer:

> As a dancer he [Uday Shankar] has the boneless grace which, with the Hindu, approaches the sinuosity of the serpent. It has been said of him that each of the four hundred and fifty muscles of his body does exactly what he wills it to do. [...] Those hands wrought frescoes on the air. The neck – only a snake charmer of the snake that is being charmed could explain that. One wondered there was no permanent dislocation.[179]

Uday Shankar's early dance presentations apparently included gestures evoking the sinuous movements popular in Western Orientalized dance performances at least since the beginning of the 20th century.[180] Mohan Khokar, biographer of Uday Shankar, here refers to the influence Western Oriental dance had on Shankar's career.[181] Most reviews, on the other hand, interpreted the movements of hands and arms in the context of the *mudras* which are understood as a distinct Indian, or even Hindu element. A German critic, while commenting on *Tandava Nrittya*, describes the *mudras* as symbolical gestures analogous to a language of movement:

> There are also dances like the big "Tandava Nrittya," whose origin disappears in the night of times, where an entire drama is acted out in symbolical gestures (mudras). The Brahmanical

---

[179] Oscar Thompson, "Music – Shan-Kar's Hindu Dancers in First events of International Festival," *Brooklyn New York Eagle* (New York), December 27, 1932; printed in: "Press Comments" 37-39; here 38.

[180] This so-called "Serpentine movement" is also mentioned as part of the Delsarte system as taught by Genevieve Stebbins and obviously made use of by Ruth St. Denis in her dance *The Cobras*. See Genevieve Stebbins, *Delsarte System of Expressions*, New York 1902: 180; quoted in: Brandstetter & Ochaim 91, footnote.

[181] "In no small measure his inspiration came from the west where other dancers were undertaking 'oriental themes' and often doing the snake routine. Whereas these protagonists were to shape up later, Shankar breathed the same air or explorations and his exposure must have led him to this vast, bountiful journey." Quoted from Ashish Mohan Khokar, "Uday Shankar: An Appraisal," in: *Nartanam* (Mumbai), no.4, October-December 2001: 39-42; here 39.

people brought this language of movement to a refinement and perfection which verges on the miraculous.[182]

The above description of the *mudras* as a main element of Indian dance is apparently based on a text written by Alice Boner, the Swiss artist and initially the main financial supporter of the group. Prominently included in the detailed programs accompanying the European performances, Boner with her writing prepares the reception of Indian dance as based on traditional gesture that serves the enactment of mythical subject matter:

> Classical Indian dance, more precisely the art of the Mudras, is a language of movement which comprises the entire diversity of life, outer as well as inner occurrences, nature and soul. Its gestures rest upon traditional convention and are immediately clear to such an extent that they are partly even used in everyday life. Their main purpose though is the plastic-mimetic portrayal of the ancient legends of the gods and the sacred dramas, as they have been exercised in the temples for centuries. This dramatic demonstration is not, as one might easily assume, a drastic simplification and watering-down of the sacred texts for the utilization of the people. On the contrary, it is as if the dramatic language of dance possesses even more delicate nuances and a wider range of expression than the word, as if it stretches even further into the ramification of feeling and thought.[183]

In this passage, Boner locates the *mudras* in everyday Indian life and thereby once again points to a holistic worldview commonly identified with primitive society. It is not the individual that expresses himself in the *mudras*. The symbolical gestures of the "dancer-actor" are stylized and based in a tradition above the personal level: "There are no contingencies, each detail of the composition of these artists is laden with meaning, and in the trance-like brightness of sight they become part of a

---

[182] "Zum Gastspiel des Indischen Balletts" 3 (see Chap.1, footnote 24).
[183] Boner, "Der Indische Tanz" n.p. (see Chap.2, footnote 129).

supra-personal reality."[184] She further elevates the Indian gestures to a language far surpassing the word due to their wider range and shading of expressions. Boner traces this tradition back to antiquity, to Bharata's *Natyasastra*, when she claims: "Indian dance rests upon a thousands-of-years old, highly developed science."[185] Finally, she reinforces the reception of Indian dance movements as statuesque when she names the rich sculptural tradition of India as one of the main sources for the dance and as a sign for the huge importance this art always had had in India's past. In the "plastic expressivity and the sophisticated grace of movement, which still today appertains to the Indian people" she sees a residue of the past, however pale, in the present.[186]

Boner's writing is also reflected in other sources. Eduard Szamba writing for the German *Der Tanz* not only states the high degree of stylization in Indian dance apparent in *Tandava Nrittya*, but also repeats Boner's claim of the high expressiveness of each single gesture: "Each gesture (*mudras*) not only signifies a sentiment, a thought, but often even a single word. This shows to what extent the Indian dancer is compelled to conventionalize his movements."[187]

Detailed information on the Indian *mudrās* apparently also reached French reviewers. Gérard h'Houville writing for *Le Figaro* similarly stresses the use of symbolic gestures in order to communicate the antique and holy content of *Tandava Nrittya*: "But it is the last dance, the most beautiful, the archaic and sacred drama in which the symbolical gestures compose a pantomime perfectly comprehensible – even beyond the dance."[188]

The praise for the Indian movement or gesture language seems to be unanimous. On the one hand, Fritz Böhme in the *Deutsche Allgemeine Zeitung* describes how "exceedingly cultivated the hand and arm movements are, which often dominate the entire movement and turn it into a

---

[184] Ibid.
[185] Ibid.
[186] Ibid.
[187] Szamba, "Tanzbriefe: Paris," April 1931: 14 (see Chap.1, footnote 79).
[188] Houville n.p. (see Chap.1, footnote 72).

frail delicate ornament."[189] On the other hand, a writer for the German *Hamburger Anzeiger* sees its origin in ritual and proof thereof in ancient sculptures: "Cultic dance with a definite language of ritual gesture already appears in old Indian sculptures that are thousands of years old."[190] Indian dance mainly consists of detailed, symbolical gestures, continues another German reviewer who stresses the "rich utilization of the speaking hand:" "It is the dance of the hands, the muscles, the shoulders, the eyebrows. Each movement – Shankar calls them in English 'moment' – has a deeply determined symbolical meaning."[191] This is repeated by a reviewer in *Theatre Arts Monthly*: "Students may know that every slightest gesture in the Hindu dance has its own meaning."[192] Indian dance movement is thus marked by stylized convention and tradition: "The realistic gesture may be implied here and there, generally though rigorous stylization and apparently also tradition prevail."[193] Others combine their praise with a degree of critical regret regarding the lack of traditional symbols in western dance and theater:

> Each gesture is in concordance, which is prescribed by an old tradition, with the words and the music. Thereby an entirely unique aesthetic value emerges right before our very eyes. This training strictly by the book and the firmly regulated ceremony, the set hierarchy and symbolism of the colors, facial expressions, gestures, forms and groups has been lost in European theater and in European art all together.[194]

This view is repeated by other German writers, stressing the "discipline of gestures" in Indian dance, "of an aloofness and nobility which only an

---

[189] Fritz Böhme, "Indische Tänze. Theater des Westens," *Deutsche Allgemeine Zeitung* (Berlin), April 20, 1932, evening edition: n.p.

[190] Sdt. n.p.

[191] Heinz Neuberger, "Der Tänzer. Zum Tänzer geboren," *Singchor und Tanz. Fachblatt für Theatersingchor und Kunsttanz* (Berlin), vol.49 no.23, 1932: 193.

[192] "The World and the Theatre," *Theatre Arts Monthly* (London), January 1933: 94-95; here 94.

[193] Brunck n.p.

[194] Adams n.p. (see Chap.2, footnote 153).

ancient, firmly established tradition can form."[195] This leads, according to the reviewer, to a high objectivity of movement since every gesture derives its meaning from an overall language of the body:

> In every single image as in the overall view the highest degree of objectivity and boundedness becomes apparent. Every time of day, every season, age and sex, birth, illness, fate, death, they all have their specific gesture or pose, manifold nuanced, never stereotype, a rich differentiated alphabet of the corporal, cosmos of the physical.[196]

In a review by the famous dance critic and advocate of the modern dance scene, John Martin, the author clearly describes how difficult it is for a Western audience to understand an Indian dance performance due to the stylization and symbolism of the gesture language. His claim is combined with a link to the writing of Coomaraswamy, who with his *Mirror of Gesture* is named as almost the sole source of information:

> When the Westerner approaches the dance of the East it is useless for him to attempt to 'understand' it; to do so is merely to raise a barrier that cannot be penetrated. There are countless movements of the body and gestures of the hands which have specific meanings in the highly involved vocabulary of the Hindu dance, and their meaning varies as they are combined and recombined with each other. The 'mudras' or symbolic gestures comprise a veritable language comparable almost to words. It is completely impracticable for a Westerner to grasp them, for with the exception of Coomaraswamy's 'The Mirror of Gesture' and a little brochure by Ragini entitled 'Nritanjali,' there is practically nothing on the subject in English.[197]

---

[195] Tidemann 596.

[196] Ibid. 596ff.

[197] John Martin, "The Dance: Hindu Art for the Western World. Uday Shan-kar Interprets a Culture Far Different From Ours – Other Programs," *The New York Times* (New York), January 1, 1933: X2.

He then examines what he regards as significantly new in the Indian dancers' movements: the use of the whole body instead of a focus on the legs, as common in Western ballet. This way he counters the supposed lack of jumps in Indian dance: "The Hindu dances with his whole body – his eyes, his neck, his shoulders, his torso and his marvelous hands, as well as his legs and feet. There is a constant flow of movement in him, progressing in perfect coordinated rhythmic sequences."[198]

Martin's above reference to Coomaraswamy might also originate from one of the accompanying programs. An American *Playbill* edition from the second half of the 1930s includes a text by Basanta Koomar Roy entitled "Bronze God." In it, Roy presents his readers with details on the artistic education of Shankar primarily from the court musicians and dancers at the Royal Court of Jhalawar, giving the dancer's performance a profound basis in India's classical traditions. But Roy further links the Indian dance positions to ancient sculpture and painting and stresses the importance of the *mudrās*, an example of which appears in a subtitle of a photograph showing Uday Shankar with a prime focus on his hands: "In infinite configuration, Hindu hands denote more than abstract dance pattern – they are a code telling specific stories in Hindu lore."[199] Roy then refers to two of Coomaraswamy's writings, *The Dance of Siva* and *The Mirror of Gesture*, as prime sources for writers on Indian dance and its gestures.

The reference to Coomaraswamy is also repeated by Annabel Learned, author of a text named "The Hindu Dance" in another program from the 1930s printed in *Playbill*. She here describes the gestures in Indian dance as an "eloquent language, in which meaning is conveyed by every movement of head and hands," and refers to Coomaraswamy's *The Mirror of Gesture* in order to present the readers or theater audiences with some examples, such as the "peacock hand" or the "half-moon hand."[200] These hand gestures she defines as *mudras*: "Each has a multitude of meanings, depending on the way it is moved or held. These attitudes are called **mudras**."[201] The *mudras* are, according to Learned,

---

[198] Ibid.
[199] Roy n.p. (see Chap.1, footnote 210).
[200] Learned, "The Hindu Dance" n.p. (see Chap.1, footnote 207).
[201] Ibid.

ways to transport meaning, while "emotion is chiefly expressed by head and eyes."[202]

Plate 1. Uday Shankar depicted as presenting Indian *mudrās*.
(Photo in: "S.Hurok presents Uday Shan-Kar and His Hindu Ballet,"
[season 1937/38:a]: n.p. / Courtesy of Dartington Hall Trust Archive)

Learned then refers to the artistic and spiritual tradition Indian dance gestures were built on, stressing their link with nature and tradition, and basing it firmly in what could be from a Western perspective described as the fine arts of India:

---

[202] Ibid.

To understand the naturalness and beauty of this art one must realize its age-old background in Indian life. Frescoes at Ajanta and elsewhere, Rajput painting, religious sculpture of every period, all record speaking attitudes of the most consummate grace.[203]

Learned also mentions continuous expressive quality up until the present in Indian dance: "Far from being a dusty language of archaic symbols, Hindu gesture is a vigorous idiom, derived from genuine impulses of expression to which it has given form and continuity."[204] She finally describes, as Boner has done it, the non-personal, detached character of Indian dance and music: "[A]rt to the Hindu is selfless, impersonal, detached. The artist submerges himself in order to evoke something of universal quality, unmarred by his own peculiar traits."[205]

As the examples show, the writings of Ananda Coomaraswamy were main sources of information for writers, artists and students interested in Indian dance in the 1930s. Coomaraswamy's books were obviously read not only by the English speaking community, but they also reached German researchers, including the dance expert Curt Sachs who in his *World History of the Dance* refers to Coomaraswamy in a footnote.[206] Coomaraswamy seems to have successfully directed *The Mirror of Gesture* (1917) at an international or even predominantly Western audience: it is written in English and complemented with an introduction that not only delivers an overview of the basics of Indian art and dance, but also – like the bibliography cited at the end – it refers to a number of European and only a few Asian sources.[207] As a translation of a treatise on dance, namely the *Abhinaya Darpana* written between the 5th and 10th

---

[203] Ibid.

[204] Ibid.

[205] Ibid.

[206] See Sachs's *Eine Weltgeschichte des Tanzes* 158ff. The English translation at hand doesn't include the reference; See Sachs, *World History of the Dance* 233 (see Chap.1, footnote 46).

[207] His importance in the field still in later times is also proven by the fact that he wrote a foreword to La Meri's book on *The Gesture Language of the Hindu Dance* first published in 1941.

centuries by the author Nandikésvara, it delivers the reader with important information on movement.[208] In his introduction Coomaraswamy presents his readers with a short definition of the *mudras*: "Certain of the dance poses possess not merely a general linguistic, but also a special hieratic significance. These poses, chiefly of the hands, are spoken of as *mudrās* (seals)."[209] The book further contains a number of footnotes giving more detailed descriptions of the material presented. In *The Mirror of Gesture* one can also find an explanation of the difference between *Nrtta* and *Nrtya* in dancing, stating the sole importance of the latter in the context of Indian dance gesture:

> Nrtta and Nrtya constitute dancing as a separate art. The ordinary performance of a *nācnī* (nautch-girl, *bayadère*) consists of alternate Nrtya and Nrtta, the former consisting of a set dances with some special subject, and accompanied by varied gesture, the latter merely moving to and fro, marking time with the feet, and so forth. Nrtta is here dismissed with a merely negative definition, as the object of the Abhinaya Darpana is to explain how to express by gesture definite themes.[210]

The main part of the small book consists of a translation of a catalogue of different gestures of the head, the eyes, the neck and the hands with the latter engaging the biggest part of the work.[211] Coomaraswamy then includes a list of plates showing dance positions mainly in sculpture and also in painting, drawing and actual dance. He apparently intends to reinforce the connection between these arts, as one can infer from the statement below: "It is, however, scarcely realised how closely connected are the dancing and the sculpture."[212] Coomaraswamy thereby also becomes an important reference regarding the common link between Indian dance and sculpture generally hinted at by reviewers.

---

[208] See "India IX. Dance,"in: S. Sadie (ed.), *The New Grove Dictionary of Music and Musicians*, vol.12, London: Macmillan 1980: 260-271; here 261.
[209] Coomaraswamy, *The Mirror of Gesture* 8 (see Chap.2, footnote 127).
[210] Ibid. 14, footnote 1.
[211] See ibid. 17-51.
[212] Ibid. 8.

Coming back to the reviews, the ability of the Indian dancers to dance with their whole body while keeping aloofness is also taken up by a German reviewer writing for a journal named *Singchor und Tanz*. In it, the reviewer adores the artistic possibilities which emerge from the "magnificent bodily movement of the women, who dance with their entire bodies and still radiate a sacred calm."[213]

The American critic W.J. Henderson is similarly enthusiastic about the company's dancing. Yet he claims that it is almost impossible for someone coming from the West to judge the Indian technique due to the exoticism of the movement: "It is not for a barbarian of the west to essay comment on such dancing; its technic is not in the motion idioms to which we are accustomed."[214] He nevertheless urges his readers to acknowledge the refinement of the gestures of arms and hands, the *mudras*, as well as the dance postures:

> Not can one overlook the magic of the arm and hand technic of the dancers. Terpsichoreans of the older schools may learn much from observing the amazing fluidity which these dancers seem to impart to the muscles and joints of the arms and wrists. They do some remarkable things with their necks also. All their body postures are worthy of study and will assuredly win the admiration of any dance lover.[215]

Writing of the female dancers Simkie and Kanaklata, Oscar Thompson further praises "the refinement, the fluidity, the ethereal quality" of the Indian dancers' movements."[216] Like others before him, he presupposes the Indian dancers' close bond with nature and compares parts of their bodies with plants while at the same time stating their floating, hardly earthly-bound, poised character: "Their arms, hands, fingers were like the tendrils of plants, air-plants, drifting or spinning with no such tedious en-

---

[213] Neuberger 193.
[214] W.J. Henderson, "Hindu Dances Performed Here. Shan-Kar and Assisting Group Appear in Exhibition at New Yorker Theater," *The New York Sun* (New York), December 27, 1932; printed in: "Press Comments" 41-42; here 42.
[215] Ibid.
[216] Thompson 38.

cumbrance as earthly roots. There were no forced climaxes, no whip-cracking closes. All was insinuating, effortless, poised."[217] A very similar description had already been published a few months earlier in the German language paper *Prager Presse*, where the reviewer noticed about Simkie: "Clung to Uday Shankar the fragile, liana-like Simkie. A marvel of hands and feet. She, too, like Uday Shankar, entirely dissolved, entirely loose and free of any earthly severity. These hands and feet like butterflies."[218]

The ethereal character of the dancers similarly moves other critics, such as H.T. Parker writing for the *Boston Evening Transcript*. He delivers a very detailed and inspiring description of the movements involved and formulates a paradox he himself confronts in Uday Shankar's performance: the physical presence of the moving body as opposed to the almost "bodyless" character of the dancing. Parker elaborates:

> So also with Shankar and the dancers themselves. More plasticity of body were hard to imagine. From head to heel every muscle moved as both an independent and a co-ordinated means. There was a new and strange technique of the neck; a play of arms marvellous in range and implication; a super-refinement of the hands in arabesques and in counterpoint; an exhaustless diversity and significance of torso-movements; the legs, the feet, as final, if subordinate, complement. Usually the faces of these dancers remained immobile as they danced; but from their eyes flashed, or in their eyes lurked, a battery of glances. Whatever the bodily instrument, it had been subtilized; whatever the use to which it was put, it remained poised. What seemed casual was actually born of studied mastery; from sophistication flowed spontaneity. The mood, the passion of the moment, was indeed a sensation by the body projected. Yet paradoxically, it seemed bodyless.[219]

---

[217] Ibid.

[218] K. 8 (see Chap.2, footnote 142).

[219] H.T. Parker, "Dancing Arts From India As Far As Boston," *Boston Evening Transcript* (Boston), January 20, 1933; printed in: Holmes 263-266; here 264.

Reviewers identify the perceived bodyless character or, as others describe it, the aloofness of Uday Shankar's presentation, with a spiritual or philosophical background of Indian dance. A writer for the German paper *Germania* elaborates on this while comparing Indian dance with its Japanese counterpart. Describing Japanese dances as rather aggressive, Uday Shankar's style of dancing is seen to reflect the quintessence of Indian thought, which is the never ending, harmonious circle of life as deeply rooted in nature:

> The quintessence of Indian thought superbly finds expression in the form of the dances. In contrast to the static Japanese world-view, to the combative, heroic sword-plays, the becoming and the run of events are here depicted matchlessly. The motif of the snake movement, the movement of the bird's head, the striding of the birds, the theme of the flow of the waves and the freezing of the face, the hands, arms and legs in meditation always recurs, determines the evening.[220]

Following this reviewer, such perfection of gesture is, due to its strong spiritual or philosophical basis, only intelligible for members of the Hindu priest caste:

> One does not have to say a word about the technical perfection; only a Brahman could provide information or deliver judgment on the hundreds and thousands of nuances of the fingers, the hands, the eyes, the eyelashes, the shoulders, the feet, the head.[221]

Critics are repeatedly careful to identify a broad Eastern style of dancing. In a review printed in the *Stuttgarter Neues Tageblatt*, the author names certain parallels between Indian and Japanese dancing with regard to body control. He nevertheless describes a distinct Indian style of dancing, explicit in content and theme of the dance pieces, and compares their

---

[220] Adams n.p.
[221] Ibid.

peaceful, harmonious and devoted outlook to the aggressive themes illustrated in Japanese dancing, for example:

> Regarding the discipline and the body control of these dancers, one feels often reminded of the Japanese, who also start very early in youth, if they want to be a dancer or an actor. It is only that the Japanese dance out of a totally different attitude towards life than the Indians. The Indians dance devotion, atonement, harmony, love. The Japanese dance combat and hatred.[222]

The devout, harmonious outlook of Uday Shankar's dances is also acknowledged in the Austrian *Reichspost*, where a reviewer declares that the dance "never loses measure and harmony, the gestures, the steps are always composed and full of dignity."[223] It is exactly the calmness, harmony and dignity of the composition, or in other words, the static character of the group's dance movements, which brings other critics to state a supposed closeness with nature. Claiming to have found "rudiments of an old dance culture," one reviewer locates the authenticity of the performance "in Eastern feeling's immense affinity with nature and in the graceful aloofness of the presentation of the passions."[224] Fritz Böhme thus names the "oscillating way of movement" of the dancers which allows "no severities and no prolonged strains."[225] In Shankar's movements, which are distinct from the styles of Western dance performances, he sees a sign of its authenticity and ancient origin. This is only partly comprehensible for Western audiences:

> Many a part remains incomprehensible, the only effect that remains is a beautiful line in space, but the overall style in its swaying and sinuous buoyancy leaves an unforgettable impression. The form in which Uday Shankar and his female partners move, makes one feel that these are people coming from foreign land-

---

[222] D. 2 (see Chap.2, footnote 14).
[223] *Reichspost* (Wien), undated; quoted in: Khokar, *His Dance, His Life* 57.
[224] Sdt. n.p.
[225] Böhme n.p.

scapes who present themselves in the way of their race without noticeable concessions to the European way of movement; thus one is dealing with nothing whitewashed or replicated but with something original.[226]

The claim of authenticity combined with the distinct otherness of the Indian dance performance regarding theme and movement is repeated in several reviews, such as in the German *Münchner Neueste Nachrichten*. Here the writer qualifies the dance as "untouched by our fashionable civilization art."[227] John Martin from the *New York Times* further confirms the originality of Uday Shankar's dance and states that it, though presented on Western stages, never loses its authenticity:

> Though the dances are absolutely authentic, the theatrical quality has not been lost. [...] Shan-Kar, a deep student of his country's ethnology and of its iconography as well, has collected his material from all over India and from all periods of its history. He has made no adaptations whatsoever except those that are indispensable when presenting, on a stage with artificial lights and curtains and an arbitrary two hours of time, dances which in their natural condition are performed about a great fire and last all night, growing into a perfect frenzy before they are ended.[228]

Trying to describe and understand "the unusual range and scope of the movement," John Martin contends that the "dancing is first of all rhythmic," meaning not only its "utmost precision in accent and phrasing," but also "the much rarer dynamic rhythm of coordinated muscular action."[229] He detects the main impulse for Shankar's dance movements, like others before him, in its rich thematic philosophical background:

---

[226] Ibid.
[227] P. n.p. (see Chap.2, footnote 183).
[228] Martin, "The Dance: Art of India" n.p.
[229] Ibid.

The mental and spiritual background of the theme is translated into movement that completely animates the body in spite of the formality of the traditional attitudes and transitions. Head, eyes and neck dance, as well as feet, legs, torso and those singularly eloquent arms, hands and fingers. It is impossible to indicate by words the vitality which underlies this delicate, perfectly ordered refinement of movement. Even in its most vigorous and its most humorous moment, there is always the poise that characterizes the arts of the East, whether it be the acting of Mei Lan-fang, of the prints of Hiroshipe, or some ancient Persian miniatures.[230]

Other reviewers apparently regard Uday Shankar's "Oriental poise and aloofness" as a theatrical means that authentic Oriental dancers simply have a better command of, when mentioning "that indescribable effect of detached passion which no Westerner may ever hope to simulate."[231]

A reviewer writing for *Cue* identifies this poise as a racial characteristic, in the same detached manner surrounding Uday Shankar: "Blessed with a beautiful body and exhibiting the poise and detached passion of his race, he dances not only with his feet, his hands and arms, but also with his body and facial muscles."[232]

In a small booklet written in the context of Uday Shankar's tour in Germany by Hermann and Marianne Aubel, the authors further elaborate on the philosophical and spiritual background of Indian dance as they see it exemplified in the performances. They here claim the Indian dancers to be particularly able to represent the spirit in their movements. The reason for this lies in the spiritual education the dancers go through. Indian dance is not solely a physical exercise, but instead:

the result of a thorough spiritual education which affects the respiration and from there on the entire physiology in such a way, so

---

[230] Ibid.

[231] Watkins, "Uday Shan-Kar and troupe offer Program of ancient rituals at New Yorker" 36.

[232] "East come West," *Cue* (New York), undated; quoted in: Khokar, *His Dance, His Life* 71.

that it is able to lead to that highest natural law by which alone the immaterial can manifest itself effectively and convincingly.[233]

This spiritual education is essential to the Brahmanical caste and supposed to start in early childhood leading to "the ultimate wraithlike and animated movement of the Hindu dancer."[234] The authors further elaborate on the repose of Indian dance movements and the harmonious unity of body and spirit or physical movement and spiritual theme:

> In the most vigorous dances we experience an immense spiritual fire, a blaze of all forces in masterly embrace, without confusion, without haste in breathing or movement. The Hindu dancer can express everything [...], [N]othing disrupts the coherence between the mental will of the artist and the moving body as his instrument.[235]

Even a seeming lack of movement, which might be perceived as monotony, leads in the end to the expression of inner spiritual insight by means of facial expression or breathing:

> In the absence of every outer movement, the inner is all the more expressive. Especially then the spiritual glow is often strongest. For the spectator it becomes apparent and can be witnessed because of the calm but immensely expressive features and the deep, moving and animated way of breathing.[236]

It is not only the unity of body and spirit that Uday Shankar's Indian dances seem to evoke, but also a unity of the various body parts versus a division into its separate fractions: "There are never sole isolated move-

---

[233] Aubel 6 (see Introduction, footnote 2).
[234] Ibid.
[235] Ibid. 6ff.
[236] Ibid. 7.

ments of the limbs, always plays the whole instrument."[237] The entire body, the unity of body and spirit, might even be exemplified by the tiniest movement, such as by a finger, further identified with nature, such as when certain movements are described as "floral," namely "toward the flowery."[238]

It is then the spiritual inspiration of every movement, "the mental-spiritual and therefore natural origin of movement," that elevates Shankar's Indian dance movements above those of a Western (ballet) dancer, "who just rips out the same movement out of his organism in a random, technical or solely outward virtuous manner."[239]

The strong expressive abilities of the Indian dancers prompt the authors to the conclusion that there is, besides their apparently Oriental appearance, a distinct Indian or Brahmanical-Indian element overrunning the Oriental one:

> Even if numerous facial structures seemingly call to mind the Oriental [element] of the Middle East, the observant spectator will not miss the specific Indian element, which first and foremost resides in the substance. The Brahmanic-Indian element is indeed entirely different from the Oriental one.[240]

Other authors as well find differences between Indian or Hindu dance and the wider field of Asian dance forms. One such reviewer writing for the German dance magazine *Der Tanz* observes "that the Hindu dances are less rigorously stylized and ritualized than the Javanese ones and leave the dancer more individuality. They are closer to the Balinese ones and are also more comprehensible for Occidental eyes."[241]

The close examination of the reviews not only confirms the mainly positive reception of the company in various Western countries. It first of all shows that reviewers obviously detected a profound difference

---

[237] Ibid.
[238] Ibid.
[239] Ibid.
[240] Ibid. footnote.
[241] Herbert A. Polak, "Tanzbriefe: Den Haag," *Der Tanz* (Berlin), vol.5 no.7, July 1932: 12.

between a supposed Western and an Eastern style of moving in dance. It is, importantly, the new and extensive use of the arms, hands and the upper body and the comparatively lesser inclusion of jumps that made reviewers describe Uday Shankar's performances as rather static and sculptural. The Indian *mudrās* or hand gestures, and similarly the different facial expressions, did, besides some criticism of their stylized nature, mainly cause enthusiasm in the reviewers. This reception is, furthermore, strongly based in the self-presentation of the company in its programs which in turn often refer to the aesthetic writings of Coomaraswamy. As contemporary remains of an ancient hieratic language of gesture, the *mudras* are perceived as a distinct Indian element and open up a hitherto unknown command of the body. Although several critics, as mentioned before, observe an extensive use of the limbs of the upper body in Uday Shankar's Indian dance, a few writers, such as John Martin, instead point towards the harmonious inclusion of the entire body in Indian dance. Asian or, more precisely, Indian dance and music are once again identified with a unifying approach combining art, religion and nature, body and spirit. Exceeding former Oriental or Asian categories of movement, reviewers increasingly distinguish and claim to discover a distinct Indian – or Hindu and in some cases even specifically Brahman – element in Uday Shankar's performances. This mainly refers to the spiritual or philosophical traditions of India, an attitude of calmness and aloofness that observers discover in both the dancing and in the enactment of mythology in dance. Repeating the Romantic view of India as the cradle of humanity, Indian dance is even perceived as the prototype of Asian dancing, the birthplace of an ancient, continually persisting, sophisticated language of gesture based in religion and myth. It is the declared spiritual basis of the presentation which finds expression in the highly developed, elaborate technique of the *mudrās* which initially attracts audiences and critics, but, which subsequently leads an increasing number of reviewers to discuss to what extent Western onlookers are able to understand the Indian performance in its depth.[242]

---

[242] Furthermore it is interesting and rather curious to note that Uday Shankar in later years stated the relative irrelevance of the *mudrās* for his dances or dance dramas. In an interview led by Mohan Khokar he declared, following Khokar's observation that there is little evidence of *mudras* in his work: "That is true. I have not adopted mudras in my

The examination of the material eventually shows that, at the beginning of the 1930s, reviewers obviously moved away from applying the category of Oriental dance to Uday Shankar's declared Indian or Hindu performance. As Joan Erdman proffers: "The West had enthusiastically received India's dance as authentic, and had been converted from 'oriental dance' as variety show, to 'Hindu dance' with Indian music by Indian performers."[243]

Finally, concerning questions of movement and authenticity, it is interesting to observe how audiences and critics reacted to Simkie. Early reviews show that in the beginning it was not known that Simkie was actually French, a fact that even if it was not hidden consciously, also was not announced directly in the presentation of the group. Some reviewers nevertheless detect a difference in the dancing of Shankar and Simkie: "On a par with him [Shankar], though at times almost European refined, seems the female dancer Simkie, whose purest form is doubtlessly epitomized in the 'Spring Dance'."[244] The success of the group did not decrease when Simkie's nationality became known, a point to be noted as the company at least in the beginning built a lot of its success on the supposed authentic Indian background of its members. The fact that Simkie was French or, which might be even more important, that she was not Indian, still became a topic in a number of reviews wondering if and how it was possible for her to dance and appear Indian. The German critic J. Lewitan wrote for the London *Dancing Times*: "Next to Uday Shan Kar, Simkie asserts herself. Although European, she has adapted

---

dance or dance dramas unless it is very necessary. Let me tell you: when a dance or dance drama is going on, perhaps vigorously and with much feeling, and the dancer suddenly stops and starts 'talking' with *mudras*, it breaks. I tell you, it breaks for me the continuity. Somehow this doesn't go with me. I like to show what I want to show with the body, with the body in emotion. For instance, when saying 'I feel angry' the dancer flutters his hands and takes leaps. Why not just show the anger? When the body is capable of showing anger why not let it do that? I try to avoid *mudras* as much as possible. *Mudras* are beautiful, and nice, but in my kind of dancing I go for movement of the whole body to express what I want, and with no exaggeration." Khokar, *His Dance, His Life* 167ff.

[243] Erdman, "Towards Authenticity" 89 (see Introduction, footnote 9).

[244] c.a.l., "Indischer Tanzabend," *Hamburger Fremdenblatt* (Hamburg), September 30, 1931, evening edition: 3.

herself to the Indian style and did not spoil anything."[245] John Martin also discusses her French background and its possible implications for the dance presentation:

> Simkie alone is not a native of India, but a French woman. Knowing this in advance, one fanices that there is a difference between her dancing and that of her colleagues, but in so unfamiliar an idiom it is difficult to tell on viewing one performance. She is, at any rate, exquisite in her art, and is apparently as heart-whole in her devotion to its tradition as any of those for whom it is inbred.[246]

A reviewer for *Time* magazine, though repeating all the clichés of Oriental sinuosity, even more directly concluded from Simkie's performance that the different ways of moving are culture-bound and therefore learnable by extensive studies: "He [Uday Shankar] is a flirtatious lover, coquettishly throwing his neck out of joint to impress his Partner Simkie, an almost equally sinuous Frenchwoman (the only Occidental in the troupe) who can throw her neck out of joint too, now that she has lived and danced with Orientals."[247]

3.3 Pressing Gender and Racial Boundaries: The Male Indian Dancer Uday Shankar

In his biography of Uday Shankar, Mohan Khokar stresses how the bodily presence of the dancer on stage, his sex-appeal or physical beauty, helped a great part in his international promising career: "What was of crucial importance in the overwhelming success of Shankar with audiences – and of his influence on choreographers – was his phenomenal and intensely sex-appeal, his great energy, and his powerful stage presence."[248] The focus on Uday Shankar's body was surely enhanced by the

---

[245] Lewitan, "The Month in Berlin" 257.
[246] Martin, "The Dance: Art of India" n.p.
[247] "Music: Radio Favorites ... Dancer from Hindustan" n.p. (see Chap.1, footnote 81).
[248] Khokar, *His Dance, His Life* 151.

costumes chosen for the performances usually leaving his upper body free and showing a great part of his legs.[249]

Khokar further reinforces his above observation with a number of comments from reviews dating from the 1930s, such those from the Italian *Il Lavoro*. But Shankar is here described not only as a "rare, yet mysterious personality of Modern India."[250] The reviewer further states: "For Uday Shan-Kar himself there are no words, he has such a physical beauty, such a transcendental expression, such grandness in his attitude, such a command of his muscles, that his presence alone has a unique significance."[251] The German *Reichpost* similarly cannot help but mention "the transfigured, remote expression of his beautiful face;"[252] and also a critic in the Swiss *Tages Anzeiger* comments on Shankar's astonishing physical appearance: "Admirable among all was Uday Shan-Kar, who years ago was in America as a partner of Anna Pavlova. His body and composed face of bronze framed by black and glossy hair, are of a perfect harmony."[253]

It is in fact striking how reviewers from various countries comment on the bodily appearance of the Indian dancer, some of them seemingly having problems integrating him into common gender categories. The "slender body of the leading dancer Shan-Kar which hardly shows any muscles" almost seems to disturb a German reviewer writing for the *Hamburger Anzeiger*.[254] Others even call him feminine, such as is the case with a reviewer writing from Prague who perceives the Indian dancer as of feminine beauty: "Before a dark background floats the feminine figure of Uday Shankar. [...] Uday Shankar has the marvelous body of an ephebe, delicate joints of hands and feet, the world-enraptured head of a woman with a tragical mask."[255] Also a writer of the *Time* magazine

---

[249] See, for example, plates 1 and 2 on pages 175 and 231 of this book.
[250] Khokar, *His Dance, His Life* 56.
[251] Ibid.
[252] Ibid. 57.
[253] Ibid.
[254] Sdt. n.p.
[255] K. 8.

describes Shankar as "a perfectly proportioned male with a sensitive, feminine face."[256]

Reviewers often seem unsure how to react to this "feminine" beauty of Uday Shankar and are thus searching for elements in the performance, which are connoted as male. A critic from Berlin declares:

> Uday Shan-Kar, this seemingly feminine man with these ostensibly rather womanly movements. From the second view on there is no longer anything feminine, nothing suspicious, nothing soft, but instead something magnificent, manly, even cruel and brutal. These are his dances which are danced and they are of such an expressive power which a feminine nature could neither find nor cope with.[257]

The observed androgyny of Shankar is also repeated by an American reviewer from the *New York City Post*: "Mr. Shan-Kar has a splendid, flexible physique and a handsome face, expressive and sensitive. His every gesture and movement is fascinating, and, although feminine in their softness, show power and firmness."[258]

The reception of Uday Shankar as being of a slightly feminine appearance parallels the image of the Orient as a feminine space linking questions of gender and race.[259] Preconceptions of the Indian people as being comparatively weak, powerless and ruled by despotism were already developed by James Mill in his *History of British India* and similarly spread by Hegel in his *Philosophy of History*. Shankar's reviewers, by contrast, look for and find further proof of his manliness. Some sources give us the impression that critics desperately searched for a masculine, rather aggressive side in Uday Shankar's dances in order to acknowledge him as an artist. This might also be due to the fact that stage dancing in the first half of the 20th century was still observed as a predominately female activity. A male dancer was easily rendered effeminate.

---

[256] "Music: Radio Favorites ... Dancer from Hindustan" n.p.

[257] Hi. n.p.

[258] A. 40.

[259] See Boer 407 and Antliff & Leighten 222ff (see Chap.2, footnote 161).

Serious Indian dance, as described before, was still first of all connected with the image of the female temple dancer.

The Western image of dancing as a feminine activity is also described by Max von Boehn in *Der Tanz* (1925). The author here names the prejudices still prevalent among the middle class concerning male dancers: "that by a dancer a middle-class man understands a slightly awkward man, of feminine impact, an unmanly man, a man of abnormal disposition, an unpleasant man."[260] Von Boehn, however, uses this opportunity to claim the importance of male dancers already emerging in the course of the German *Körperkulturbewegung* (body culture movement), when he declares that the art of dance had been in danger "to degenerate as such alarmingly, to perish of the abundance of the female element, when the male dancer emerged."[261]

As the above example already shows, the reception of Uday Shankar runs parallel to a recently emerging trend (mainly in modern dance) towards the male dancer who sought to surpass his second-rate role in classical ballet and the according image. In the United States, where Ted Shawn should be named as one of the first male modern dancers, the masculinity of Shankar is stressed by a reviewer who presents the dancer as a possible role model for other male dancers. According to the review, Shankar could represent an entirely masculine dance aesthetic:

> The reasons for his enormous appeal here were psychological as much as artistic. The dance, in common with most other arts, has seldom recognized the division of the sexes, and in America male aesthetics have always been held up to scorn. Whatever virility a male dancer possessed was not, due to the very nature of the art, apparent in his work. Shan-Kar upset the deeply-rooted conviction that dancers of his sex were necessarily effeminate. His work exhibited a strength, a forcefulness, that was entirely masculine.[262]

---

[260] Boehn 125ff (see Chap.2, footnote 157).
[261] Ibid. 126.
[262] "East come West," *Cue* (New York), undated; quoted in: Khokar, *His Dance, His Life* 71.

Modern dance was in turn strongly influenced by or even accounted for as part of the reform movements focusing on the body in the German context at the turn of the century generally summarized under the term *Lebensreformbewegungen* (life reform movements).[263] An American equivalent can be found in Delsartism.[264] It is not only important that Isadora Duncan and other so called barefoot dancers had freed the body in ways of floating costumes allowing new movements.[265] Various reform movements, such as the German *Kleiderreformbewegung* (dress reform movement) and the *Freikörperkulturbewegung* (nudist movement), strove towards a more free, healthy and sensual, and thereby even a more beauty-oriented, approach to the body. Following Esther Sophia Sünderhauf, German reform movements interested in the body often found inspiration in ancient Greek sculpture. Photographs in aligned magazines show various naked or half-naked models appearing in poses reenacting Greek statues.[266] A similar phenomenon can be found in the statue posing of American Delsartism, once again inspired by classical Greek and Roman models.[267] The sometimes sparingly dressed body of Uday Shankar performing Indian dance, an art which apparently had ancient roots and a close affinity to sculpture, might for that reason have appealed to those audiences familiar with current reform tendencies.

The growing interest of audiences and critics in the physical presence of dancers was certainly also prepared for by the various Oriental or exotic dancers on Western popular stages. It must, however, have been

---

[263] See, for example, Kerbs & Reulecke (see Chap.2, footnote 61).

[264] See Nancy Lee Chalfa Ruyter, *The Cultivation of Body and Mind in Nineteenth-Century American Delsartism*, Westport & London: Greenwood Press 1999.

[265] John Schikowski stresses the importance of Isadora Duncan in the liberation of the body regrading dance costumes: "Die Duncan war die erste, die es wagte, das Korsett, das steife Gazeröckchen, ja sogar die Trikots der Ballettänzerinnen abzulegen. In einem leichten, schleierartigen Gewande, das sich den Formen der Körpers anschmiegte und feine Umrisse durchscheinen ließ, trat sie auf. Füße und Beine waren nackt." Schikowski 135.

[266] See Esther Sophia Sünderhauf, *Griechensehnsucht und Kulturkritik. Die deutsche Rezeption von Winckelmanns Antikenideal 1840-1945*, Berlin: Akademie Verlag 2004: 173ff.

[267] See Nancy Lee Chalfa Ruyter, "Antique longings: Genevieve Stebbins and American Delsartean performance," in: Susan L. Foster (ed.), *Corporealities*, London & New York: Routledge 1996: 70-89; here 73.

even more compelling to look at the bodies of the Indian performers whose exotic beauty was seen as a part of nature:

> The dance of these strange beautiful people, in whose eyes is velvety mildness and the gentle demonism of internalized faith, [...] is of such a natural refinement, which does not, like our art, seek "liberation" from the earth by means of spiritual energy and mental combat, but apparently finds salvation in the eternal recurrence to itself, like nature in the cycle of seasons.[268]

The Oriental performers were thus perceived as having a more direct, more natural, or more sensual access to the body. This was contrasted with a detected western focus on the mind and reason. Vaguely resuming Friedrich Nietzsche's address to the "despisers of the body" in *Thus Spake Zarathustra*, a German reviewer looks upon the Indian performers as representatives of the Orient and takes the opportunity to call for a full humanity meaning a union of East and West:

> We Occidentals are men of listening and seeing, of thinking and feeling. The mind has primacy, everything should be instantaneously pitted against it. And we thought that this being, put out to such an extent, represents now the entire human being, or at least that which matters. The word of Nietzsche that the body is our capital reason admittedly met with applause, but hitherto remains rather opaque. And now these Orientals arrive. [...] What lay in our selves concealed and buried: the knowledge of the entire human range of movement in all its glory, in its proud and in its humbleness, the knowledge of the God-given instrument of one's own limbs – here it lights up. And we understand how only from East and West the entire realm of human existence rounds off.[269]

---

[268] P. n.p.
[269] See Friedrich Nietzsche, *Thus Spake Zarathustra* (1883-85); quoted in and translated by: Amelia Jones, "Body," in: *Critical Terms for Art History*, R.S. Nelson & R. Shiff (eds.), Chicago & London: The University of Chicago Press 2003[2]: 251-266; here: 251; Tidemann 597.

Some reviewers, however, depreciate the physical appearance of the dancers on the grounds of supposed racial differences: "With the exception of the slightly female looking, gorgeously bodied solo dancer Uday Shan-Kar are these overly slim people with their lean slightly curved legs and flat feet by our standards not exactly beautiful, the women plain."[270]

It is still the majority of reviewers, however, who show themselves very impressed and comment positively on the physical beauty of Shankar:

> It is a fact that on stage Uday Shankar appeared as an artist with the grandest temperament, tremendous skill, and a penetrating charm of personality. That he, in addition, is also beautiful, even very beautiful, will indeed only be held against him as a fault in Germany, a fault which allegedly sentimentalizes his art.[271]

A French reviewer for *Le Figaro* similarly praises the beautiful appearance of the Indian dancer. Describing his movements and expressions as partly female, partly male and sometimes even "reptilian," he additionally compares his with a god and attests that there is a natural spirituality inherent in the entire presentation:

> This great dancer, Shan-Kar, with gestures encompassing both the sweet and terrible, who has the refinements of a woman, serenities of a god and the primitive skills of a warrior, is one of the most beautiful artists we have seen for a long time. The facial expressions, the majesty, the nobility of postures, the strength of the leaps, the reptilian flexibility of the arms, shoulders, hands, the natural hieratic character of all is fascinating; the spectators, emotionally moved, are captivated.[272]

---

[270] Brunck n.p.
[271] J. Lewitan, "Tanzaufführungen: Uday Shan-Kar, Simkie und Hindu-Tanzgruppe, Theater des Westens, 19.-25. April 1932," *Der Tanz* (Berlin), vol.5, June 1932: 13.
[272] Houville n.p.

The conflicting view of Shankar's androgynous appearance is thereby to a certain extent solved by activating a third category: the divine body. An American critic goes one step further and elevates the discussion on Shankar's body to the ranks of the disembodied: "But Shan-Kar's entire art is remote from anything suggesting effort, much less violence. It might be feminine if it were not so sexless. It is rarefied to the extent of suggesting the disembodied."[273]

Comments such as those above verify the trend towards a differentiation of Indian from Oriental dance and confirm the image of the former as a traditional ancient art form of spiritual impetus. Though Shankar's apparent beauty, his androgynous physical appearance, might have confused audiences as it stood in conflict with the general Western perception of men at the beginning of the 20th century, the religious context of the Indian performance as well as probably its perceived exoticism surely helped its serious reception by Western art critics and artists. The link between dance, music, and religion and the enactment of mythological stories of the Indian gods on stage, will further be explored in the following chapter. It will treat once again the prime importance of the Indian aesthetician Coomaraswamy for the reception of Indian arts in the West at the beginning of the 20th century.

---

[273] Thompson 38.

4. Art, Religion and Mythology

4.1 Filling the Lack of Religion: Mythology and the Spiritual in Western Modern Dance

In his writings on "Religion and Art" (1880), Richard Wagner described the important function of art as activating mythology in order to fill the lack of religion that had emerged in modernity:

> One might say that where Religion becomes artificial, it is reserved for Art to save the spirit of religion by recognising the figurative value of the mythic symbols which the former would have us believe in their literal sense, and revealing their deep and hidden truth through an ideal presentation.[1]

Wagner further concluded that art "could only fulfill her true vocation when, by an ideal presentment of the allegoric figure, she led to apprehension of its inner kernel, the truth ineffably divine."[2]

Nietzsche, at the time of his early writings a follower of Wagner and later a distinct opponent, similarly described the special role of art. According to Nietzsche, art comprises the stream of religious feeling that has no outlet in modern rational society. His following claim, however, was intended only in order to target the Wagnerian Romantic attempt to revive the symbols and practices of a decaying religion in art:[3]

> Art raises its head where religions decline. It takes over a number of feelings and moods produced by religion [...]. The wealth of religious feeling, swollen to a river, breaks out again and again, and seeks to conquer new realms: but growing enlightenment has shaken the dogmas of religion and generated a thorough mistrust

---

[1] Richard Wagner, "Religion and Art," transl. by William Ashton Ellis, Lincoln: University of Nebraska Press 1994:213-252; here 213; originally published: London: K. Paul / Trench / Trübner 1897.

[2] Ibid.

[3] See Williamson 274 (see Chap.2, footnote 34).

of it; therefore, feeling, forced out of the religious sphere by enlightenment, throws itself into art; in certain instances, into political life, too, indeed even directly into science. Wherever one perceives a loftier, darker coloration to human endeavors, one may
assume that the fear of spirits, the smell of incense, and the shadow of churches have remained attached to them.[4]

As hinted above, the urge to fill the perceived spiritual discontent or to
oppose the growing "disenchantment of the world", as Max Weber has
coined the phrase, by means of art, has its basis in the Romantic concept
of *Kunstreligion* (religion of art), which fuses aesthetic and religious aspects and reintegrates them with public social life.[5] From the era of early
Romanticism in the late 18th century, German philosophers and thinkers
such as Friedrich Schelling and Friedrich Schlegel challenged the dogmas of Protestant Christianity and the doctrines of the church when they
called for a "new mythology" in order to transform modern society with
the help of poetry.[6] According to George S. Williamson, mythology in its
19th-century use, which still had topicality at the beginning of the 20th
century and therefore will be used in the context of this thesis, refers to
"a system of sacred images, narratives, and rituals that reflects the values
of a community."[7] Myth, in contrast a more limited term, describes "a sacred narrative of gods, heroes, or cosmogony that reflects the fundamental values and beliefs of a community or nation."[8] At the beginning of the
19th century the growing interest would lead scholars to further research
on ancient mythology and enable Friedrich Creuzer to write his influential but much debated work *Symbolik und Mythologie der Alten Völker*
(1810-12). In this text, Creuzer claimed to have found the origin of Greek
religion and mythology in the Orient, especially in India, hereby following a new enthusiasm with all Oriental installed mainly by the works of

---

[4] Friedrich Nietzsche, *Human, All Too Human. A Book For Free Spirits*, transl. by
Marion Faber, with Stephen Lehmann, Lincoln: University of Nebraska Press 1996:
105.
[5] Max Weber, "Wissenschaft als Beruf" (1919), Berlin: Duncker & Humblot 1967[5]: 17.
[6] See Williamson 56ff.
[7] Ibid. 6.
[8] Ibid.

Sir William Jones.[9] Creuzer's path would be modified and taken up by the linguists Adalbert Kuhn and Friedrich Max Müller. Exploring the connections regarding structure and etymology among Indo-European languages from the point of view of comparative philology, they, too, located an original mythology or religion in India.[10] At the beginning of the 20th century, the striving to fill the religious gap also rendered possible various new religious associations, organizations and movements, such as the Free Religious Communities, Ernst Haeckel's Monist League, Theosophy or Rudolf Steiner's Anthroposophy, some of them loosely linked to the German life reform movement.[11]

In the early 20th century the longing towards religion and spirituality, often linked with mythology, also reached the field of dance. At this time we find references to the topic and claims of a lack of religious dancing in modernity – especially in German dance writings. Authors therefore looked at primitive dance cultures because they, in accordance with evolutionary approaches, stood for an earlier, original and sometimes more desirable, stage of dancing. Following Max von Boehn in his chapter on "The Dance of the Indigenous Peoples," dance is not only the first, most natural and original form of art, but it also emerged from religious practice.[12] And from there on, over the course of centuries, it degraded to its current level of profanity:

> The customs and traditions of dance of the current indigenous peoples are all the more important for the universal history of civilization, because they cast a light on the views of the primitive peoples, which one may assume they have developed in an analogous manner to. One may be all the more confident, as in that moment, when the light of history falls on antiquity, all accounts agree therein, that dance for the ancient peoples as well played the same important and significant part, that for them as well it arose

---

[9] See ibid. 127ff.
[10] See ibid. 213ff.
[11] See ibid. 285ff.
[12] See Boehn 7 (see Chap.2, footnote 157).

from religion, in order to end, only after the course of centuries, in the profane.[13]

Other writers, in contrast, saw the link between art and religion as already fulfilled and lifted out dance as the one art form that could lead to god and the spiritual. Curt Sachs, for example, identified an already-accomplished step towards god and the soul in the current tendencies of modern dance. Without providing names he describes how dancers in general, and especially the practitioners of modern dance, are able to direct modern man, caught in times of crisis, towards the ever-present aim of all humanity, which is to enter into a unity with the spiritual:

> In the midst of a period of conflict over new forms, where the other arts have floundered uncertainly, it has been their good fortune to express the joys and sorrows, the fears and hopes of mankind today in rapturous form. And yet not only of mankind today, but of men of all races and in all ages. For that to which they give living expression has been the secret longing of man from the very beginning – the victory over gravity, over all that weighs down and oppresses, the change of body into spirit, the elevation of creature into creator, the merging with the infinite, the divine.[14]

He backs up his statement with a quote from the Persian dervish poet Rumi: "Whosoever knoweth the power of the dance dwelleth in God."[15] Due to the fact that the dance of the dervishes had also been a main source of inspiration for Rudolf von Laban, Sachs's quote indirectly refers to the modern German dancer as having realized the deep-rooted connection between dance and the divine.[16]

---

[13] Ibid. 28ff.

[14] Sachs, *World History of the Dance* 448 (see Chap.1, footnote 46).

[15] Ibid. See also David Michael Levin, "Balanchine's Formalism," in: Copeland & Cohen 123-145; here 134 (see Chap.2, footnote 9).

[16] The German version of this quote uses the expression "Reigen" which can be translated as "round dance." See Sachs, *Eine Weltgeschichte des Tanzes* 301. The theme of the round dance is also taken up by Rudolf von Laban in his book *Die Welt des Tänzers.*

In his last chapter of *Der Tanz der Zukunft* entitled "Tänzerische Weltanschauung" (Dancing Worldview), Fritz Böhme similarly describes dance as allowing access to god: "In other arts God pours out into man; Man as a dancer flees out of his innermost to God, stretches himself towards God."[17] Through dance man further finds his place in the cosmic arrangement: "To dance is to touch upon God, the becoming of a succession that takes shape in time and is part of the essence of the overarching and determined framework."[18] Leaning towards "Entpersönlichung" (depersonalization) and at least partly giving up his individuality, man instead follows a higher order and hereby becomes one with the cosmic rhythm.[19] The unity with god can then also be felt by the audience participating: "The experience of the world through dance means, for the dancer and for the onlooker, to enter undivided into God, to experience God in the form of the space-filling movement of the human body."[20] Böhme ends his chapter with a "Prayer of the Dancer" which once again presents the dancer's movements as being directed towards god.[21]

One author who explicitly combines the stated religious origin of dance with India is Rudolf Bode. His book *Rhythmus und Körpererziehung* (1923) contains a chapter entitled "Vom Wesen des Urtanzes" (On the Essence of the Primordial Dance) in which he also comments on Oriental dance. In this text he accentuates the Indian tradition: "All true dance wells out of religious affinity, and from the depth of this basic feeling, which formerly captured the entire human race, is rising as a mysterious resemblance between all genuine artistic creation the *ease of appearance*."[22] Bode then not only locates the origin of dance in religious practice, but also highlights the role of Indian dance as part of this religious primordial tradition. As an advocate of the German branch of

---

Fünf Gedankenreigen (1920) where it serves as a bridge connecting dance and the writing on it (see Chap.2, footnote 98).
[17] Fritz Böhme, *Der Tanz der Zukunft*, München: Delphin-Verlag 1926: 50.
[18] Ibid. 50ff.
[19] Ibid. 52ff.
[20] Ibid. 54.
[21] Ibid. 54ff.
[22] Rudolf Bode, *Rhythmus und Körpererziehung. Fünf Abhandlungen*, Jena: Eugen Diederichs 1925 (1923): 88.

Lebensphilosophie (philosophy of life) and especially of the writings of Ludwig Klages, he opposes – as Böhme had done before – modernity's focus on personality.[23] Conversely, he promotes the basis of Indian dance in "Selbstvergessenheit" (absent-mindedness), "Ichlosigkeit" (selfless-ness), and "Entpersönlichung" (depersonalization).[24] This established identification of Indian dance with religion and the spiritual would then, in the future, inspire a number of Western modern dancers and thereby gain popularity in the dance scene.

It was especially modern dance which was, in its emergence, closely aligned with notions of religion and spirituality. Vaguely follow-ing Wagner and the early writings of Nietzsche, dance was understood as functioning as a substitute for religion, as evoking the desired unity be-tween body and spirit. In the views of a number of early modern dancers, the art of dance allowed a return to its supposed divine origins, which in turn led to a number of religiously-inspired or quasi-religious dance con-ceptions.

It was not only Loïe Fuller who had her first inspiration for her dances while seeing the light and the colors in the Notre Dame Cathedral in Paris, but Isadora Duncan also followed the aim of reconnecting dance and religion, or body and soul.[25] She described the case in ancient Greece:

> But the dance of the future will have to become again a high reli-gious art as it was with the Greeks. For art which is not religious is not art, is mere merchandise. The dancer of the future will be one whose body and soul have grown so harmoniously together that the natural language of that soul will have become the move-ment of the body. The dancer will not belong to a nation but to all humanity. She will dance not in the form of nymph, nor fairy, nor coquette, but in the form of woman in her greatest and purest

---

[23] See Georg Bollenbeck, *Eine Geschichte der Kulturkritik. Von Rousseau bis Günther Anders*, München: Beck 2007: 240.
[24] Bode 87.
[25] See Fuller 13 (see Chap.2, footnote 91).

expression. She will realize the mission of woman's body and the holiness of all its parts.[26]

Duncan apparently further pursued the theme of the sacredness of the body, especially the female body, and gave lectures in Germany on the subject of "The Religion of the Body."[27]

Other of the founding figures of the German *Ausdruckstanz* also referred to ideas of religion or spirituality in their writings. One of them was Rudolf von Laban. Similarly influenced by the German life philosophical writings of Ernst Haeckel, Wilhelm Wundt and Ludwig Klages, which were in turn based in Romantic *Naturphilosophie* (natural philosophy), Laban proclaimed a holistic approach to the human being as he saw it ideally reflected in dance.[28] Following Klages, he declared the threefold unity of body, spirit, and soul whereby he opposed modernity's single focus on reason.[29] He had already described his "dance worldview" in *Die Welt des Tänzers,* published in Germany in 1920. In a religiously connoted language Laban here elaborates on the "faith of the dancer" and highlights the worldwide universal connection between dance, myth and religious belief:

In his "Timaeus" Plato conveyed the cosmogony of Pythagoras, which is a form of dance's confession of faith. The successors of the Dschella-eddin-Rumînû (son of the founder of the order of dancing dervishes), whose poetry and worldview is known under

---

[26] Isadora Duncan, "The Dancer of the Future," in: I. Duncan, *The Art of the Dance*, New York 1928; quoted in: M. Huxley & N. Witts (eds.), *The Twentieth-Century Performance Reader*, London & New York: Routledge 2002: 171-175; here 175.

[27] See Gunhild Oberzaucher-Schüller, "Vorbilder und Wegbereiter. Über den Einfluß der 'prime movers' des amerikanischen Modern Dance auf das Werden des Freien Tanzes in Mitteleuropa," in: G. Oberzaucher-Schüller (ed.), *Ausdruckstanz. Eine mitteleuropäische Bewegung der ersten Hälfte des 20. Jahrhunderts*, Florian Noetzel: Wilhelmshaven 1992: 347-366; here 363; footnote 15.

[28] See Evelyn Dörr, "Rudolf von Laban. Tänzerische Identität im Spannungsfeld von Kunst, Wissenschaft und Politik," in: S. Karoß & L. Welzin (eds.), *Tanz–Politik–Identität*, Hamburg: LIT Verlag 2001:103-132; here 104; See Laban, *Die Welt des Tänzers* 3ff.

[29] See Bollenbeck 242.

the collective term "Sufism," sang about world affairs as the dance of the spheres around God. In the Middle Ages numerous leagues existed, which, in their ritual gatherings, praised the dance as the source of all knowledge and as the essence of Being. In the mythologies of all peoples the dancer is ascribed his own faith and a particular nature.[30]

For Laban movement itself becomes the main principle of the world, the direct expression of all worldly affairs. The dance work, able to represent the eternal Being, is then already in itself a total work of art representing religious or spiritual aspects.[31]

This concept of the dance work coincides with Laban's focus on cult, ritual, and feast as means of general education in dance. Laban claims that every human being has the disposition to be a dancer and he aims at the implementation of so-called "cultic dance instructions" open for every human being.[32] These instructions, due to dance's cultural impact, should serve as means to enhance the sense of cultural community. Besides his interest in mystic Sufism mentioned above, Laban's approach to dance as established in *Die Welt des Tänzers* further reflects his involvement in the German life reform movement as exemplified in his work at Monte Verità near Ascona in Switzerland in summer 1912.[33]

Also in his later book *The Mastery of Movement on the Stage* (1950), Laban stresses the important basis of movement in worship and prayer and refers to the still-existent variety of ritual and sacred dances in other cultures or ancient societies:

> The European has lost the habit and capacity to pray with movement. The vestiges of such praying are the genuflexions of the worshippers in our churches. The ritual movements of other races are much richer in range and expressiveness. Late civilisations

---

[30] Laban, *Die Welt des Tänzers* 7.
[31] See ibid. 239.
[32] See ibid. 8; Ibid. 106.
[33] See Preston-Dunlop 89 (see Chap.2, footnote 100). See also Gabriele Brandstetter, "Ausdruckstanz," in: Kerbs & Reulecker 451-463; here 454ff (see Chap.2, footnote 61).

have resorted to spoken prayer in which the movements of the voice-organs become more important than bodily movements. Speaking is then often heightened into singing. It is, however, probable that liturgical praying and ritual dancing co-existed in very early times; and so it is also probable that the spoken drama and the musical dance have both developed from worship; from liturgy on the one hand and ritual on the other.[34]

Similarly Mary Wigman, a former student of Rudolf von Laban, seems to have approached dance as in its basis a religious art. This is not only reflected in her interest in the meditative circular movements of the Sufi-monks which she also integrated into her work, but even more in her self-declaration as a "priestess of dance:" "I am the dance. And I am the priestess of dance. The impetus of my body speaks to you of the movement of all things."[35] Some of the titles of her works, such as *Visionen* (1925) or *Das Opfer* (1931), might attest for her involvement with ritual and the sacred.[36]

Some authors further regard Rudolf Steiner, founder of the so-called movement system of *Eurhythmie* (eurhythmics), as another possible representation of a dance that might close the religious gap in modernity. In an article published in *Musikblätter des Anbruch*, Ernst Müller first declares pedagogy, and here especially the movement branch of "rhythmic gymnastics," as a means to reach and refine the spirit by means of the body in a time when religion obviously cannot fulfill this task:

> In a time where religious tradition is mainly attributed to the past, the most serious question is [...] that of pedagogy. Thus rhythmic gymnastics seeks to, as formerly in Greece, integrate dance once

---

[34] Rudolf Laban, *The Mastery of Movement on the Stage*, London: Macdonald & Evans 1950: 4ff.
[35] Mary Wigman, "Vom Wesen des künstlerischen Tanzes," in: R.v. Laban & M. Wigman et al. (eds.), *Die tänzerische Situation unserer Zeit: Ein Querschnitt*, Dresden: Reißner 1936: 10ff; here 10; quoted in: Huschka 179 (see Chap.2, footnote 59).
[36] See Brandstetter, "Ausdruckstanz" 457.

again into education as an element which is designated to harmonize and ennoble the soul by means of the body.[37]

In one of the succeeding numbers of the journal, Müller distinguishes Rudolf Steiner, a former member of the Theosophical Society, as initiator of certain current efforts of spiritual renewal.[38] Thereby "Steiner reaches an all-embracing theosophical worldview […], a concept of the essence of the human and of humanity that corresponds, on the one hand with Christian mysticism, on the other hand with the ancient doctrine of reincarnation; a concept which can also be understood as a cosmic-spiritual doctrine of evolution."[39]

The various sources of Steiner's teachings here mentioned by the author, including Steiner's interest in natural science and Goethe's theory of the metamorphoses of plants, show once again the eclectic character of spiritual endeavors in the context of dance, most prominently in modern dance.[40] The use of religiously or ritualistically connoted language obviously spread further and prevailed in the modern dance scene for years to come, as can be seen in a review on the American modern dancer Martha Graham written in the early 1950s by Eric Bentley. After having witnessed some of her dance performances in the United States, Bentley refers to Graham as a priestess: "She is a priestess. A present-day priestess of an ancient cult."[41]

The link between dance and religious or spiritual thought, however, dates back to the very beginnings of modern dance. Already the French singer and art-educationalist François Delsarte, who is generally cited as one of the main influences for the emergence of modern dance, founded his teaching system of applied aesthetics in accordance with

---

[37] Ernst Müller, "Von Tanz und Eurhythmie," *Musikblätter des Anbruch* (Vienna), no.7, April 1921: 125-127; here 127.
[38] See Helmuth von Glasenapp, *Das Indienbild deutscher Denker*, Stuttgart: Köhler 1960: 194ff.
[39] Ernst Müller, "Von Tanz und Eurhythmie. Schluß," *Musikblätter des Anbruch* (Vienna), no.9-10, May 1921: 161-163; here 161.
[40] See Eva Froböse (ed.), *Rudolf Steiner über Eurythmische Kunst*, Köln: DuMont 1983: 34-35, 103ff
[41] Bentley 202 (see Chap.2, footnote 174).

metaphysical concepts. Delsarte presented a system based on French Catholicism mixed with mystic aspects which encompassed a variety of arts such as music, mainly singing, as well as acting and dance.[42] Especially in their reference to aspects of movement, the teachings of the educationalist influenced modern dancers such as Ted Shawn, who later published a book on Delsartean movement. Shawn here also focused on Delsarte's religiosity and even comes to the conclusion: "Delsarte could not have evolved this system had he not been a deeply religious man."[43] Following Shawn, the system of Delsarte is built on two principles continually working simultaneously: the Law of Trinity and the Law of Correspondence. The former, based on humanity's existence as an image of God, states that "as God is triune in nature and essence, so is Man."[44] Expanding on Delsartean thought, Shawn sees this principle encompassed not only in the Christian religion, but also in Hinduism, in the trinity of Brahma, Siva, and Vishnu, as well as in daily life, such as in the trinity of father, mother, and child.[45] He also quotes a passage of the educationalist as handed down by one of his followers, Genevieve Stebbins, which underlines Delsarte's belief in the trinity of life, mind, and soul as a universal world formula – a conception arising from the metaphysical supposition of a trinity of body, mind, and soul which is also reactivated by Ludwig Klages in his philosophy of life.[46] Stebbins conveys the basic assumption of Delsarte's approach as follows:

> The principle of my system lies in the statement that there is in the world a universal formula which may be applied to all sciences, to all things possible. This formula is the trinity. What is the requisite for the formation of a trinity? Three expressions are requisite, each presupposing and implying the other two; there

---

[42] See Claudia Jeschke & Gabi Vettermann, "François Delsarte," in: Oberzaucher-Schüller, *Ausdruckstanz* 15-24; here 16.
[43] Shawn, *Every Little Movement* 21 (see Chap.2, footnote 70).
[44] Ibid.
[45] See ibid. 29.
[46] See Ruyter, "Antique longings" 70-88; See Bollenbeck 242.

must also be an absolute co-necessity between them. Thus the three principles of our being, life, mind, and soul, form a trinity.[47]

The Law of Trinity is then complemented by the Law of Correspondence which claims a correspondence between the spiritual and the material world: "To each spiritual function responds a function of the body; to each grand function of the body corresponds a spiritual act."[48] Accordingly, each gesture or movement is expressive of an inner emotion, feeling, or motive and therefore has a meaning of its own. Nancy Lee Chalfa Ruyter summarizes the approach and stresses the link between the body and the spirit: "The Delsarteans equated art with religion, the physical with the spiritual; and they identified their expressive arts with the glories of ancient Greece and the mystical East."[49]

Herself also a follower of François Delsarte, Ruth St. Denis strongly understood dancing as a spiritual experience and regularly presented religious topics in her dance performances. In one of her journals she even compared herself to "a priestess in the Temple of Dance."[50] Influenced by her mother, St. Denis was "part of a nineteenth-century American spiritual tradition that included Unitarianism, Universalism, Transcendentalism, and Christian Science."[51] Her self-understanding as a dancer was founded on a conception of the unity of body and spirit, which she saw endangered due to the modern focus on "the language of the intellect – speech."[52] Dance, as the "word of the living spirit" coming from "divine sources," became her solution to close this gap.[53] Based on natural bodily gesture as "the first communication of the simple needs of primitive man," dance, in her understanding, opens up the vision to "live

---

[47] Genevieve Stebbins, *The Delsarte System of Expression*, 1st edition 1885; quoted in: Shawn, *Every Little Movement* 24.
[48] Ibid. 31.
[49] Ruyter, "Delsarte System of Expression" 372 (see Chap.2, footnote 71).
[50] Schlundt, "Into the Mystic with Miss Ruth" 25 (see Chap.3, footnote 25).
[51] Jack Anderson, *Art Without Boundaries. The World of Modern Dance*, Iowa City: University of Iowa Press 1997: 39.
[52] St. Denis, "The Dance as Life Experience" 23 (see Chap.2, footnote 83).
[53] Ibid; Ibid. 22.

life in its finer and higher vibrations."[54] It also reconnects modern people with the spiritual and accordingly with the whole cosmos: "To dance is to feel one's self actually a part of the cosmic world, rooted in the inner reality of spiritual being."[55] In another article which is entitled "Religious Manifestations in the Dance," she describes a scene from her past when she was standing at night in the moonlight on a hill behind the family's farm house in New Jersey at the age of sixteen. This night becomes the initial moment for her orientation towards and understanding of religious dancing:

> I believe that my whole creative life stemmed from this magic hour under the stars on that hilltop. It was then that my religious consciousness emerged to flower years afterward into definite forms of religious dancing in which there is no sense of division between spirit and flesh, religion and art. It is this same unity that inspires and governs my every vision for the votary dance of the future.[56]

Also in a text printed in a Souvenir Program of the Denishawn Dancers (the company she built up with her husband the American modern dancer Ted Shawn) her dance is presented as a means for divine expression:

> Thruout [sic] the whole career of Ruth St. Denis there has been unfolding but one great plan – the expression of God through the dance. At the beginning of her great fame in Europe she announced that her East Indian dances were but the first of a series of dance productions dealing with the religious beliefs of all Oriental peoples. *Radha, The Incense Dance, The Yogi* gave rhythmic and plastic form to the religions of India. [...] In the coming years she will continue to give to the world the idea of Truth, as expressed through feminine divinities, by all peoples of

---

[54] Ibid. 23; Ibid 22.
[55] Ibid.
[56] Ruth St. Denis, "Religious Manifestations in the Dance," in: W. Sorell (ed.), *The Dance Has Many Faces*, Pennington: A cappella books 1992³: 3-9; here 3ff.

all times – for Ruth St. Denis has but one great message, the expression of God through the Dance.[57]

St. Denis, who, among other factors, named "formal religions" as responsible for the "inert mass of humanity," paints a utopian vision of a new art of dance that bridges nature and art.[58] According to St. Denis, "the divine self is expressed" in this vision – a conception that might also be influenced by the Delsartian correspondence between man and god.[59]

As just mentioned, the spiritual approach of Ruth St. Denis not only influenced her on a theoretical level, but it also found direct expression in the presentation of her religious theme dances. Pieces such as the above mentioned *Radha*, *The Incense Dance* or *The Yogi* were concerned with non-European mythology and religion, mainly Hinduism and Buddhism. As described by her in her autobiography *An Unfinished Life* (1939), St. Denis for years always travelled accompanied by a number of readings, such as a biography of Ramakrishna, a copy of the *Bhagavad-Gita*, and Coomaraswamy's *Buddha and the Gospel of Buddhism*. Furthermore, she showed a genuine interest in the writings of American transcendentalists, namely Emerson and Thoreau.[60] Transcendentalism emerged in early 19th century in New England under the influence of German and mainly English Romanticism, the Bible criticism of Schleiermacher and Herder, and German idealist philosophy. Centered on Ralph Waldo Emerson, the movement proclaimed the importance of the individual's intuition in opposition to (Unitarian) empiricism and the skepticism of Hume. Its thinkers further showed an affinity to Indian and Chinese philosophy.[61]

After her separation from Ted Shawn that put an end to the Denishawn Company in the early 1930s, St. Denis founded the *Society of Spiritual Arts* and the *Church of the Divine Dancer* and performed with

---

[57] *Denishawn Souvenir Programm* (1923-24); quoted in: Schlundt 24.
[58] St. Denis, "The Dance as Life Experience" 25.
[59] Ibid.
[60] See St. Denis, *An Unfinished Life* 247, 285-88; quoted in: Schlundt 45.
[61] See Russell Goodman, "Transcendentalism," *Stanford Encyclopedia of Philosophy*, 2008 (http://plato.stanford.edu/entries/transcendentalism/; last accessed June 21, 2011).

her Rhythmic Choir in churches.[62] At least by 1936 she was generally known for her religiously-inspired dancing, as is confirmed by her prominent inclusion in an article named "Religious Dance" in the Los Angeles-based dance magazine *The American Dancer*. The author here describes current presentations of dances in American churches – a context in which she also mentions St. Denis and her choir – and recognizes a general worldwide trend of "dances of worship" that produce religious exaltation:

> Today a new religion has sprung up among intellectuals the world over. They worship beauty, as recreated in art. Since the dance has taken its place with the highest of art forms, it has become one of the phases through which the true intellectual feels a religious exaltation, perhaps a greater exaltation than would ever come to him through mere attendance at a church.[63]

The article also includes a quotation from Ruth St. Denis in which she requests all dancers to dedicate their talent to God:

> Not that art is a religion to the artist, but so that every artist shall lend his talent to the All-Powerful; so that it will develop from a consciousness of self to one of the universal. Some day my sacred choir will not have to do mundane things in order to exist. The members will be able to devote all their time to this movement. And when that day comes, they will all say with me 'I, the dancer, bring my body to You, Lord!'[64]

Her ideas of religious dancing and for a dedication of the dancer's body to god culminate in her vision of "The Cathedral of the Future," as described in her article "Religious Manifestations in the Dance." She here

---

[62] See the foreword to St. Denis, "The Dance as Life Experience," in: Brown 21 (see Chap.2, footnote 65).
[63] Verna Arvey, "Religious Dance – And How It is Used to Express Sacred Themes," *The American Dancer* (Los Angeles), June 1936: 13, 40; here 13.
[64] Ibid. 40.

envisions the construction of a cathedral which reflects an ideal combination of the present with past religious structures in terms of architecture, lighting, and the use of materials. This cathedral would integrate the various arts, including "Dance and drama, painting and sculpture, poetry and oratory, music and fine craftsmanship" in order to "enrich the consciousness of the celebrants, educate and inspire the congregation."[65] It is conceived as stimulating the spontaneous participation of the audience members and meant to compete with other forms of general entertainment:

> Through a new pattern of audience participation and the soul-satisfying dramas concerned with man himself rather than the constant comings and goings of his objective world, this dynamic center of wisdom and beauty should surpass in sheer attracting power and theater or other secular exposition of the arts. To state it briefly, I want to see the House of God the most fascinating and perfect creative center ever conceived, the flower of civilization.[66]

In contrast to St. Denis, her husband, the dancer Ted Shawn, seems to have followed a slightly more ethnological interest in the dances of other cultures. Shawn shares the interest in dance as a religious experience and follows St. Denis when he describes art, and therefore dance, as "vital experience" in which body and soul are united in one, adding that "in the dance we experience a rhythmic beauty, the activity of God himself."[67] In order to return to dance as a religious experience he closely looks at foreign dance cultures, such as in India, about which he gave lectures and published essays.[68] One essay entitled "Gods Who Dance"

---

[65] St. Denis, "Religious Manifestations in the Dance" 8.

[66] Ibid.

[67] Ted Shawn, "Constants – What Constitutes a Work of Art in the Dance," in: Brown 27-32; here 32.

[68] Shawn mentions a lecture entitled "Hindu Art and Religion," which he held at the Nelson Gallery of Art in Kansas City. See Shawn with Gray Poole, *One Thousand and One Night Stands* 257 (see Chap.3, footnote 30). He further wrote at least two essays concerned with dance in India, both obviously printed in the same, yet unknown, source. See Ted Shawn, "Hindu Temple Dances. Of the Rites and Customs of the

apparently was written after an 18-month tour of the Denishawn Dancers throughout Asia in 1925/26.[69] The tour was taken with the intention to "search after the forms of dance [in these countries] and the principles from which they sprang."[70] Shawn starts his essay with a quote from Nietzsche's *Thus Spake Zarathustra*: "I should only believe in a God that would know how to dance."[71] The German philosopher becomes a starting point for his elaborations on the "essential and inseparable relation between God and dance" which Shawn especially claims to find in Asian countries, such as India, Japan, Burma, Siam, or Cambodia, and strives to (re)introduce to Western or mainly American culture.[72] Based on Nietzsche and loosely on the American transcendentalist assumption "that no one person can define God, but that each had inherited or achieved his own concept of God; that there were, therefore, as many existing concepts of God as there were people alive in the universe," Shawn presents his concept of God as a "Divine Dancer" or "Infinite Rhythmic Being."[73] He accordingly claims dancing to be "God's activity" and concludes that it "could be truly great only when it was Infinite Rhythm, Infinite Beauty, Infinite Strength, Lightness, Speed, Grace and Intelligence, finding outlet through the channel of a human dancer."[74] In order to revitalize the original close relation between dancing and the Divine, Shawn requires the Western world to learn from the ancient traditions of Asian or Oriental cultures because "these ancient peoples had believed only in gods who knew how to dance, and had come to Nietzsche's conclusion thousands of years before he was born."[75] To prove his argument, Ted Shawn presents his readers with

---

Nautch Dancers of Southern India," undated, unknown source: n.p. and "Gods Who Dance. 'Now There Danceth a God in Me ...' Nietzsche," undated, unknown source: n.p.; both Deutsches Tanzarchiv Köln. The second one might at least in part coincide with a book entitled *Gods Who Dance*, New York: E.P. Dutton 1929 mentioned in Allen 90, 99 (see Chap.2, footnote 127).

[69] See Allen 88.
[70] Shawn, "Gods Who Dance" n.p. (see Chap.2, footnote 126).
[71] Ibid.
[72] Ibid.
[73] Ibid.
[74] Ibid.
[75] Ibid.

mythological stories, first from Japan and then mainly from the gods of the Hindu pantheon as related to dance; he ends with dance as linked to Buddhism and Islam. For further support of his concept of "dancing as the most appropriate activity of God," Shawn also has a look at "primitive people" as well as at dance in ancient Greece and Egypt.[76] He hereby not only draws once again a parallel between Oriental and ancient Greek dance, as it had been done before at least since the British Orientalists. His argumentation further shows that he, like other dance writers of his time, differentiates between Oriental and primitive dancing. Bringing Asian and mainly Indian dance in the foreground, he highlights the ancient spiritual basis of these traditions and introduces them as possible models for Western modernity.

Concerning his argumentation and the literature chosen, Shawn proves to be informed in the current discourse on Indian art and identified with writers whose work has been described previously in this dissertation in the discussion on music, under the subtitle "New Orientalism."[77] The two main writers that he can be identified with are Ernest B. Havell and Ananda K. Coomaraswamy.[78] For his elaborations on the religious significance of Indian dance as linked primarily to Hinduism he accordingly quotes, apart from other authors, from Havell's *The Himalayas in Indian Art* and Coomaraswamy's *The Dance of Siva*.[79] By means of a quote from *The Dance of Siva*, Shawn adopts and passes on the superior position of Indian dance as a religious art as claimed before mainly by Coomaraswamy: "Whatever the origins of Siva's dance, it became in time the clearest image of the activity of God which any art or religion can boast of."[80] It is Shiva's dance, its mythological meaning and artistic

---

[76] Ibid.

[77] See Guha-Thakurta, *The Making of a New 'Indian' Art* 8 (see Introduction, footnote 6). See also Chapter 1.3.4 of this book.

[78] For more information on the role of Havell and Coomaraswamy in the emergence of a new approach to Indian arts see also Chapter 4.3.1 of this book.

[79] Shawn here names James Woodruffe, Krishna Sastri's *Indian Images of Gods and Goddesses* and an Indian author by the name Gangoly. See Shawn, "Gods Who Dance" n.p.

[80] Coomaraswamy, "The Dance of Shiva" 84 (see Chap.1, footnote 191); quoted in: Shawn, "Gods Who Dance," n.p. The spelling of the title differs in the various editions

representation in statues which Shawn further focuses on, a topic he is familiar with and he himself has already composed a dance on.

For his remarks on the ritual significance of dancing in the lives of "primitive peoples who by dancing sought to imitate and become one with their God," Shawn refers to the book *The Dance of Life* (1923) by Havelock Ellis.[81] According to the British author:

> To dance was at once to worship and to pray ... The gods them-selves danced, as the stars dance in the sky – so at least the Mex-icans, and we may be sure many other peoples, have held; and to dance is therefore to imitate the gods, to work with them, perhaps to persuade them to work in the direction of our own desire. ... To dance is to take part in the cosmic control of the world. Every sacred Dionysian dance is an imitation of the divine dance.[82]

In the writing of Havelock Ellis, whose book he describes as a "master-piece," Shawn finds perfect support for his argumentation concerning the link between dance and spiritual life.[83] Due to the fact that Ellis, besides many other sources, also mentions the writings of Coomaraswamy – and includes the exact same quote from *The Dance of Shiva* as Shawn uses a few years later in his article on "Gods Who Dance" – it might even be possible that Shawn knew of the Indian aesthetician through Havelock Ellis.[84] The influence of Ellis on Shawn's ideas becomes more obvious when one examines how Ellis begins his chapter on "The Art of Danc-ing:"

> If we are indifferent to the art of dancing, we have failed to un-derstand, not merely the supreme manifestation of physical life, but also the supreme symbol of spiritual life. The significance of dancing, in the wide sense, thus lies in the fact that it is simply an

---

of Coomaraswamy's book. Whereas Coomaraswamy's original used the spelling "Śiva," the Indian edition from 1982 at hand spells the title as "Shiva."

[81] Shawn, "Gods Who Dance" n.p.

[82] Ellis 37ff (see Chap.2, footnote 168); quoted in: Shawn, "Gods Who Dance" n.p.

[83] Ibid.

[84] See Ellis 39.

intimate concrete appeal of a general rhythm, that general rhythm which marks, not life only, but the universe, if one may still be allowed so to name the sum of the cosmic influences that reach us.[85]

The above examples demonstrate how the connection between art, religion and mythology, which was already given its peculiar shape in the Romantic concept of *Kunstreligion*, further reached into the 20th century and there found its distinct expression in the modern dance scene. Modern dancers, dance writers and critics in Europe and the United States partly were inspired by Wagner and his united artwork, partly by life philosophy and affiliated reform movements, by Nietzsche and, last but not least new religious movements such as theosophy and anthroposophy. With these influences, they claimed that dance originated in religion and myth and proclaimed to be tracing it back to its roots. On the agenda as a main representative of an ancient spirituality since Romanticism, India became, alongside other Asian cultures, a serious artistic and cultural reference in the struggle against "the materialism and the anti-religious stance of the Enlightenment," which was still leaving its imprints on modern Western culture.[86] Concerning India, Western writers at the beginning of the 20th century strongly built on the writings of Ananda K. Coomaraswamy who here emerged as an expert on spiritual Indian arts and aesthetics and a mediator for the West. This focus is also reflected in the reception of Uday Shankar, who himself drew from the aesthetician's writings.

---

[85] Ibid. 34ff.
[86] Clarke 55 (see Introduction, footnote 4).

4.2 Dancing the Divine: Shankar, Coomaraswamy, and Shiva as *Natarāja*

4.2.1 "He Dances and His Dance Becomes a Prayer." Uday Shankar's Religious Dancing

The examination of reviews in the preceding chapter regarding Uday Shankar's dance movements has suggested that critics distinguished Asian (including Indian) dance from the broader field of Oriental performance by stressing that its ancient stylized character of movement was based in religion and the enactment of myth. As a further inquiry into the material will bear out, the religious or mythological context was increasingly understood to constitute the prime marker of an Indian compound artwork encompassing dance, often compared with pantomime, and music.

Programs and reviews of the earlier performances show that the religious background of the dancers and musicians of Uday Shankar's group were regularly included. A program of a performance in Berlin from spring 1932, for example, referred to the group as "Brahmanische Inder" (Brahmanic Indians).[87] Whereas German reviewers at the beginning of the 1930s mainly referred to the performers as Indian dancers, still a number labeled them as the "Hindu dance group."[88] In the French and English language reception encompassing England and the United States, the connotation "danse et musique hindoue" (Hindu dance and music) was even more common.[89] The American programs accompanying the group's performances accordingly advertised the company as "Uday Shan-Kar and his Hindu Ballet."[90] The denotation "Hindu," in

---

[87] See "Gastspiel der Brahmanischen Inder (Hindus) mit Uday Shan-Kar" n.p. (See Chap.1, footnote 6).

[88] See, for example, D. 2 (see Chap.2, footnote 14).

[89] See, for example,"Informations Internationales. Allemagne," *Archives Internationales de la Danse* (Paris), initial issue, unnumbered, 1932: 20ff; Deutsches Tanzarchiv Köln; "Hindu Music and Dance. Programme at Arts Theatre," *The Times* (London), April 5, 1933: 12 and Martin, "The Dance: Hindu Art for the Western World" X2 (see Chap.3, footnote 197).

[90] See, for example, "S.Hurok Presents Uday Shan-Kar and his Hindu Ballet," [season 1937/38a, b]: n.p. (see Chap.1, footnote 206, 207).

217

fact, originally derives from the Persians who used the term to designate the people living at the Indus River; the term was later adopted by the Europeans.[91] Joan Erdman mentions how "at that time [the 1930s] Hindu meant Indian, or at least characteristically Indian."[92] The denomination accordingly fulfilled audience expectations. In addition, the themes of most of the dances originated in Hindu mythology. Due to the fact that the group also had members with other religious backgrounds, such as the Muslim Ustad Allauddin Khan, who in 1935 became the music director, and the French dancer Simkie who was only at the beginning received as being Indian or Hindu, its connotation as Hindu seems disputable. Joan Erdman concludes: "We may question the use of 'Hindu' today, with our greater sensitivity to India's secularism and multi-religious tolerance, but no one questioned the usage then."[93]

From the beginning on the programs ascribe the Indian performance a major religious significance. In a text written by Alice Boner which is prominently included in a program for Uday Shankar's tour in Germany in 1931/32, the Swiss sculptor and early financial supporter of the group presents audiences and critics with an overview of what Indian dance – as represented by Shankar – is supposed to be. Beginning with a short reference to Gottfried Keller's *Das Tanzlegendchen*, in which Musa offers the Virgin Mary a prayer in the form of a dance, Boner detects the deep rootedness of Indian dance in religious service, in contrast to its European counterpart:

> Whereas devotions of this kind are not common in Europe, dancing has all along been part of the practices of church service in India. Dance can be lyrical prayer, dramatic representation, or erotic rapture; nothing is excluded from the temple, because everything that is part of life is sanctified through cosmic insight. The Indian regards dance as a language, the chant of the body, and thus cherishes it equally and offers it to the gods, just as we

---

[91] See Axel Michaels, *Der Hinduismus. Geschichte und Gegenwart*, München: Beck 1998: 28.
[92] Erdman, "Performance as Translation" 77 (see Introduction, footnote 8).
[93] Ibid. 86, footnote 28.

offer music in our churches. He does not know any other direct expression of his religious emotion than the dance.[94]

In accordance with the Indian religious worldview described in this passage, Indian dance is basically religious dance. Program texts published in the New Yorker *Playbill* in the 1930s similarly put religious or mythological aspects in the forefront, such as when they prominently include drawings or photographs of the god Shiva, as well as of Uday Shankar in the role of Shiva, an aspect to be further examined in the subsequent sub-chapter.[95]

Reviews of Uday Shankar's first tour in Germany in 1931 and 1932 indeed confirm the classification of the Indian performances as being of genuine religious or mythological significance. This even led to a hesitation to talk about them as art performances. A German reviewer for the *Hamburger Nachrichten*, for example, described Uday Shankar's dancing as "Gottverleibung" (divine embodiment).[96] This description obviously refers to the German poet Stefan George (1868-1933) who at the beginning of the 20th century strove to reinitiate the "Vergottung des Leibes" (which might be translated as "deification of the body,") as combined with its counter-concept, the "Verleibung des Gottes," (literally the "embodization" of the deity,) meaning an increased human or bodily presence of the deity. For these ideas he found inspiration in Greek antiquity.[97] George proclaimed god to be directly accessible in the beautiful human body (Leib). Ancient Greek sculpture ideally embodied the divine and therefore served as the model in the present for a new interest mainly in the young, male body.[98]

Returning to the reviews, the same German writer further stresses the continuously enduring holistic worldview of the Indian dancers. While highlighting the ritualistic character of the performance he spots a

---

[94] Boner, "Der indische Tanz" n.p. (see Chap.2, footnote 129).
[95] See "S.Hurok Presents Uday Shan-Kar and his Hindu Ballet," [season 1937/38a,b]: n.p.
[96] Mk. n.p. (see Chap.1, footnote 74).
[97] See Sünderhauf 219 (see Chap.3, footnote 266).
[98] See ibid. 219ff.

parallel with ancient Greek cults of Dionysus and thereby creates a link between current India and the European past:

> It was a miracle of nature, a revelation of the creative powers, a dance of the deity in a human body in all forms and on every level of incarnation, dance of the deity and dance of the human being before the deity, service at the image of the deity, worship of Vishnu not in the act of theatrical presentation, but in magical identification. [...] This wasn't a play, as it had not been one for the Greeks; whoever has seen the victory dance of Shiva after the death of the demon knows that Dionysus had once been there in the flesh.[99]

The group's performance is perceived as authentic Indian religious cult. It represents a return to the origin of what dance supposedly once had been in the West. It stands for a holistic ideal toward which German modern dancers obviously seemed to strive. The same writer in the following refers to the writing of Ernst Cassirer on myth and mythology, mainly in *The Philosophy of Symbolic Forms* (1923-29), when he describes the Indian dance performance as primarily marked by the "mythical consciousness" of the dancers and musicians.[100] Thus, yet again, he situates Indian dance in the context of the primitive:

> This dance has nothing in common with that of the occident. After the arts were displaced and became independent in the 18th century, the dance of the occident went its own way up until the century's end: to virtuosity and the cult of "personality." It was exactly the real personalities which intended to finally bring dance back to its conceptual foundation; the dancing of Laban and Mary Wigman once again strove towards that foundation from which emerges the dance of the people of India as well as all primitive people: the closed world view identified with a state of

---

[99] Mk. n.p.
[100] Ibid.

consciousness which we have to call (following Ernst Cassirer) the mythical consciousness.[101]

The reviewer's reference to Ernst Cassirer, whereas cursory, is a clear sign of the ongoing significance of myth in Western and especially German discussions on art. In continuation of the Romantic interest in mythology, Cassirer locates the origin of all mental culture in the mythical consciousness.[102] This leads him to include mythology as part of his system of symbolic forms, together with, among others, language, art, religion, and science. Cassirer identifies mythology as the very foundation of science and thereby opposes the positivism of Auguste Comtes and Kantian as well as Neo-Kantian thought, which seeks to totally banish myth from the present intellectual world and locate it in a primitive bygone past.[103] In Cassirer's conception, more sophisticated symbolic forms, such as art and religion, evolved from mythical thought in a dialectical developmental process.[104] Myth therefore must be acknowledged as an inevitable basis of theoretical science. It has its very own necessity or reality and furthermore it represents a form of objectification, though at a lower level.[105]

In accordance with the earlier-assumed predominance of mythical consciousness in India, the German reviewer describes India as a place "where cult and form still constitute an inseparable unity."[106] This puts it in stark contrast to the Western modern secularized world, "whose most urgent ceremonial still chases away the gods."[107] The Indian dancer, while dancing, does not distinguish between himself and the deities he embodies, whereas Western dancers have to make use of artistic means in order to express a mythological theme: "Because all that modern dance

---

[101] Ibid.

[102] See Ernst Cassirer, *Philosophie der Symbolischen Formen. Zweiter Teil: Das mythische Denken*, Oxford: Bruno Cassirer 1954 (1923): ix.

[103] See ibid. xi.

[104] See Michael Friedman, "Ernst Cassirer," *Stanford Encyclopedia of Philosophy*, 2004, (http://plato.stanford.edu/entries/cassirer/; last accessed June 21, 2011).

[105] See Cassirer 7, 18ff.

[106] Mk. n.p.

[107] Ibid.

wanted to accomplish out of nothing, simply on the strength of expression, is naturally provided there without any expression."[108] Besides this profound difference in consciousness and perception between the Indian dancers and their German audiences, the reviewer nevertheless shows himself convinced that Western spectators can recognize the authenticity of Shankar's mythical embodiment: "How natural, how cheerful and unforced Uday Shankar strides and dances in the great dance drama; yet still: this is Shiva with his entire authority; we all felt it."[109] Cassirer's conception of mythical thought as the very basis of all sophisticated cultural forms theoretically opens up the possibility of linking cultures globally due to their common foundation in myth. This idea is partly reflected in the German reception. The link between German spectators and Indian performers leads back to a European mythical past as represented in the ancient Greek cult of Dionysus. Yet the reviewer states: "We do not stand on mythical ground; we reinterpret the magic realities into mental symbols."[110] The Indian dance and music presentation nevertheless offers modern Western audiences a point of connection with their bygone mythical past, a past still existent at the very foundation of Western culture. At this point, the reviewer once again utilizes the concept of "Gottverleibung," of a deity descending amongst the humans, as he finds it in the Indian performance as well as in ancient Greek cult:

> It was this ecstasy of the sounding world, of the whirring and droning guitars, the raving drums, the frenzy of the god in the battle of the unbound universe and in the triumph over the beast; it was the fading away of this frenzy into the silence of contemplation, when song and flute reinstate and the deity sits down for reflection – it was this embodization of the deity which imposes on us the image of Greek cult, which underlies our own occidental history; the image of Dionysus, which has never appeared so vividly before our mental eye as it here appeared before our corporeal eye.[111]

---

[108] Ibid.
[109] Ibid.
[110] Ibid.
[111] Ibid.

Other reviewers similarly hesitate to interpret the group's presentation merely as a successful artistic performance. A writer for the *Stuttgarter Neues Tageblatt* states that dance and music surpass their artistic significance due to their basis in cult: "One almost feels apprehensive to talk about a success with an art, which thus avoids all splendid stardom and whose gesture of the body and music are so deeply rooted in cult, as is the case with these Indians."[112] The reviewer further stresses the Brahmanical background of the company members, dancers and musicians, which are "descendants of Brahmins and thus possess the sacerdotal tradition which gives all their dances their distinct imprint."[113] This description corresponds with a review that was published on the following day in the *Schwäbischer Merkur*:

> The artists, musicians and dancers, all masters of their discipline, are young Brahmin sons; for dance and music are the arts of the priests, they originated in cult and, up until today, first of all serve cult. And thus one may compare these ineffable stylish, cultic or mythological dances, which are incorporated into every movement and presented in splendid Indian national garment, with a superb liturgy; a liturgy which, in every word, tone and gesture, emerged from the ultimate powers of creation and has grown organically over centuries.[114]

The reviewer especially accentuates Shankar's embodiment of Indian gods, such as Shiva and Indra, and points to the dance drama *Tandava Nrittya* as a highpoint of the performance. He not only acknowledges the influence Indian dance has exerted on Western or German modern dance, but declares that *Tandava Nrittya*, the piece "that most of all dates back into Indian primordial times," allows German audiences authentic insights into Indian culture, a culture which is still signified by its religious or mythological worldview.[115] The German reviewer is obviously deeply

---

[112] D. 2.
[113] Ibid.
[114] W. 6. (see Chap.2, footnote 181).
[115] Ibid.

moved by the intensity of the "mysterious" experience. Due to its profound religious significance, the performance seems to touch humanity at its core: "It is as if a piece from a distant world and a distant humanity was unveiled, a play of religious awe und human mystery, which stirs us from the inside. This art is the servant of the ultimate – religion."[116] In the end, the performance is not received as an ordinary performance but, once again, as authentic Indian cult enacted on a western stage: "None of these artists thinks of himself, none acts for "the audience;" they only serve the work and the work serves the gods."[117]

In *Der Kreis* Wilhelm Tidemann deplores the poor and lean character of the Christian cultic apparatus in contrast to the Hindu performers whose entire life and art is equally pervaded by the divine: "And this appears to me to be the significance of the Indian dances of salvation: that in them the sacred is lived before an audience as tangible, magically operating cultic force, radiating and penetrating into everyday life, affixed to and active in the presentation of the corporeal."[118] The German critic Heinz Neuberger further distinguishes between Indian and Western performers and hereby follows a strict racial essentialism:

> Uday Shan-Kar [...] is not a dancer like the dancers and leapers from Russia, not a dancer like Laban or Jooss, but a dancer by birth, by ways of the millenniums-old tradition of the Indian caste of priests, which he descends from. He was not trained to be a dancer, did not attend any kind of dance education; instead the cultic and national elements of his dance are innate.[119]

Dancing, accordingly, is not a career to choose but a vocation linked to the racial and religious background of the Indian performers. Deeply pervaded by the "Brahmanical worldview," to dance means to pray, as stated by Hermann and Marianne Aubel, authors of a small booklet on Uday

---

[116] Ibid.
[117] Ibid.
[118] Tidemann 597 (see Chap.2, footnote 8).
[119] Neuberger 193 (see Chap.3, footnote 191).
[119] Ibid.
[119] T

Shankar's Indian dance: "We here recognize the seriousness behind the dance of the Hindus. It is religion; that is to say reunion of the human with the Devine; to dance is religious service."[120] The liturgical significance of the dance performance of Shankar is also acknowledged in the *Prager Presse*: "He dances and his dance becomes a prayer."[121]

For other reviewers, however, the cultic significance of the performance does not meet with their expectations. A critic in the *Vossische Zeitung* misses the "Asian soul" and observes only a superficial existence of "something primeval Indian-Asian."[122] While acknowledging the performance of one of Shankar's brothers as Gajasura in *Tandava Nrittya* as "something original, fundamental," Uday Shankar in his role as Shiva is criticized for the theatricality of his dancing and the (false) pretense of ecstasy obstructing the anticipated passage to the divine: "[...] whereas Shankar as Shiva, besides all severe bodily agitation, gets stuck in the theatrical and only pretends the ecstasy which should bring him and us closer to the divine."[123] Negative reviews of that kind, however, remain scarce.

The British press also elaborates on the spiritual powers the Indian performance set free, but less frequently and enthusiastically than the German. Writing for the London magazine *Everyman*, C.B. Purdom inquires after the apparent difference between Indian and British artists:

> It is the spiritual mystery of physical form so complete that form and substance, body and spirit, are realised as one. When you see these dancers on the stage you do not think of technical excellence, you do not say, here are movements fully controlled by mind; you perceive an integrity of artist and the thing done which admits of no questioning, which you have to accept as it exists or not at all. You cannot say, these are clever dancers: you must admire or reject as your attitude to the drama may determine. What

---

[120] Aubel n.p. (see Introduction, footnote 2).
[121] K. 8. (see Chap.2, footnote 142).
[122] A.M., "Indische Tänzer. Theater des Westens," *Vossische Zeitung. Berlinische Zeitung von Staats- und gelehrten Sachen* (Berlin), morning edition, April 20, 1932: n.p.
[123] Ibid.

they do has a hidden cause and is subject to secret powers, which one is bound to acknowledge, whatever one may think of them.[124]

It is once again the holistic worldview, the perfect unity of body and spirit the Indian dancers represent. For Western audiences it thus remains on the verge of the incomprehensible. The performance is accordingly qualified as "mystic" with "secret powers" at work during the Indian dancing.

American reviewers as well acknowledge the cultic significance of the Indian dances. Whereas Mary F. Watkins, in a review on Uday Shankar published in *Theatre Arts*, only briefly hints at the topic when she states that Eastern dancing is "almost entirely religious or ceremonial in scope," H.T. Parker writing for the *Boston Evening Transcript* refers to the apparent gap between Western and Eastern dancing exemplified in Shankar's embodiment of the gods of the Hindu pantheon.[125] He writes that:

> the rapturous and contemplative, the symbolic and quasi-hieratic, dances left strangest and deepest impression. For they remained essentially of Hindu cult and art, unalterable by contacts with the West or propaganda before it. In conception of Indra, Shankar draws as close to sublimity as mortal dancer may come; in execution touches this lord of all the gods with a celestial grace.[126]

He further concludes how Western audiences will only perceive the divine embodiment from an outside position, unable to really enter into the spiritual experience: "In all these dances of the gods we Westerners see the outer symbols, illuded and possessed."[127]

---

[124] C.B. Purdom, "Mystic East and Psychic West," *Everyman* (London), April 15, 1933: 457.

[125] Mary F. Watkins, "Five Facets of the Dance," *Theatre Arts Monthly* (London), February 1934: 135-143; here 136ff.

[126] H.T. Parker, "Shankar at Peak of Old-New Powers," *Boston Evening Transcript* (Boston), October 28, 1933; in: Holmes 266-268; here 268 (see Chap.3, footnote 36).

[127] Ibid.

The above examination of source material confirms the view that Western critics generally located the Indian dance and music presentations in the context of an ancient religious cult continually and unchangeably passed on to the present. Shankar's performance, surpassing the realm of art, visualizes images of Dionysian cult as prominently revived by Nietzsche and functions as a vivid example of a mythical consciousness, a term coined by Ernst Cassirer. Transporting Romantic longings into their time, (especially) German writers in the 20th century, see here the ideal embodiment of an original unity between art, life and religion (in this case Hinduism) revealed. The performance also serves as a direct link to the perceived origins of European artistic culture in ancient Greek religion and myth. Spiritualized Indian arts are hereby ideally opposed to Western art as based on the individual personality in modernity as guided by rationalism.

One can add here that in an article published in *The Illustrated Weekly of India* in 1935 Uday Shankar indirectly repeats and confirms the prime spiritual impetus of his Indian presentations. Under the more general title "Reawakening of India's Classical Dance," he describes the ancient roots of dance as lying in religion and rite which in turn evolved from nature: "In India, however, the art of dancing and drama has, since time immemorial, formed an essential part of religious rites and a special feature of all auspicious occasions. Its roots were embedded deep in religion and the holy scriptures and its inspiration came from the whole of nature."[128]

It should further be noted that the religious contextualization, namely in Hinduism, which was appearing in the years to follow, is the prime marker in other writings on Indian dance apart from Shankar. Around 1940 the Los Angeles-based dance magazine *The American Dancer*, for example, published at least two articles on Indian or "Hindu" dance; one in 1938 by Dorathi Bock Pierre on the dancer Ram Gopal and a second one in 1941 written by the American-born dancer Ragini Devi. Ram Gopal is here introduced as being trained as a temple dancer. Whereas the article rather focuses on the rigorous dance training he obviously went through, there is a constant reference to the temple and the

---

[128] Uday Shankar, "Reawakening of India's Classical Dance," *The Illustrated Weekly of India* (Bombay), June 30, 1935: 19, 59; here 19.

spiritual aspects of dance. Besides, dance is described to have derived from a mythological age, from the god Shiva who, as the author writes, "[t]wo thousand years ago [...] dedicated the fourth chapter of the Veda to the science of the dance and the temple dancers still follow his laws."[129]

Ragini Devi in her article on "Hindu dance" also bases dancing in antiquity and describes its continuous, unchanging, existence in the temples of South India. While focusing primarily on aspects of movement and expression she ends her article by stressing dance's "sacred purpose in the life of the people," a comment which once more highlights the holistic worldview of the Indian people.[130]

The fundamentally different character of Indian as compared to Western or European dance is also affirmed by the German dancer Grete Wiesenthal. She not only detects its strong religious ties, but also qualifies Indian culture as a whole as being deeply mysterious from a Western perspective:

> A part by itself will always form the Oriental dance. I do think here first of all of the national dances of the people from India. Their elements remain mysterious, like the entire people. Everything is linked with religion. Dance stops meaning to act out oneself, to manifest one's own soul, and is almost without exception a cult of the gods. Dance is elevated to religious devotion, strives towards the uppermost and is stripped off any terrestrial meaning of life.[131]

As late as 1945, Indian dance is still being presented as having been born primarily out of spirituality. This view appears in an article by Shirada Narghis published in the New Yorker *Dance Magazine*:

---

[129] Pierre, "Ram Gopal" 25 (see Chap.3, footnote 76).

[130] Devi 32 (see Chap.3, footnote 92).

[131] Grete Wiesenthal, "Tänze der Nationen. Freier und gebundener Tanz. Der Wiener Walzer," in: *Der Tanz* (Berlin), vol.8 no.5, May 1935: 19-21; here 19.

The spiritual dedication which was the source of the dance in antiquity had not changed. Mystics and philosophers, who observed the rhythmic progression of all phases of universal life, regarded that rhythmic pattern of time, movement and development as evidence of specific laws or principles governing nature and which the sciences are continually proving. From the personification of these principles came India's dancing gods and goddesses. Out of profound reverence and respect for universal laws, the dance, reproducing rhythmic pattern and movement, was a sacred art. This relation to the cosmic ideology caused the rules of dance to become set; its forms, subjected to an intensive analysis in relation to the possibilities of movement and expression, expanded on the basis of these rules, into a complete and perfect stylized art.[132]

Current Indian dance is here described as being based in ancient philosophy and science and is equipped with a perfect form, which has developed long ago in accordance with natural and cosmic laws. It is this specific, sophisticated, and ancient spiritual background which also built the fundament of Ananda Coomaraswamy's theoretical conceptions of Indian arts. Beyond that, it would be Coomaraswamy who apparently first brought the divine figure of Shiva into the spotlight of Indian dance performances on international art stages.

4.2.2 Shankar as Shiva

The dance presentations of Uday Shankar commonly included, as mentioned before, dances in which he or other members of his group embodied deities from Hindu mythology. Besides pieces on Indra and Krishna, the depiction of Shiva gained prime importance. This can be seen in his often mentioned dance drama *Tandava Nrittya*, which told the mythological story of Shiva's rescue of his wife Sati, reincarnated as Parvati, from the elephant-demon Gajasura. Due to Shiva's manifestation

---

[132] Shirada Narghis, "India's Dance in America," *Dance Magazine* (New York), no.19, August 1945: 10ff; here 11.

as *Natarāja*, or Lord of Dance, the deity gained an important position in Shankar's dancing as well as in Indian dance and arts in general.

Already in a German program of 1932, Alice Boner stressed the main significance of Shiva for Indian dance and explained the role of the Hindu god in creating and destroying the universe by ways of his movements to German audiences. From an unnamed source she quotes:

> 'In the night of Brahma the universe is idle and only awakes to dance at Shiva's command. He awakes from his stillness and in his dance he sends pulsating waves through matter, waves of awaking sound, which he produces with his drum. The rhythmic movement of his feet, the sway of his limbs permits worlds to arise und vanish, creates solar systems, form and names and once again treads them down to dust. Life and death, joy and sorrow, triumph and downfall, everything emerges out of the dynamics of his body. The rhythm of the spheres, the atomic cycle, evolution and involution, everything is the dance of Shiva. There are one hundred and eight different ways of his dance which correlate with certain cosmogonic aspects of his doing. He is the master of Sangit, the threefold art of drama, music and dance, which in India forms an inseparable unity.'[133]

American programs as well stressed the importance of Shiva for Indian dance. In a *Playbill* from the late 1930s we find a full-page photograph of Uday Shankar as the "Divine Dancer." The photograph is subtitled as follows: "Around the god Shiva is spun an intricate Hindu mythology. Shiva is the Divine Dancer – his mystic dance is the rhythmic movement of the universe."[134] Uday Shankar is shown sitting in a position of mediation on top of a leopard skin. He wears little clothing but various metallic ornaments on chest and arms as well as a huge head ornament.

---

[133] Boner, "Der indische Tanz" n.p.
[134] "S.Hurok Presents Uday Shan-Kar and his Hindu Ballet," [season 1937/38a]: n.p.

Plate 2. Shankar as Shiva in a position of meditation.
(Photo in: "S.Hurok presents Uday Shan-Kar and His Hindu
Ballet," [season 1937/38a]: n.p. / Courtesy of Dartington Hall
Trust Archive)

Another program on Uday Shankar from *Playbill*, obviously from the
same season, presents a drawn depiction of a statue of Shiva as *Natarāja*
on its front cover.[135] The article printed therein – "The Hindu dance"
written by Annabel Learned – accordingly starts out by referring to
Shiva's rhythmic divine dance which "sets forth through many aspects,
benign or terrible, the dance of the universe and of life: creating, sus-
taining and destroying from age to age."[136] Continuing her article,

---

[135] See "S.Hurok Presents Uday Shan-Kar and His Hindu Ballet," [season 1937/38b]:
n.p.
[136] Annabel Learned, "The Hindu Dance," in: ibid.: n.p.

231

Annabel Learned goes into detail about the gods of Hinduism, starting out with a passage on Shiva as the creator and destroyer of the universe. Regarding the content of the dances, Shiva is not only presented in *Tandava Nrittya*, but also becomes the focus of a second dance drama entitled *Shiva-Parvati Nrittya Dwandva* circling around the dance competition between Shiva and his wife Parvati, with both pieces one after another well-positioned at the end of the performances.

Plate 3. Cover of an American program.
("S.Hurok Presents Uday Shan-Kar and His Hindu Ballet,"
[season 1937/38b]: frontispiece / Courtesy of Dartington Hall Trust Archive)

Constant and often detailed remarks on Shiva in the reviews further indicate that the mythological background of the dancing god must have generally been elaborated on in the written programs accompanying the group's presentations in the 1930s. In the German newspaper *Germania*, for example, Paul Adam refers to *Tandava Nrittya* as "the Shiva episode" and describes it as the major and most meaningful item of the whole evening.[137] John Martin from the *New York Times* sees the link between Indian dance and religion or mythology primarily indicated in the figure of the dancing god Shiva. Due to a holistic Indian worldview, dance in its deep connection with myth is once again described as a part of everyday Indian life:

> The dance is no mere amusement medium in India. In the person of Shiva, one of the three manifestations of the Absolute, it enters the rarefied atmosphere of the celestial hierarchy itself. Shiva, lord of creation and destruction, of whom all other deities are merely emanations, is a divine dancer whose movement is the rhythm of the universe. It is natural, therefore, that for a people for whom the cosmic rhythm is no esoteric abstraction but the actual basis of life-movement the dance should contain and reveal much that is vital to them for all that is too intangible for rationalizing.[138]

The reference to Shiva as a cosmic dancer similarly appears in the writing of the French reviewer René Daumal. Under the heading "The Dance of Him who Dances the Worlds," Daumal presents a detailed explanation of the content of *Tandava Nrittya* as a dance drama on Shiva complemented by much praise for the dancers and musicians, their "attitude of sustained attention, of continual reality," as well as the "truth" of the whole presentation.[139]

---

[137] Adams n.p. (see Chap.2, footnote 153).
[138] Martin, "The Dance: Hindu Art for the Western World" X2.
[139] Daumal 291ff (see Chap.2, footnote 152).

Plate 4. Figure of Shiva as *Natarāja.*
(Photo in: Coomaraswamy, *The Mirror of Gesture* plate 1)

Uday Shankar himself elaborates on the very impact which the figure of Shiva exercised on him. In an interview with Mohan Khokar he mentions how he saw for the first time a picture of a sculpture of *Natarāja* in Coomaraswamy's *The Mirror of Gesture*. Coomaraswamy himself had given him the book during Shankar's tour with Pavlova in the United States.[140] In a current reprint of *The Mirror of Gesture*, the photograph subtitled "The Cosmic Dance of Śiva (Natarāja)" is included as the first plate at the end of the book and shows a copper figure from the Madras Museum.

---

[140] See Khokar, *His Dance, His Life* 42 (see Introduction, footnote 8).

For Uday Shankar the image obviously was groundbreaking for his dance choreographies and his approach to movement:

> Then I discovered that this was not merely a pose but the centre of hundreds of movements that moved from one to another and finished with that pose. I invented movements which I thought emanated from the Nataraja pose. Of course, at that time I did not know at all who Nataraja was or what he represented. Later, this idea of movements radiating from a source and merging back into it I used in a number of my compositions.[141]

The mythological background of Indian dance also becomes a starting point in a written outline of the Uday Shankar Art Centre in India from 1937 which would be opened in Almora in 1938. The text starts with a description of the eternal dance of Shiva manifesting the cosmic background of Indian dance:

> DANCE has kept in India from time immemorial a most important place in the cultural achievements of her people. Having a background of cosmic symbology, and drawing inspiration from the whole of nature, it has been a constant source of inspiration to great sculpture and painting in the past. In the rhythmic revolution of the universe India sees eternal dance – the dance of Shiva, Lord of Dancers, the Creator and Destroyer, who dances in the heart of the world, releasing those who love him from earthly bondage and bestowing on them eternal bliss.[142]

In an article published in the New Yorker magazine *ASIA* in 1941, Gertrude Emerson Sen, in contact with Shankar through his English financial supporters, the Elmhirsts, introduces her American readers to the Centre. Shankar and his work are here once again identified with a timeless mythological tradition. She stresses the link between Almora as the

---

[141] Khokar, *His Dance, His Life* 42.
[142] "India and the Dance. The Need for Action," in: *Uday Shankar's Project for an Art Centre in India*, 1937: n.p.; Dartington Hall Trust Archive.

location of the Centre and the legend around the dancing god Shiva. Describing the Himalayan setting of the town Emerson Sen continues: "There, among the eternal snows, is the traditional home of Siva, India's God of Dance, and it is within sight of the snows that India's premier dancer of today, Uday Shankar, has lately founded at Almora a new school of dance and music, known as the Uday Shankar India Culture Centre."[143] She then elaborates on Shiva's prime role for Indian dance whose roots are detected in antiquity: "Whether or not Brahma was the creator of dance, it is Siva who has always borne the proud title of Nataraja, or Lord of Dance, and in Indian sculpture and painting the theme of Siva's breath-taking cosmic dance of destruction, the *Tandava*, has been a favorite one for hundreds of years."[144] Emerson Sen continues with a summary of the mythological background of Shiva's *tāndava*-dance and refers to its famous sculptural depiction in the temple of Chidambaram in South India. Indian dance (represented by Uday Shankar's dancing) is once again identified with a rich body of ancient sculpture by which it is given a firm and respectable basis: "Sculptured tradition thus amply proves the antiquity of the art of dance in India, and from the multiplicity of similar poses found in sculptures from widely separated areas, it is evident that dancing had already been systematized fifteen hundred years ago, if not before."[145]

Though Shankar's dances were widely commented on as part of an ancient continuous tradition of Indian dance rooted in sculpture, Uday Shankar's representation of Shiva's mythological *tāndava*-dance were apparently new for Indian audiences at that time as well. This can be concluded from an article published in 1934 in the New Delhi art journal *Roopa-Lekha*. Here the author writes:

> I was aware of the ancient prescriptions in the celebrated chapter – Chitrasūtra of *Vishnudharmottarapurana* that dancing is the parent of all plastic and graphic arts. Uday-Shankar's performance was the first concrete proof of the ancient text that I expe-

---

[143] Gertrude Emerson Sen, "A Beacon on the Himalayas," *ASIA* (New York), December 1941: 690-694; here 690; Dartington Hall Trust Archive.
[144] Ibid.
[145] Ibid. 691.

236

rienced. His interpretation of *Nataraja* – His *tandava* – was something unique. The great conception of the *Nataraja* image, one of the greatest creations of Indian plastic genius, was but as it were a representation of the finale of the *tandava*.[146]

Uday Shankar's representations of Shiva as well as of other gods of the Hindu pantheon obviously fascinated and convinced reviewers and audiences and led to his denomination as a divine dancer. European and American reviewers recognized his dancing as exceptional, as surpassing common Western dance performances due especially to Shankar's divine embodiment which was perceived as derived from an authentic living spiritual tradition. This is, for example, expressed by a reviewer from the *Prager Tagblatt*: "I've never seen a dancer like Udaj-Shank-Kar before, one who floats across the stage like a young, incarnate god."[147] H.T. Parker from the Boston Evening Transcript comments: "When Shankar danced as the great gods – Krishna and Indra and Shiva – the divine presence seemed to illuminate the scene, the godhead to permeate it."[148] Also Samuel S. Modell in the *New York City American* claims to detect "something of godly impressiveness in the appearance of Shan-Kar."[149] The silent film actress Pola Negri is quoted by Basanta Koomar Roy as having emphatically referred to Uday Shankar as "simply divine."[150] Similarly, several friends or acquaintances of Shankar at Dartington Hall, after having attended his performances there in the 1930s, enthusiastically described his divine appearance. Not only Beatrice Straight, daughter of Mrs. Elmhirst and a close friend of Shankar, described him as "godlike on the stage," but also Paula Morel, who worked, studied and lived at Dartington Hall for several years, later remembered: "When the

---

[146] Nanalal Chamanlal Mehta, "The Dance of Uday-Shankar," *Roopa Lekha* (New Delhi), vol.4 no.13, 1934: 10-14; here 10.
[147] L-r., "Indische Tänzer," *Prager Tagblatt* (Prague), March 23, 1932: 7.
[148] Parker, "Shankar at Peak of Old-New Powers" 266.
[149] Samuel S.Modell, "Hindu Dancers win applause in Debut," *New York City American* (New York), undated; printed in: "Press Comments" 39-40; here 39 (see Chap.2, footnote 5).
[150] "Pola Negri praises Uday Shan-Kar," *The International Literary Exchange* (New York), undated; printed in: "Press Comments" 43-44; here 44.

curtain went up, it was as though the Gods had come to Devonshire. I shall never forget the experience. [...] I have seen many dancers in my time, but none except Uday Shankar seemed to bring Gods to the earth."[151] Deidre Hurst, a close friend of Beatrice Straight, confirmed this impression regarding a performance of the group at Dartington Hall in 1933: "Many people have said that he seemed to be transformed into a god or some unearthly deity when he performed."[152] Although enthusiastic comments of this kind might be a common tone in the dance and art scene, the context in which they were uttered speaks for their reading as a confirmation of the image of Indian dance as being of divine and spiritual significance and inspiration. In his biography of Uday Shankar, Mohan Khokar furthermore includes the following episode to have taken place in Austria in the early 1930s:

> A little story: Uday Shankar was performing in Salzburg, in 1932. The show was over but the applause would not stop. Shankar came out again and again before his audience, and acknowledged the cheering with his usual grace. The bravoing choked him. Struggling, he could utter only two words: "Thank you." A matronly lady, sitting in front, was startled. From her lips escaped two words: "He speaks ..." She was still under the spell of Shankar as Shiva, as Indra, as ... .[153]

The outstanding stage appearance of Uday Shankar, his mere divinity, is similarly described by an Indian reviewer in *Theatre Arts Monthly*. Uday Shankar's dancing is here firmly based in Hindu cosmology and reflects necessary and almost unique spiritual insight:

> According to Hindu cosmology, the hidden beauty of nature has only one name – spirituality. And the expression of spirituality in the human body is grace. But it is not in a day that a man is likely to feel and respond to spirituality. In order to become a star on the

---

[151] Khokar, *His Dance, His Life* 91; Ibid.
[152] Ibid. 90.
[153] Ibid. 165.

stage, one must let the starlight flow through his body. Those who have seen Shan-Kar's performance know that it makes little difference what Shan-Kar dances as long as he is on the stage, for his appearance breathes as electric joy and a radiant peace.[154]

Although Shankar at the beginning of his career clearly was not familiar with the mythological background spun around Shiva as dancing god, he himself describes the deep spiritual link he experienced while dancing in a late interview in 1976 with his biographer Mohan Khokar:

> [US:] Dance is my life. When I dance I am nearer to God. I am not myself. What else is God? Or prayer? [...] [MK:] *When you did the dance of Shiva, Kartikeya or Indra, did you also inwardly identify yourself with these deities?* [US:] No, not that. But I completely went out of myself. It was like something possessed me. I forgot myself. I was no more Uday Shankar.[155]

As other Western sources from the early 20th century indicate, the figure of Shiva as *Natarāja* had already entered the field of Indian or Oriental dance before Uday Shankar's international appearance. One early example is linked to Mata Hari. A photograph taken at her performance on 13 March, 1905 at the Musée Guimet in Paris shows that she performed her so-called Indian dance before the background of a famous *Natarāja* sculpture from the museum's collection positioned on the stage.[156] A French review of this performance by the theater critic Édouard Lepage describes the statue while mentioning its destructive forces and suggests a connection with the content of the dance pieces.[157]

Several years later the American modern dancer Ted Shawn composed a dance piece entitled *Cosmic Dance of Siva* which premiered

---

[154] Nirmal A. Das, "The Hindu Dance," *Theatre Arts Monthly* (New York), December 1938: 904.

[155] Khokar, *His Dance, His Life* 165ff.

[156] See Brandstetter, *Tanz-Lektüren* 85, plate 12 (see Chap.3, footnote 18).

[157] See Édouard Lepage, "Les Danses Brahmaniques au Musée Guimet," undated, unknown source: n.p.; Deutsches Tanzarchiv Köln.

during a trip to various Asian countries in the Grand Opera House in Manila on 17 September 1926.[158] Shiva's *tāndava*-dance is a vigorous, male dance in contrast to its complement called *lāsya*-dance, which refers to graceful and feminine dance elements, and thus it must have been especially attractive to Shawn to choreograph a dance piece, because it was ideally in accord with his interest in "healthy masculine elements" of movement.[159] Following Suzanne Shelton, the dance piece, which he obviously developed out of his knowledge and associations linked to the sculpture of *Natarāja*, became a huge success with audiences:

> Ted scored a major triumph with his *Cosmic Dance of Siva*, which electrified his American audiences as it had in the Orient. As the Hindu sculpture of Nataraja or the dancing Siva, he wore only body paint, brief trunks, and a towering crown and stood on a pedestal within a huge upright metal ring that haloed his entire body. Moving in plastique, he mimed five cosmic stages: creation, preservation, destruction, reincarnation, and salvation. The dynamics of the solo ranged from still balances on half-toe to violent twists of the torso and furious stamping of the feet, all confined within the hoop that represented the container of the universe.[160]

In 1929 his choreography would be followed by a publication named *Gods Who Dance* which focused on the close connection between dancing and the divine in different Asian or Oriental cultures. Here Shiva is once again presented as the deity in Hinduism most closely linked to dance. As indicated before, one major source for his knowledge of Shiva was Ananda Coomaraswamy's *The Dance of Shiva* (1918). Similarly, Curt Sachs includes a photograph of a bronze of *Natarāja* from the Madras Museum in his *World History of the Dance*, whose subtitle indicates

---

[158] See Allen 90.
[159] Ibid. 80, 87.
[160] Shelton, *Divine Dancer* 213 (see Chap.3, footnote 32); quoted in: Allen 91.

240

that it is taken from a publication by Coomaraswamy.[161] In his studies on the revival of dance in India Matthew Harp Allen also stresses how the link between Indian dance and the *Natarāja* sculpture with its background in Hindu mythology must be examined in close connection with the Indian art specialist and aesthetician:

> The central figure in promoting Nataraja as the symbol of the synthetic grandeur of ancient (specifically Hindu) Indian art, science, and religion was Ananda Kentish Coomaraswamy. [...] Coomaraswamy's essay "The Dance of Shiva" [...] has been the most influential publication in the phenomenal 20th-century popularization of the Nataraja image.[162]

Allen further describes how at the very beginning of the 20th century the *Natarāja*, hardly connected with dance or the arts as "a primarily South Indian manifestation of the Hindu god Siva, [...] became the central icon and master metaphor for the revival of dance and, arguably, for the Indian nationalist movement as a whole."[163] This development Allen also strongly ascribes to the Indian dancer Rukmini Devi and the Theosophical Society to which she was strongly attached.[164] Although Ananda

---

[161] See Sachs, *World History of the Dance* n.p., plate 10 (see Chap.1, footnote 46). Whereas the English edition only mentions Coomaraswamy as the source of the photo of the *Natarāja* sculpture, the German edition gives more details. Following Sachs, *Eine Weltgeschichte des Tanzes* n.p. plate 12, the picture is taken from Auguste Rodin / Ananda Coomaraswamy / Ernest B. Havell / Victor Goloubeu, *Sculptures Çivaïtes de l'Inde*, Ars Asiatica III, Brussel and Paris: G. van Oest et Cie 1921.

[162] Allen 83.

[163] Allen 63. Anne-Marie Gaston contradicts the "modern tendency to think of Natarāja as essentially a south Indian deity [...] since images of Śiva in dancing poses come from all parts of the Indian subcontinent, including Kashmir and the Himalaya." She nevertheless acknowledges that after 1450 Natarāja images are only found in South India and show a smaller variety of poses. See Anne-Marie Gaston, *Śiva in Dance, Myth and Iconography*, New Delhi: Oxford University Press 1982: 56.

[164] Allen states how the renaming of South Indian temple dance as Bharata Natyam in the 1930s, a process in which Devi strongly took part, was "evoking a connection with a presumed glorious Hindu golden age." Allen 79.

Coomaraswamy was no decided nationalist, his influence here remains pivotal.

The role Coomaraswamy had in the success story of the *Nataraja*-sculpture representing Shiva's cosmic dance is also acknowledged by the Indian author V. Subramaniam. Subramaniam attests that it exceeded dance circles and reached the broader international art world: "Lord Siva is the Lord of Dance and Coomaraswamy's exegesis of the Ananda Tandava pose is well-known in all art circles."[165]

By integrating his various essays under the heading *The Dance of Shiva* Coomaraswamy from the beginning on singled out the deity as prime symbol of Indian arts, aesthetics, and culture. The inclusion of a picture of a bronze of *Nataraja* from the Madras Museum on the inside front cover of his book further supports Shiva's prominence and gives his readers a visual point of connection to start off from. His essay of the same name standing in the middle of the publication accordingly becomes the core piece of his writing and delivers his readers with the mythological and philosophical background and meaning of Shiva's cosmic dance as represented in imagery as well. One should note here that Coomaraswamy obviously singled out the sculptural depiction of one specific pose of the dancing god which then became Shiva's most famous representation worldwide. Anne-Marie Gaston identifies it as "the south Indian bronze Natarajas of the Cola period, the pose generally referred to as *Ananda Tandava* 'the dance of bliss.'"[166] In spite of its international propagation she points out that this image of Shiva which is linked to the temple at Cidambaram is not the only one in existence and also may not be the most common one in India:

> Coomaraswamy and other scholars have discussed this pose at such length that it is often accepted as the typical form of Nataraja. The images are usually of bronze and have four arms, the two main or foremost pair of hands in *gajahasta*, and *abhaya*,

---

[165] V. Subramaniam, "The Sacred and the Secular: Symbiosis and Synthesis," in: V. Subramaniam (ed.), *The Sacred and the Secular in India's Performing Arts: Ananda K. Coomaraswamy Centenary Essays*, New Delhi: Ashish Publishing House 1980: 1ff; here 1.

[166] Gaston 47.

242

while the other two hold the fire and the *damaru*. It is in this form that Śiva is the presiding deity of the temple at Cidambaram, and it was in such temples that the Bharata Nātyam style originated. According to mythology it was at this spot that Śiva performed his dance of *Ānanda Tāndava* at the request of his devotees. Practically all Bharata Nātyam items invoking Natarāja refer to Cidambaram, or Tillai as it is also known. Although this pose is the form of Natarāja most familiar to most people, it is not in fact the most widespread, being more or less confined to south India.[167]

In his essay "The Dance of Shiva," Coomaraswamy stresses the outstanding impact Shiva's dance and its sculptural representation had and continually has on linking people worldwide with the divine in art:

A great motif in religion or art, any great symbol, becomes all things to all men; age after age it yields to men such treasures as they find in their own hearts. Whatever the origins of Shiva's dance, it became in time the clearest image of the *activity* of God which any art or religion can boast of.[168]

Shiva's dance accordingly becomes a universal symbol that ideally signifies the unity between religion and art. It thereby surpasses, according to the author, other religious imagery worldwide. Coomaraswamy goes on describing three different representations of Shiva's dance but mainly focuses on, as hinted at by Gaston, one to be found at the famous *Natarāja* temple at Chidambaram in Tamil Nadu. Here Shiva is represented with four arms: "One right hand holds a drum, the other is uplifted in the sign of do not fear: one left hand holds fire, the other points down upon the demon Muyalaka, a dwarf holding a cobra; the left foot is raised."[169] This image of Shiva as *Natarāja* dancing his cosmic dance would be the one

---

[167] Ibid.
[168] Coomaraswamy, "The Dance of Shiva" 84.
[169] Ibid. 86.

which gained such international popularity.[170] Coomaraswamy goes on naming Shiva's five cosmic activities – creation, preservation, destruction, embodiment and release – in reference to Tamil Śaivite sources which focus on the worship of Shiva as Supreme Being, such as the *Unmai Vilakkam*, the *Chidambara Mummani Kovai* and the *Tirumantram* of Tirumular.[171] Having introduced his readers to the conception of thought surrounding Shiva as Lord of Dance, he closes his essay by stressing the universal timeless power of attraction of the *Natarāja* image. Representing by itself a "synthesis of science, religion and art" it allowed the ancient prophetic artists "no division of life and thought:"[172]

> How amazing the range of thought and sympathy of those rishi-artists who first conceived such a type as this, affording an image of reality, a key to the complex tissue of life, a theory of nature, not merely satisfactory to a single clique or race, nor acceptable to the thinkers of one century only, but universal in its appeal to the philosopher, the lover, and the artist of all ages and all countries.[173]

The *Natarāja* image therefore represents a universal alternative to the modern secular world of the West with its specialization, although the image is of Indian or more exactly Hindu origin. In his last sentence Coomaraswamy suggests the existence of a community of *Natarāja* worshippers from past times through the present, including himself and his readers: "It is not strange that the figure of Nataraja has commanded the adoration of so many generations past: familiar with all scepticism, expert in tracing all beliefs to primitive superstitions, explorers of the infinitely great and infinitely small, we are worshippers of Nataraja still."[174]

---

[170] Coomaraswamy labels this dance the "Nadanta dance of Nataraja before the assembly (*sabha*) in the golden hall of Chidambaram or Tillai, the centre of the Universe, first revealed to gods and rishis after the submission of the latter in the forest of Taragam, as related in the *Koyil Puranam*." Ibid. 85.

[171] See ibid. 87ff.

[172] Ibid. 93; Ibid. 94.

[173] Ibid.

[174] Ibid. 95.

The figure of Shiva and its representation in sculpture and dance is further addressed in an article by Coomaraswamy on "Uday Shankar's Indian Dancing," which was published in the New Yorker *Magazine of Art* in 1937.[175] Ananda Coomaraswamy here once again includes a full-page photograph of a *Nataraja* Bronze, at this time an item of his collection at the Boston Museum of Fine Arts.

Plate 5. Bronze of Shiva as *Nataraja*.
(Photo in: Coomaraswamy, "Uday Shankar's Indian Dancing" 613)

---

[175] For further examination of this article see the Conclusion.

On the preceding page we find a smaller picture of Shankar showing him as the meditating Shiva in *Tandava Nrittya*. In the subtitle Coomaraswamy stresses the dancer's thematic concern with the *Natarāja* and further encourages a comparison of Shankar's ornaments with the bronze on the following page: "Shankar as Shiva in the dance, 'Tandava Nrittya.' Compare the dancer's poised head with that of the deity dancing on the opposite page."[176]

Coomaraswamy's intention obviously is to highlight Shankar's detailed approach, such as in his use of authentically inspired costume in dance, while at the same time he reinforces the art's rootedness in ancient Indian sculpture. He furthermore once again manifests his expertise in the discussion of Indian arts and aesthetics.

Besides this, the same picture of the Indian dancer is also included in a *Playbill* edition accompanying Shankar's tour in the United States in 1937/38 while a drawing of the very same *Natarāja* bronze is used as cover image of another program from the same season.[177] This also speaks for Coomaraswamy's acknowledged and influential position regarding what would be understood as serious or authentic Indian artistic presentations in the West.

Another even more obvious example that demonstrates Ananda Coomaraswamy's influence on Uday Shankar can be found in a picture showing Shankar and his French partner Simkie as Shiva and Parvati. The picture is taken during a season at the Gaiety Theatre in London in 1937. The Indian dancer here uses a head ornament which is almost ex-actly modeled on that of the *Natarāja* image from the Madras Museum which is included both as a photograph in Coomaraswamy's *The Mirror of Gesture* and in the drawn or photographed version on the first page of *The Dance of Shiva*.[178]

---

[176] See ibid. 612.
[177] See plates 2 and 3 on pages 231 and 232 of this book.
[178] See plate 4 on page 234.

Plate 6. Uday Shankar and Simkie as Shiva and Parvati,
Gaiety Theatre London 1937. (Photo Gordon Anthony /
© Victoria & Albert Museum, London)

247

Plate 7. Drawing of a *Natarāja* Bronze in an edition of Coomaraswamy's *The Dance of Shiva* from 1971, front inside cover.

Plate 8. Photo of a *Natarāja* Bronze in an edition of Coomaraswamy's *The Dance of Shiva* from 1982, front inside cover.

In the general field of Indian dance one can conclude that the *Natarāja* image went on to keep or even extend its international popularity. One example is an advertisement found in the dance journal *The American Dancer* of July 1940 for the New York "School of Natya," a center "for the study of the Dance, Song, Drama and Music of the Orient," here mainly encompassing India, Java, and Japan, founded by Ruth St. Denis and La Meri. This advertisement prominently displays a picture of a *Natarāja* sculpture.

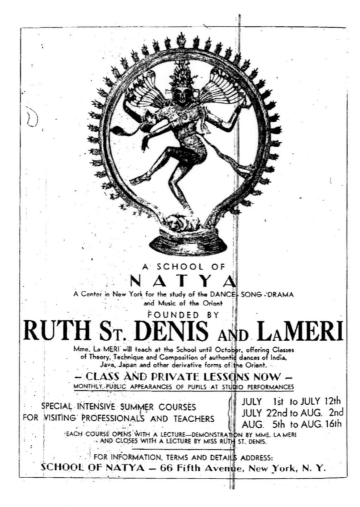

Plate 9. Advertisement of "A School of Natya."
(In: *The American Dancer* (Los Angeles), July 1940: n.p.)

Initiated mainly by Coomaraswamy, its dissemination through the present surpassed the world of dance where Shiva became a "standard patron deity for dance, a niche he occupies on dance stages around the world to this day."[179] According to Matthew Harp Allen the *Naṭarāja*

---

[179] Allen 79.

image also reached the greater context of Indian arts and life "as an ubiquitous symbol for everything majestic and noble in Indian culture."[180] V. Subramaniam writing for an Indian centenary publication in honor of Coomaraswamy even points to the international vulgarization of the image:

> The Nataraja image itself, almost unknown outside South India round the turn of this century, is now found in all the posh lounges of Indo-Philic Western homes, offices and universities all over the world and practically in every Western museum either as an original or in a good replica. The dramatic story of the recent theft of the Sivapuram Nataraja, its detection by a British art critic, its valuation at over 4 million dollars, the well publicized legal action and its impending restoration to India have all highlighted the glory of the Nataraja image beyond all doubt. We may also add that through a study of this icon and that of Sivakama Sundari, the consort of Nataraja, Western artists and art critics have come to appreciate the basic principles and standards of Indian sculpture more than through any other means. On the other hand, we cannot also forget the story of vulgarization. The icon has become a prestige symbol, regardless of the quality of the casting and as a result, these icons are made in every State of India and with all sorts of alloys and even the Tibetan refugees in Janpath, Delhi, do a roaring trade with ugly icons of the dancing lord.[181]

Though Coomaraswamy clearly intended the opposite of an international vulgarization of Indian sculpture, it remains undebateable that he had a main part in the propagation of the *Natarāja* image.

As the above examination has shown, at the beginning of the 20th century Ananda Coomaraswamy had a profound influence on the work and the reception of Uday Shankar and Indian dance in general. He

---

[180] Allen 83.

[181] V. Subramaniam, "The Kalayogi, Art and Religion," in: Subramaniam, *The Sacred and the Secular in India's Performing Arts* xiiv-xx; here xviii; quoted also in Allen 84.

strongly participated in the spreading of the image of Shiva as *Naṭarāja* and herewith had a major influence on Shankar, his catalogue of movement, his choreographies and last but not least his costumes and ornamentations. Reviewers of Indian dance further referred to him as main source of knowledge in the field, reason enough to further investigate Coomaraswamy's conception of Indian arts as well as main streams of thoughts he had been subjected to and influenced by in the shaping of his approach.

4.3 Indian Arts and Aesthetics on the Rise: The Impact of Ananda K. Coomaraswamy

4.3.1 From Arts and Crafts to Fine Arts in India

It has been mentioned before that after the death of his father, Coomaraswamy grew up in England where he came into contact with the last phase of the Arts and Crafts movement strongly represented by William Morris and the architect Charles Robert Ashbee.[182] In its profound criticism of modern society's basis in industrialism and materialism this movement would bring Coomaraswamy close to the wider field of cultural criticism. Yet Coomaraswamy's approach to and view of Indian arts would soon take a different turn, namely towards Indian arts as fine arts with a profound spiritual basis, a change which apparently happened in accordance with the British arts administrator Ernest Binfield Havell (1864-1937). Their approach has already been identified as "New Orientalism" due to the fact that it developed in direct reaction to the before established arts policy of the British Orientalist officials in India.[183]

After the Great Exhibition in London in 1851, which had aroused a fascination with Indian design and craftsmanship, a number of British Governmental art schools were set up in Indian cities such as Madras (1853), Calcutta (1854) and Bombay (1857). These schools came into existence for economic and commercial reasons as they were established with the intention of "increasing the market for Indian handicrafts abroad by adapting to European taste household items fashioned with Indian de-

---

[182] See Lipsey 44 (see Introduction, footnote 10).
[183] See Guha-Thakurta, *The Making of a New 'Indian' Art* 8. See also Chapter 1.3.4.

sign and craftsmanship."[184] For the training of the students, Greek sculptures and European paintings were imported; the latter had to be copied accurately by the students in order to become familiar with color and form and the Renaissance canon of objective representation of the visual world.

In 1884 Ernest Havell became Superintendent of the Madras and later of the Calcutta branch of the Government School of Arts (1896-1906). At that time the European classical and Renaissance canons of representation were still seen as the model for any judgment of Indian art – since Henry Cole the Buddhist sculptures at Gandhara were regarded as the highpoint in Indian art due to their "classic simplicity," which was attributed to Greek influence.[185] In accordance with the notion of historical progress as mainly derived from Hegel, arts in India were regarded to be in decline or even to be non-existent. A quote from an earlier appeal for financial assistance to employ British instructors in Indian art schools suggests as much: "there are no persons born or educated in this country to be found available for instruction in the industrial arts above-named, for the arts themselves may be said to be *unknown* in India."[186] In the beginning, Havell was exclusively an art educationalist who was interested – following the ideas of the Arts and Crafts movement – in re-linking art and industry. He came to Calcutta with the aim of implementing new classes in decorative design in the school's curriculum in order to strengthen the applied arts or handicrafts as the only living art tradition in India. When he bought a number of "fine old specimens of oriental art industries," such as metal-works and textiles, for support of his teaching method, he also purchased single Mughal miniature paintings.[187] In 1904 he had obviously changed his position and decided to sell all European

---

[184] Mahrukh Tarapor, "Art Education in Imperial India: the Indian Schools of Art," in: K. Ballhatchet & D. Taylor (eds.), *Changing South Asia. Vol.III: City and Culture*, London: Asian Research Service 1984: 91-98; here 92.

[185] See Mitter, *Much Maligned Monsters* 258, 263 (see Chap.1, footnote 187).

[186] "Society for the Promotion of Industrial Art, Calcutta," Prospectus and Circular of Colonel Goodwyn, President, *Journal of the Royal Society of Arts* (London), no.3, 1854/55: 752; quoted in: Tarapor 92.

[187] "Havell's scheme for the reorganisation of the Government School of Art, Calcutta," BGP/E, May 1897, no.49-50: 5; quoted in: Guha-Thakurta, *The Making of a New 'Indian' Art* 151.

paintings from the Calcutta Art Gallery with the intention of using the money to acquire more Indian art. This move was accompanied by several articles by him in which he was describing fine arts in India, such as on the historical development of Indian painting, culminating in the publication of *Indian Sculpture and Painting* (1908) after his return to England. The preface included the following dedication: "To Artists, Art Workers and Those Who Respect Art, This Attempt to Vindicate India's Position in the Fine Arts is Dedicated."[188] According to Roger Lipsey, by the time of the publication – Coomaraswamy had published *Mediaeval Sinhalese Art* in the same year – Havell and Coomaraswamy were already friends.[189]

To summarize their art approaches one can say that both Havell and Coomaraswmy found an aesthetic basis in Platonism and followed Neo-Platonic arguments for the primacy of the idea referring to the ideal world beyond that of appearance. Their views emerged in response or even in opposition to the supremacy of classical art and the ideal of exact imitation of nature or reality which placed Indian art in an inferior position. The ideal world was seen to lie in the spiritual world as described in the *Vedānta* school of Indian namely Hindu philosophy, where the world of perception was regarded as an illusion or *māyā*.[190] From a statement from Havell's *Essays on Indian Art, Industry and Education* (1910) it can be seen that he regarded Indian aesthetics with their close link with spirituality as being generally inscrutable to the West. Havell intended to manifest the superiority of Indian art: "The spirituality of Indian art permeates the whole of it, but it shines brightest at the point where we cease to see and understand it."[191] During an address on "Art Administration in India" delivered at the Royal Society of Arts in London on January 13, 1910 in which Coomaraswamy was also present, Havell criticized British training methods in India and called for a revival of India's heritage in fine arts. A number of the Society's members denied the mere existence

---

[188] Lipsey 63.

[189] Ibid. 65.

[190] See Mitter, *Much Maligned Monsters* 273ff; Guha-Thakurta, *The Making of a New 'Indian' Art* 162.

[191] E.B. Havell, *Essays on Indian Art, Industry and Education*, Madras 1910: 2ff; quoted in: Guha-Thakurta, *The Making of a New 'Indian' Art* 157.

of a fine arts tradition in India and Sir George Birdwood, chair of the meeting, finally made a denouncing statement about the statue of a Dhyani Buddha from Indonesia by saying: "A boiled suet pudding would serve equally well as a symbol of passionless purity and serenity of soul."[192] After the publication of the meeting's minutes, on February 28, 1910, a number of artists and art critics published a letter in *The Times* in defense of the Buddha statue further stating their sympathy and admiration for an Indian fine arts tradition. This letter – signed, among others, by William Rothenstein, the later art teacher of Uday Shankar – can be regarded as a manifesto of the New Orientalism as it describes Indian art as a sophisticated and living art of antique origin and mainly religious, divine inspiration. Indian art is here described as possessing a certain Indianness and, as part of the wider field of Eastern art, opposed to the Western art tradition:

> We find in the best art of India a lofty and adequate expression of the religious emotion of the people and of their deepest thoughts on the subject of the divine. We recognize in the Buddha type of sacred figure one of the great artistic inspirations of the world. We hold that the existence of a distinct, a potent, and a living tradition of art is a possession of priceless value to the Indian people, and one which they, and all who admire and respect their achievements in this field, ought to guard with the utmost reverence and love. While opposed to the mechanical stereotyping of particular traditional forms, we consider that it is only in organic development from the national art of the past that the path of true progress is to be found. Confident that we here speak for a very large body of qualified European opinion, we wish to assure our brother craftsmen and students in India that the school of national art in that country, which is still showing its vitality and its capacity for the interpretation of Indian life and thought, will never fail to command our admiration and sympathy so long as it remains true to itself. We trust that, while not disdaining to accept whatever can be wholesomely assimilated from foreign sources, it will

---

[192] *Journal of the Royal Society of Arts*, February 4, 1910; 287; quoted in: "Fine Art in India," *The Times* (London), February 28, 1910: 6.

jealously preserve the individual character which is an outgrowth of the history and physical conditions of the country, as well as of those ancient and profound religious conceptions which are the glory of India and of all the Eastern world.[193]

This manifesto further evokes the notion of an Indian national identity in referring to an already existent national art, more precisely the so-called national school of art identified with the painter Abanindranath Tagore, nephew of Rabindranath Tagore and main protégé of Havell who became Vice-Principal of the Calcutta School of Art in 1905.[194] Havell, following the former British Orientalists' interest in a classical Hindu golden age, more and more equated Indian with Hindu. In his coming writings and already in one of his earlier books named *Benaras the Sacred City: Sketches of Hindu Life and Religion* (1905) he increasingly ignored the Mughal past with its art and focused on a unchanging Hindu civilization deeply marked by spirituality.

The focus on the spiritual versus the material world brought Coomaraswamy as well as Havell both closer to the spiritual discontent of critics of Victorian industrialism, such as Ruskin and Morris, and also allowed them to find a parallel in the Theosophical society (from the Greek *theos* = god and *sophia* = wisdom) as founded by the Russian Helena Blavatsky and the American Colonel Henry Steel Olcott in 1875.[195] Themselves distinct critics of Western materialism, science, and Christianity, the theosophists believed in the Indian doctrine of reincarnation and combined it with ideas of universal brotherhood, the occult and comparative religion. After the death of Madame Blavatsky, her successor Annie Besant further joined the movement with Indian nationalism.[196] Although Coomaraswamy, as remarked before, was not a major defender of Indian nationalism, a number of his early writings, brought together in *Essays in National Idealism* (1909) and *Art and Swadeshi*

---

[193] "Fine Art in India" 6. See also Guha-Thakurta, *The Making of a New 'Indian' Art* 163ff.
[194] See Guha-Thakurta, *The Making of a New 'Indian' Art* 155.
[195] See Allen 95.
[196] See Partha Mitter, *Art and Nationalism in Colonial India 1850-1922. Occidental Orientations*, Cambridge: Cambridge University Press 1994: 244ff.

(1912), treated the relationship between Indian art, aesthetics, and natio-nalism. Furthermore, several of his writings, as well as those of E.B. Havell, were reviewed in Bengali by Sister Nivedita (1867-1911), an Irish disciple of Swami Vivekananda (formerly named Margaret E. Noble), who was an important activist in the Indian nationalist move-ment.[197] Yet as a close acquaintance of the Tagore family, he was soon disillusioned by the violence which emerged in the course of the Swadeshi movement.[198] He firmly retreated from politics, stating that In-dian nationalism could only gain real significance as "an idealistic move-ment" to be fulfilled best in art.[199]

Although not a decided Hindu nationalist, Coomaraswamy's work still shows, besides an interest in Buddhist art, a main concern with Hindu sources on which he builds his view of an Indian arts tradition based in antiquity. Allen concludes:

> As with Havell before him, Coomaraswamy's attention evolved in the first decade of the 20th century from an emphasis on crafts towards an overriding concern with Hindu India's 'classical' heritage in the arts – a concern both to demonstrate the existence of an ancient, sophisticated heritage based on ideals of *Vedanta* and *yoga* and to revive that heritage in the present day.[200]

Following Allen, at the beginning of the 20th century Coomaraswamy's "emphasis on a high art grounded in a specifically Hindu spirituality" would be reflected in his mayor works *Rajput Art* (1916) and *The Dance of Shiva.*[201] Since its publication in 1918 the latter became, as we have seen before, a major source of information for modern dancers, dance

---

[197] See Guha-Thakurta, *The Making of a New 'Indian' Art* 167, 174.

[198] The Swadeshi movement was a "nationalist movement to boycott imports from England while encouraging Indian manufactures" which started in Bengal in 1905 and spread all over India. Lipsey 67; see also ibid. 77ff.

[199] A.K. Coomaraswamy, *Essays in National Idealism*, Colombo 1909; Indian Reprint New Delhi 1981: 1-2; quoted in: Guha-Thakurta, *The Making of a New 'Indian' Art* 162ff.

[200] Allen 85. See also Guha-Thakurta, *The Making of a New 'Indian'Art* 178.

[201] Allen 85.

experts and reviewers interested in Indian dance. In his introduction to *The Mirror of Gesture* (1917) he would also refer to the mythological origin of drama, including dance and music, in the fifth Veda as created by the god Brahma.[202] As one of the first Indian authors on Indian art writing in English his publications circulated worldwide and reached international acclaim and were also a source of inspiration for Shankar himself in his search for an Indian basis for his dance choreographies.

In addition to his essay "The Dance of Shiva" (examined in detail above), there is another article which should be considered as part of the wider Western discussion on Indian arts at the beginning of the 20th century. Although Coomaraswamy elaborates on his art theory in several book size publications, "Oriental Dances in America" ideally summarizes his spiritualized approach in the context of the more popular debate on dance.

4.3.2 "Oriental Dances in America"

Coomaraswamy's theoretical approach to art as strongly focused on the spiritual had been elaborated on by him throughout his life in a number of his writings. In what is likely his most famous work, *The Dance of Shiva*, there are, for example, two essays which both appear under the main title "The Hindu view of art." Coomaraswamy here elaborates on the "concept of Art as Yoga" as one of the most important approaches in Indian art;[203] he also argues that the basics of the process or ritual of art making are deeply rooted in religion and worship and thereby he explores the deep relationship between art and religion, namely Hinduism, in India. In the second essay he adds the concept of *rasa* to his introduction to Indian art and aesthetics which is described as the "equivalent of Beauty or Aesthetic Emotion."[204] Coomaraswamy in-

---

[202] See Coomaraswamy, *The Mirror of Gesture* 2 (see Chap.2, footnote 127).

[203] Ananda K. Coomaraswamy, "Hindu View of Art I. History of Æsthetic," in: *The Dance of Shiva* 39-51; here 42. In the edition at hand the title slightly differs between the essay itself and the table of contents, where it is named "Hindu View of art: Historical."

[204] Ananda K. Coomaraswamy, "The Hindu View of Art II. Theory of Beauty," in: *The Dance of Shiva* 52-60; here 52ff.

cludes the artist, together with the lover and the philosopher, in the circle of "those of penetrating vision" who have access to the Absolute: "Precisely as love is reality experienced by the lover, and truth is reality as experienced by the philosopher, so beauty is reality as experienced by the artist: and these are three phases of the Absolute."[205] On the concept of rasa he goes into further detail in a third essay named "That Beauty Is a State." Beauty he defines as absolute and as such identifies it with the Devine: "in so far as we see and feel beauty, we see and are one with Him."[206] In addition to this, *The Dance of Shiva* opens with a preface by the French dramatist, writer and Nobel Prize winner Romain Rolland. Rolland presents India as a main representative of Asia which, as a whole, becomes a model for spiritual and cultural renewal in the West. Asia or India is identified with "a thousand wisdoms," with the place from where "have always come to us our gods and our ideas" and marked by "the universality of her great thought."[207] Rolland, positively reinterpreting clichés of a passive, stationary East versus an active, progressive West, introduces Europe and Asia as matching opposites which should unite for the emergence of a full humanity.

Yet already before *The Dance of Shiva* and years before the start of Uday Shankar's international career, Coomaraswamy introduced the basics of his art theory in an article which even made it into the fashionable American Magazine *Vanity Fair*. While only a short essay, "Oriental Dances in America" must, due to its wider appeal, have paved the way for his book publications to come in which he drew a more distinct picture of Indian arts, aesthetics, and culture. Despite what the title suggests, the essay is mainly concerned with Indian dance and surely has to be examined in the context of the debate on Oriental and Indian dance. Published in the same year as his *The Mirror of Gesture*, Coomaraswamy's choice of title is noticeable. The popular discussion of Western Orientalized dance performances here becomes a point of departure to introduce for the first time the topic of Indian dance and arts to wider American audiences. Then curator of the Indian Section in the Boston Museum of

---

[205] Ibid. 59; Ibid.

[206] Ananda K. Coomaraswamy, "That Beauty Is a State," in: *The Dance of Shiva* 61-70; here 70.

[207] Romain Rolland, "Foreword," in: ibid. 5-11; here 5.

Fine Arts, he uses a dichotomist approach when he opposes basic aspects of oriental dance including Indian dance with fundamentals in western dance and art.

Coomaraswamy opens the essay by emphasizing the current importance of dance and observes that in the United States "it is perhaps in dancing, more than in any other art, that one sees the expression of contemporary and national feeling."[208] He thus names three current tendencies in dance in American: the folk-dancing of the ballrooms and cabarets, the revival of Greek movement, and the imitation of oriental dance on the stage. While he outlines that the folk-art is the most "artistic" or the "most definite, conventional, and expressive" one of these three, he regards the latest derivative Oriental and Greek dance forms as much more "realistic and human" or free in their form than their "supposed prototypes."[209] This observation becomes a starting point for his theoretical implications which he expands onto the field of music and drama. Building on the aesthetic opposition between idealism and naturalism, Coomaraswamy elaborates on the distinction between the "theme" and the "artist" or "personality" in art:[210]

> Those who succeed in the free forms of the dance, or in music, free verse, or in the realistic drama, do so by the force of their personality, rather than by art – it is themselves that they exhibit, rather than the race [...]. But the greatest and most enduring art (the No dance of Japan was perfected in the 14th century, and the Indian Nautch before the fifth) has never been developed in this way: it has arisen when men have felt a need that some great thing should be clearly and repeatedly expressed in a manner comprehensible to everyone. In other words, the inspiration of great art has always been fundamentally religious (in the essentials, rather

---

[208] Coomaraswamy, "Oriental Dances in America" 61 (see Chap.1, footnote 190).
[209] Ibid.
[210] Coomaraswamy elaborates on this opposition in his later book *The Transformation of Nature in Art* striving to develop a general theory of art by bringing together Eastern spiritual art with Western art from the Middle Ages. See Ananda K. Coomaraswamy, *The Transformation of Nature in Art*, New York: Dover Publications 1956 (1934).

than the formal meaning of the word) and philosophic: under these conditions the theme is more important than the artist.[211]

Coomaraswamy thus distances himself from concepts of naturalistic representation in Western classical or Renaissance art as well as from mainstream tendencies in Western dancing at the beginning of the 20th century. Instead, he stresses the importance of a religiously or philosophically inspired theme as fundamental to his idealistic art theory. He carries on with the statement that ancient art – either Oriental or Greek – may be useful as an inspiration, but "ought not to be regarded as a model for our exact imitation."[212] Opening up the field for his own theoretical implications he states: "It is rather the theory than the practise of oriental art that has a real significance for us at the present moment."[213]

From here on he leaves the general field of oriental dance and draws a more specific connection between his remarks and Indian dance. Dance in India is first of all established as an activity which originated in the world of the gods, as it "is the gods who are the primal dancers of the universe."[214] Following Coomaraswamy, dance as a human art has to be learnt from the gods and only then does it have the ability to reveal life in all its essential and true meaning. This brings him to the comparison of "*cultivated* or *classic*" and "*popular* or *provincial*" dance. The former is defined by its definite theme – which comes from religion or mythology, – while the latter is identified with mere rhythm and spectacle.[215] The Indian tradition is then compared with the ancient Greek due to their compound character of arts: "Indian culture – like that of the old Greeks – employs a single name for the common art of acting and dancing; and this word *Natya*, in its Indian vernacular form, becomes *Nautch*."[216] Regarding the state of Indian dance in America he follows: "authentic Indian acting does survive in the Nautch, where instrumental music, song,

---

[211] Coomaraswamy, "Oriental Dances in America" 61.
[212] Ibid.
[213] Ibid.
[214] Ibid.
[215] Ibid.
[216] Ibid.

and pantomime are inseparably connected."[217] He refers to the gestures of the classical Indian tradition as still alive in the Nautch and comes to its mystical content, the love between Radha and Krishna. It is this "drama of seduction," which is, according to Coomaraswamy, "so near to the realities of life, and reflects the spiritual experience of Everyman" so much so, that it can be of great relevance for current audiences.[218] Coomaraswamy concludes his essay with a short description of the myth spun around the love between Radha and Krishna as represented in dance.

It is Indian dancing, inspired by an ancient mythology, which comes to the forefront in this essay by means of Oriental dance. While Coomaraswamy takes up the common thread established by the British Orientalists when he compares Indian with Greek compound arts, it only leads him to elevate the spiritual and symbolic basis of Indian arts above everything currently to be seen on American and probably also European stages. Indian arts are strongly identified with spirituality which, due to its universality, can on a basic level appeal to audiences in the entire world. Yet his growing occupation with a distinct Indian art theoretical approach as rooted in ancient Sanskrit writings and Hindu philosophy at the same time elevated Indian arts to a level beyond the reach of Western audiences, a tendency reflected once again in the reviews on Shankar.

4.4 "Replete with an Unknown Beauty." The Incomprehensibility of Indian Dance and Music

European and American reviewers of Uday Shankar's perfor-mances were in many cases undecided as to how deeply they and the public were able to understand and appreciate the Indian dance and music presentation. In accordance with the presupposed general opposition between Oriental and Occidental art as located in different kinds of movement and themes as well as aesthetic approaches, they clearly dis-tinguished between Western and Eastern, or in this case explicitly Indian art. A German reviewer writing for the German newspaper *Schwäbischer Merkur* refers to the influence Indian religious dancing had already had

---

[217] Ibid.
[218] Ibid.

on Western (especially German) modern dance. He nevertheless states the pointlessness of any attempt to truly understand the Indian performance, since it is so deeply based in Indian culture:

> Although we are familiar with some of the forms, though in their European variation – one has the strong feeling to face a world which is in its essence foreign, a world of an extraordinarily developed culture, with respect to which we remain in the outmost realm of comprehension and which to discuss is hopeless.[219]

Other German reviewers basically follow this pronouncement while at least allowing the possibility that German audiences are able to learn:

> India's landscape – its flora and fauna – remains exotic for us; exotic and partly opaque the people, their religion, their customs and their concept of beauty; their art therefore appears to us strange and mostly difficult to access. One needs time and preparation to relate to it.[220]

This writer attributes the foreignness of Indian dance mainly to the symbolic gestures representing Hindu myths that spectators are unfamiliar with. Repeating the Coomaraswamian opposition between Indian symbolism versus Western realism in art, he accordingly welcomes the inclusion of background information with the content of the dance pieces in the programs:

> The realistic gesture admittedly is suggested here and there; but strict stylization and apparently tradition as well generally prevails, and so the meaning of the gestures is not always readily understandable – particularly concerning the expression of content concerning Indian divine mythology, which we're not familiar with and often even do not understand. (It was for that reason

---

[219] W. 6.
[220] Brunck n.p. (see Chap.1, footnote 78).

helpful that there were given short explanations on the progam supplement.)[221]

Hermann and Marianne Aubel prove surprised that an artistic presentation as exotic as the one by the Indian artists, which is furthermore fundamentally based in religion and mythology, can so thoroughly attract such a wide European public:

> It is worth the effort to investigate how it has been possible indeed that people from a nation and a culture foreign to us were able to captivate and thrill a large audience to such an extent. One thing is certain, the premises under which these Indian dancers and musicians work and create are fundamentally different from those of European artists. Concerning the Indian dances we are distinctly dealing with a religious background as is the case with most dances which spring from the traditions of ancient cultures.[222]

The authors partly explain this phenomenon by pointing out the primitive ability of dance to represent "a full and universal humanity."[223] Yet Indian and Western dancers work in their distinct forms and also apply different artistic means. The authors here see European artists at a disadvantage due to the lack of a continuous dance tradition from antiquity up to the present, a continuity whose existence they presuppose in India.[224]

Writing for the dance magazine *Der Tanz*, J. Lewitan experiences a basic, strangely inexplicable connection between Indian and European art and describes the dances and musical pieces as "at most fundamental level essentially the same and understandable."[225] For him the difference exists only on the outside while deep on the inside European and Indian

---

[221] Ibid.
[222] Aubel 3.
[223] Ibid. 4.
[224] See ibid.
[225] Lewitan, "Tanzaufführungen: Uday Shan-Kar, Simkie und Hindu-Tanzgruppe" 13 (see Chap.3, footnote 271).

arts are related to each other. This experience of "inner connectedness despite outer disparity" [226] he though doesn't explain further. One might here suppose a perceived affinity between Indian and European culture due to their shared Indo-Aryan background in language, a view that had been transferred to the cultural level and promoted by the philologist Max Müller.[227] Other reviewers advocate the view that the East and West are two complements of a universal humanity and thereby explain the receptiveness of European audiences to Indian arts and culture. This humanist position is decidedly taken by the German reviewer Wilhelm Tideman, who writes on the Indian performance in *Der Kreis*: "Another mankind has borne witness before us. And to the extent to which we are part of an overall humanity we are also a part of precisely this humankind."[228] He criticizes the Eurocentric, compartmentalized view on art, religion, and humanity as narrow and dogmatic and instead praises the Indian performance, which is based on the unity of art and religion and body and mind. This is presented as an opportunity for westerners to revise and overcome their limited and limiting perspectives. The Indian performers hereby represent an approach not only on par with the Europeans, but even surpassing them: "Hence a concept of composition arises from the other hemisphere which not only attains or completes the entire Occidental artistic world but basically surpasses it."[229] It is especially the presupposed opposition between East and West which calls for their unity in a universal humanity. The Indian artists:

> place [...], in their legitimate and autonomous manner, something coequal next to Occidental humanity – the other side of humankind. What was residing in ourselves covert and buried: the knowledge of the human range of movement in all its magnificence, its pride and humbleness, [the knowledge] of the God-given instrument of one's own limbs – here it shines. And we un-

---

[226] Ibid.
[227] See Romila Thapar, 'The Theory of Aryan Race and India: History and Politics," in: Thapar 1108-1140; here 1111ff (see Chap.1, footnote 85).
[228] Tidemann 596.
[229] Ibid. 597.

derstand how the entire realm of human existence emerges from both East and West.[230]

American reviewers of Uday Shankar are similarly concerned about their ability to understand and comment on Indian arts and culture. It is not only the distinctly different way that the Indian dancers move, but especially the imaginative, almost dreamy state of mind – a description reminding once again of Hegel's views on India – that makes the critic W.J. Henderson in the *New York Sun* refer to the modern American onlooker as the "barbarian:"

> It is not for a barbarian of the west to essay comment on such dancing; its technic is not in the motion idioms to which we are accustomed. Its imagination dwells in distant regions among the age old myths of Buddhism and the almost equally venerable customs of a people incomprehensible to the prosaic denizen of an American metropolis.[231]

He nevertheless seems to recommend the presentation for its new, exotic character: "But one thing may be said without hesitation, to wit, that this is one of the most interesting dance exhibitions yet placed before seekers after novelty in this city of a thousand delights."[232]

Mary Watkins offers a similar opinion when she admits to having had a feeling of ignorance during and after Uday Shankar's Oriental performance: "Faced by the contemplation of such refinement of technique, such ancient and polished ritual, the mere Occidental leaves the theater feeling gauche, raw, and untutored in the alphabet of art."[233] Watkins is nevertheless critical of the authenticity of the Indian performance and detects a certain level of Western showmanship in Shankar's choreographies, including the music:

---

[230] Ibid. 598.
[231] Henderson 42 (see Chap.3, footnote 214).
[232] Ibid.
[233] Watkins, "Uday Shan-Kar and troupe offer Program of ancient rituals at New Yorker" 35 (see Chap.3, footnote 2).

He has brought the Orient to us, but he has not forgotten that the street is Broadway. His program is well built and varied, his music is calculated in the proper emotional key, and the plan of his dances, while unquestionably orthodox, is always built to an effective dramatic climax.[234]

A writer for the *New York City Post* also declares his western ignorance when facing Indian dance, yet feels confident that this ignorance does not prevent a sympathetic reception: "Undoubtedly the many gestures must have definite meanings of which the Westerner is ignorant; but whether or not we understand them they are sufficient in themselves."[235] John Martin, dance critic of the *New York Times*, is equally convinced that American audiences will enjoy the performance, regardless of whether or not they make sense of all philosophical and symbolic implications of Indian dance:

> There is nothing for us to do, therefore, but go to Shan-kar's performances with receptive minds and allow his exquisite art to work upon us as it will. Certainly it requires no scholarship, no special esthetic equipment, to respond to such gay and charming stuff as this, however much it may mean under the surface.[236]

The title of his review, namely "Hindu Art for the Western World: Uday Shan-kar Interprets a Culture Far Different From Ours," already indicates that Martin perceives India as "a culture in many ways antipodal to our own" which furthermore "is not to be understood in any real sense by the perusal of books."[237] He is entirely convinced that people from the West are unable to understand Eastern or Indian dance due to "a barrier that cannot be penetrated."[238] It seems, however, that Martin does try to understand more as he deplores the lack of English writings on Indian

---

[234] Ibid.
[235] A. 40 (see Chap.3, footnote 178).
[236] Martin, "The Dance: Hindu Art for the Western World" X2.
[237] Ibid.
[238] Ibid.

dance, mentioning Ananda Coomaraswamy's *The Mirror of Gesture* as one notable exception:

> When the Westerner approaches the dance of the East it is useless for him to attempt to 'understand' it; to do so is merely to raise a barrier that cannot be penetrated. There are countless movements of the body and gestures of the hands which have specific meanings in the highly involved vocabulary of the Hindu dance, and their meaning varies as they are combined and recombined with each other. The 'mudras' or symbolic gestures comprise a veritable language comparable almost to words. It is completely impracticable for a Westerner to grasp them, for with the exception of Coomaraswamy's 'The Mirror of Gesture' and a little brochure by Ragini entitled 'Nritanjali,' there is practically nothing on the subject in English.[239]

According to Martin, it is because of Shankar's universal artistry that American audiences nevertheless get a glimpse of what Indian or Hindu dance is: "Because Uday Shan-kar, the Hindu dancer, is an artist in the universal sense, he is able to illuminate for the Western mind the dancing of his people – an art so delicate and with so many ramifications."[240] After a performance of Shankar in Boston, H.T. Parker from the *Boston Evening Transcript* reveals that he is not satisfied with the fact that the Indian dance performance remains "necessarily superficial" for Western spectators.[241] He still describes the sweeping and long-lasting effects aroused among the audience by Shankar and his troupe: "None the less we aliens may have our sensations, generalized but impressive; on the instant stirring; in recollection lasting and to be cherished."[242] This view is confirmed by a British reviewer from *The Times* who describes how Western audiences, confronted with a "strikingly unusual entertainment founded on a highly finished art" like the performance of Uday Shankar,

---

[239] Ibid.
[240] Ibid.
[241] Parker, "Dancing Arts From India As Far As Boston"263 (see Chap.3, footnote 219).
[242] Ibid.

are not able to grasp its inside symbolical meaning yet can enjoy the presentation as outside observers:

> There were one or two mime dances, including a pantomime play of some length, which were simple enough to be universally understood, but in the more symbolical dances Western eyes were apt to miss the significance of the symbol while remaining more than content with the beauty of the arabesques.[243]

It is then only the form or outer appearance of the dances, its apparent ornamental character as typically identified with Oriental arts, which Western reviewers feel able to appreciate, whereas the inner significance and meaning of Indian arts remains incomprehensible due to its symbolical significance being deeply rooted in Indian spirituality and myth. However, writing for the British magazine *Everyman*, C.B. Purdom detects, as others before him, a universal truth in the mythological content of Indian dance that Western dancers might learn from:

> Ideas such as were in this dance are strange to our Western world to-day, which cares nothing about gods and is concerned only with material conquests; but the truth in this symbolic drama is a universal one, which I fancy few who saw the dance would deny.[244]

A review which appeared in *Theatre Arts Monthly* pointedly summarizes the contradictory reactions Western onlookers had towards Shankar's performance when the critic describes it as "replete with an unknown beauty." The Western inability to understand the symbolical significance of the dance and to apprehend the Indian musical forms here does not form an obstacle to the enjoyment of the presentation. Though Shankar wins the praise of critics and spectators the artistic appreciation necessarily remains on a superficial level:

---

[243] "Hindu Music and Dance" 12.
[244] Purdom 457.

Uday Shan-Kar and his group of Hindu dancers and musicians were a striking feature of the International Dance Festival. The audience who greeted them expected to find in the highly stylized movement and gesture of this Oriental dance, and the unfamiliar tonalities of Hindu music, a form more satisfying to the curiosity than to the understanding or to aesthetic appreciation. But as so often happens, in things that are completely right and true, Shan-Kar's dance did not seem strange at all, only replete with an unknown beauty. The idea of the dance, and its pattern, the movement of the dancer, the costumes, the music, were of a single purpose, easy to enjoy. And this was as true of the ritual dances as of the simpler pantomimes. Student may know that every slightest gesture in the Hindu dance has its own meaning; they may be stimulated by the experience of Shan-Kar's dance to search out some of these meanings, and such curiosity may enrich their experience when they see the dancers at another time. But they will not need it to thrill to the dance as a work of art, nor will they need to know the forms of Hindu music to enjoy the playing of the artists who accompany the dancers.[245]

In the perception of the reviewers, the opinion prevails that Indian dance and music are, in its symbolical and spiritual depth, incomprehensible for American and European audiences. Indian spiritual arts are thereby strongly opposed with Western materialist artistic culture. Though some critics hint at a universalism which guarantees the acknowledgement of the Indian performance as art, various reviewers presuppose an essentialism which makes it almost impossible for westerners to further access the world of Indian dance and music. Accordingly art appreciation is described as remaining on a superficial level. The Indian arts, on the one hand, gain their fair share of recognition due to their stated ancient spiritual and symbolical character (Coomaraswamy being a strong proponent of this view); however, they still mainly remain on the level of the mysterious, obscure, and exotic.

---

[245] "The World and the Theatre" 94ff (see Chap.3, footnote 192).

Conclusion

The preceding examination of reviews of Uday Shankar and his company of dancers and musicians revealed the enthusiasm with which Western critics, dancers, and dance experts welcomed the Indian performance in the early 1930s. How was it possible that a company from India had become so successful when it presented dance, music, and myth in a traditional idiom with which Western audiences were not familiar? The answer to this question is manifold. To begin, Shankar appeared on Western art stages at a time when audiences, dancers, and reviewers had already been introduced to so-called Orientalized performances from Western artists. At the beginning of the 20th century Western vaudeville stars and modern dancers who performed Oriental dance arrived on the scene. Individuals such as Mata Hari or Ruth St. Denis, for example, would have been familiar. They competed with and sometimes embellished the 19th-century Romantic operas and ballets by incorporating Oriental themes and scenery. Their performances were paralleled by the introduction of decidedly more authentic dance and music presentations at world fairs or *expositions universelles*, important venues in the expanding globalization of the arts and former performance locations of Shankar himself. These types of performances gained the interest of the developing academic field of anthropology in Europe and the United States. Its exponents included the main representatives from the German branch of *Vergleichende Musikwissenschaft* (or comparative musicology) which was mainly concerned with non-European or non-Western music. These representatives were eager to collect material from all the cultures of the world for further classification and systematization into a universal model. At a time when both anthropologists and spectators became more and more interested in what they understood as authentic foreign art performance, Uday Shankar with his company of primarily Indian dancers and musicians reached an altogether new level of authenticity in the eyes of Western onlookers. For audiences used to the opulent scenery of popular Oriental theme dances and operas, Shankar's performances must have caught the eye and appealed as strikingly different and, in its comparative purity, more authentic because of the range of exotic instruments onstage and the use of colorful Indian dress – even thought this appeared before a

271

simple stage curtain. Furthermore, in addition to a few presentations at world exhibitions, Shankar appeared on regular European and American art stages, a novelty which had only become possible in continuation of or as an upgrade of former Orientalized art performances. In addition, the appearances on Western art stages surely enhanced the serious artistic reception of the group.

Shankar's performances at that time helped audiences in Europe and the United States to form a clearer image of Indian dance and music. From the beginning of the 20th century on this image fruitfully met with the various individual dance conceptions and philosophies Western modern dancers were developing in distinct opposition to the classical ballet. Early modern dancers regularly built their eclectic dance views on the Romantic notion of man's unity with nature and spirit, a notion that was transferred into the 20th century among others by life philosophical approaches. Coinciding with the criticism of modern life conditions offered by various life reform movements, they favored a holistic, naturebound approach to life and art. Dancers discovered this approach not only in Greek antiquity, but they also searched for inspiration in other ancient or primitive societies including India.

The Romantic ideal of a synthesis of the arts also reached the modern dance scene at the beginning of the 20th century via the concept of the *Gesamtkunstwerk*, which was primarily identified with Richard Wagner. Wagner's total work of art referred back to ancient Greek mythological drama. His view of dance as one of the three most original and human art forms strongly appealed to modern dancers. Wagner and Nietzsche, the latter of whom in *The Birth of Tragedy* conceptualized his Dionysiac principle in allusion to dance, both became common sources of reference for modern dancers who proclaimed the prime importance of dance among the arts. Early modern dancers further developed their own, more original, conceptions of a unifying artistic model by giving dance a prominent part in it. Against this background Shankar's presentation of the dance drama *Tandava Nrittya* in particular gained enormous success, as it was claimed to transfer an original unifying approach in the arts to the present. Foremost to German and American onlookers *Tandava Nrittya* appeared as an ideal example of a united artwork since it combined dance, music, and elaborate dress with an ancient mythological story depicted by symbolical gestures, the Indian *mudrās*. The reception of the Indian dance drama as a united artwork was however, like unifying artistic approaches in general, identified with a holistic worldview and primitivism. This led, among a number of sources, to the reception of the presentation, the instruments, and the performers themselves within the context of primitive arts. The fact that dancing in particular was commonly understood to be the most primitive art form further enhanced this link. This view could be read from Wagner and it was promoted by modern dancers who thereby claimed the prime position of their art in the search for origins. In this era when the search for cultural origins dominated both anthropology and comparative musicology, Shankar's Indian performance appeared to spectators to have come directly out of ancient times and thereby to open up, in accordance with common evolutionary models, a link with the Western artistic and mythological past.

Indian arts were thus understood to have maintained contact with their origins and retained their form continuously since antiquity, a view prominently shaped by the British Orientalists. Early Romantic writers, such as Herder, had already claimed that India was the cradle of humankind and religion and in so doing shaped the image of Indian arts and culture as part of the world's classical traditions. Indeed, Indian arts and culture was seen as comparable with or even as possibly surpassing Greek antiquity. Eager to retrieve what they held as the classical Hindu golden age, British Orientalist officials in their research on Indian arts and culture focused on the translation and investigation of ancient Sanskrit writings and Hindu mythology. Stating that Sanskrit India was the zenith of Indian arts and culture, they developed a model of cultural decay brought about by the Islamic impact on India from the 13th century onwards. While they degraded all Muslim influences on Indian arts in the present, British Orientalist scholars perceived themselves as modern saviors of Hindu culture. Additionally, in the context of their interest in Sanskrit India the British Orientalists had established and pursued a parallel between Indian and ancient Greek music, dance, theater, and aesthetics which encompassed Indian and Greek arts' compound character, which brought together music, dance, and mythological drama. In British Orientalist writings on music since Sir William Jones, father of the Indo-European family of languages, this link had received prominence mainly in the comparison of the Indian raga with the ancient Greek mode, a reference re-emerging in reviews on Shankar's performances. Later writers, such as the British ethnomusicologist A.H. Fox Strangeways, would even claim a common origin of Indian and European music due to their shared Indo-Aryan language background. Furthermore, the comparison between Indian and Greek arts had already stirred responses by Indian authors. Apart from Sourindro Mohun Tagore, an early defendant of Indian music's unique identity and the un-translatability of its terms and theoretical concepts, Ananda Kentish Coomaraswamy here emerged as an international expert and theorist on Indian arts and aesthetics. In his article on "Indian Music" he already located the art in its distinctly Indian spiritual context and described the difficulties non-Indians must have in accessing it.

It is also due to Coomaraswamy that reviewers, audiences, dancers, and dance experts perceived Indian dance to consist mainly of stylized, statuesque movements and gestures, primarily of the hands and the upper body. Following along the path that British Orientalists had prepared before them, they located the main sources of movement in classical Hindu writings. Welcomed further by Coomaraswamy's translation of the Sanskrit treatise *Abhinaya Darpana* in *The Mirror of Gesture*, one of very few English-language sources Western artists and writers on dance could rely on, Indian dance movement was exceedingly understood to consist of static postures and symbolical gestures strongly derived from or manifested in ancient Hindu sculptures. In the field of dance writing this meant a further distinction between Oriental and Asian, specifically Indian dance movements. Whereas the former had popularly been identified with eroticized or spectacular movements, in the course of the 1920s dance experts and theorists such as André Levinson sought to describe and systematize non-Western dance in greater detail. Levinson here developed the influential opposition between Oriental dance movements as statuesque and concentric in contrast to the outward turning, extended character of Occidental dance. A few years later, in an article on Javanese dance, he would further distinguish Asian from Oriental dance and highlight the Indian religious dance tradition, a distinction and new emphasis one can find in other international dance writings of the time as well. Reviewers of Uday Shankar took up this same line of argumentation. Whereas Indian dance was generally still allocated to the wider field of Oriental performances, it was increasingly disengaged from the former's erotic suggestiveness and linked with the spiritual, philosophical, and mythological tradition of Hinduism. The figure of the Indian temple dancer here functioned as a junction bridging the erotic with the religious spheres. Critics of Shankar's company were therefore undecided if Indian dance could at all be described as primitive and they tended increasingly more towards its denomination as classical fine art. This estimation was, of course, also backed up by the propagation of the group in accompanying programs which stressed its use of ancient symbolical gestures, the role of mythology, and the Brahmanic background of its members, including Shankar's education at royal Indian courts. Modern dancers looking for new movement idioms in contrast to Western classical ballet thus not only found inspiration in the stylized gestures of Indian dance, but also in its decided mythological and philosophical background further stressed by Coomaraswamy. In addition, both Shankar's androgynous appearance and the apparent beauty of his body – half-naked in his Indian costumes – not only confused and fascinated audiences, but surely met with the dissemination of male dancers in modern dance who exceeded the traditional supportive roles of classical ballet. Although Indian dance was classified as a classical, stylized art, Western modern dancers in their opposition to the cataloged movements of classical ballet still discovered various points of contact.

The above-mentioned link between Indian dance and sculpture found further expression particularly in Coomaraswamy's emphasis on the god Shiva incarnated as *Natarāja* (Lord of Dance) as described in his influential publication *The Dance of Shiva*. Program texts on Uday Shankar often directly referred to or rephrased the writings of Ananda Coomaraswamy and thus they similarly stress the link between dance, ancient sculpture, and the *Natarāja* image. Their authors also gave the dances of Shankar that included Shiva special attention. In particular, one distinct sculptural representation of the deity performing his cosmic dance not only profoundly influenced Shankar's own choreography of movement and choice of garment and adornment, but it also directly entered the modern dance scene and became a widespread symbol for In-

275

dian arts and culture in general.[1] Through its link with mythology, its origin in and ongoing connection with the Hindu pantheon, Indian music (and especially dance) was thus almost exclusively identified with an ancient spiritual tradition. In stark opposition to common views of Oriental dance as erotically suggestive or spectacular, Asian (especially Indian) dance was considered religious dance. This perceived spiritual and philosophical basis became the prime marker of Indian arts and gave Indian dance and music its very distinctive character. At a time when modern dancers postulated a return to the connection between dance and the spiritual, thereby recalling the Romantic concept of art religion and a firm basis of the arts in mythology, Shankar's dance and music performance with its stated mythological and religious basis not for that reason alone appealed to European and American audiences.

Ananda Coomaraswamy's profound impact on the international propagation of the spiritual image of Indian arts in the 20th century has been pursued and brought to light over the course of this investigation. His approach, however, remains contradictory. While he on the one hand states the universality of a religious symbol such as the sculptural representation of *Naţarāja*, he on the other hand develops a distinct Indian image of Indian arts which is positioned in direct opposition to Western arts since the Renaissance. Similarly, as seen already in "Oriental Dances in America," Coomaraswamy himself mentioned parallels between ancient Greek and Indian music, dance, and theater traditions and therewith drew on the Western fascination with Greek antiquity and questions of origin in the arts in order to stress the classicality and the fine arts status of Indian arts. At the same time, namely in the field of sculpture, he had yet to demarcate clearly Indian from ancient Greek arts and aesthetics with the aim of highlighting the independence of the two traditions. He here sought to refute the view that the Gandhara School of the early Christian era had represented the highpoint of Indian sculpture, to which British Orientalists attested a profound Graeco-Roman influence.[2] His early publication *Mediaeval Sinhalese Art* from 1908 had already included an essay on "The Influence of Greek on Indian Art," in which he declared "that the influence of Greek on Indian Art, however extensive at

---

[1] Ted Shawn's piece *Cosmic Dance of Shiva* is a modern example.
[2] See Guha-Thakurta, *Monuments, Objects, Histories* 186 (see Introduction, footnote 6).

a certain period, was ultimately neither very profound nor very important" and degrades the works of the Gandhara school as "effeminate and artistically unimportant."[3] He then irreconcilably opposes Greek and Indian art when he discerns a lack of the mystical and transcendental element in the former:

> The philosophies of Greek and Indian art are poles apart. [...] Greek art, as has been said, has in it no touch of mysticism. The gods are but grand and beautiful men; sometimes, as in the case of many Apollos, it is uncertain even whether the representation is of a god or of an athlete. Indian art is essentially transcendental. Indian art is concerned not with the representation of perfect men, but with the intimation of Divinity.[4]

Following Guha-Thakurta, the struggle to differentiate between Greek and Indian aesthetics – "between the former's commitment to naturalistic representation and the latter's emphasis on idealized perception" – in the end was a main step in "the self-positioning of Indian art" and was instrumental in establishing a uniquely Indian point of view.[5]

The concept of art as "a modern European episteme" could only be applied to an Indian heritage if some of its Western aspects were rejected.[6] Guha-Thakurta concludes: "It was not enough, therefore, for Indian art to acquire a fine arts pedigree on par with the West; it also had to be empowered by an aesthetic content that was distinctly separate from that of Western art and unique to itself."[7] This would lead to the contraposition of Indian and Western arts and aesthetics with the former mainly characterized by its spiritual theme:

---

[3] Ananda K. Coomaraswamy, "The Influence of Greek on Indian Art," in: *Mediaeval Sinhalese Art*, New York: Pantheon Books 1956; originally published: Norman Chapel: Essex House Press 1908: 256-261; here 256.
[4] Ibid. 257.
[5] Guha-Thakurta, *Monuments, Objects, Histories* 220.
[6] Ibid. 185.
[7] Ibid. 186.

Indian art could come into its own only through posing of a sharp East-West dichotomy in aesthetics: though a construed opposition between Western "realism" and Indian "idealism," between the European Renaissance mode of "objective" representation and the Indian mode of "spiritual" and "symbolic" perception. Henceforth, the spiritual and the transcendental became the defining marks of India's fine arts heritage, the code that could reduce and compress its complex history around a common essence.[8]

In terms of Western reception, the pointed spirituality of Indian arts both led to its journey of success among modern artists and audiences who longed for unity, myth, nature, antiquity or just a new motion idiom for artistic expression, and at the same time it resulted in the perception of Indian arts as incomprehensible. As the final part of the examination of reviews on Uday Shankar has shown, Indian dance and music as ancient Hindu religious arts were elevated beyond the level of Western audiences' ability to understand them. One British critic pointedly summarized it thus: "Western eyes were apt to miss the significance of the symbol while remaining more than content with the beauty of the arabesques."[9] Coomaraswamy, denominated by Guha-Thakurta as "the period's most influential ideologue of Indian art," must be considered influential regarding this tendency to obscure Indian arts.[10]

As already seen, both Coomaraswamy's and Uday Shankar's success in Europe and the United States was in a large part made possible by the emergence of modern dance at the turn of the century, most importantly in Germany and the United States. Yet modern dancers were profoundly influenced by notions of India as derived from Romanticism and British Orientalism. One might further question the novelty or originality of the new spiritual image of Indian arts, an image that had been identified with Coomaraswamy and which became an emblem of the Indianness of Indian arts. Is it not possible that it was, in the end, essentially a revived, updated, popularized and Indianized version of an older Roman-

---

[8] Ibid.
[9] "Hindu Music and Dance" 12 (see Chap.4, footnote 89).
[10] Guha-Thakurta, *Monuments, Objects, Histories* 155ff.

tic ideal of mystic India? Certainly, Coomaraswamy formed his approach by adopting, rejecting, and altering parts of already-existent Western images of Indian arts and aesthetics. Already in *The Dance of Shiva* his reference to various Western authors, including, among others, William Blake, Nietzsche, Wagner, Goethe and Benedetto Croce, suggests his preoccupation with Romantic thought and idealism. Indeed European and American audiences would be presented with this perception of Indian arts in the specific context of religion and mythology, a perception that had its roots in Romanticism and British Orientalism and was transplanted into the 20th century. And thus provided with Coomaraswamy's Indian aesthetical insights and the authentic Indian appearance of Uday Shankar and his company, this perception surely continued its influence, at least on a more popular level, for a much longer time to come. Even in 1980 the Indian author Subramaniam points out a trend in the West and partly in India that attempts to explain Indian dance and music solely in reference to religion, a tendency that thereby prevents a serious inquiry into the arts. Stating that "Westerners have come to associate Indian art with religion more than Indians do themselves," he hints at the deep rootedness of this impression in the history of Western perceptions of India and holds Coomaraswamy accountable for its further international circulation in the 20th century:[11]

> [T]here is a persistent tendency to label Indian music and dance as religious – as improvisation or whatever and avoid all serious effort to understand the art as such. In India, too, the umbrella of Bhakti is often used in discussion to keep out the sunlight of analysis and criticism. Coomaraswamy cannot be blamed directly for all that but he must at least bear part of the blame indirectly. [...] We need not take refuge behind high spirituality to impress the West and indeed we need not seek to impress the West at all.[12]

---

[11] Subramaniam, "The Kalayogi, Art and Religion" xviii (see Chap.4, footnote 181).

[12] V. Subramaniam, "The Editors Postscript," in: *The Sacred and the Secular in India's Performing Arts*: 181-185; here 184 (see Chap.4, footnote 165).

However, there still remains one article, inevitable in the context of this work, which has yet to be discussed. In 1937, when Shankar was receiving international acclaim, Coomaraswamy published an essay entitled "Uday Shankar's Indian Dancing" in the New Yorker *Magazine of Art*. In it, he summarizes his approach to Indian art theory once again and he also points to certain topics which would come to occupy the discussion on Shankar in subsequent years up through the present.

Coomaraswamy commences with a short outline of what he presents as the major current tendencies in modern dance, namely its sole focus on movement and feeling: "It has been said that the substance of the dance should consist not of story, nor pantomime, nor music, but movement – motion only expressive not of ideas, but of emotion."[13] He criticizes this approach as being spectacular and having "nothing specifically human about it" and it becomes the model against which he develops his traditional view of art.[14] Traditional arts, Coomaraswamy remarks, are "conditioned as to their nature and end by the general good of the whole, and not merely the sensitive, man."[15] Opposing a sensual modern versus an intellectual traditional approach, he introduces Indian dance as an ancient art, a representation of the divine: "We need hardly say that Indian dancing is a traditional art, of immemorial antiquity, and referred, as are all traditional arts, to a superhuman prototype."[16] This brings him to the topic of mime. While he states that Indian dance is substantially mimetic he urges his readers to distinguish between imitation as can be found in naturalistic art and imitation as "an embodiment of the ideal form of reality."[17] In Indian dance, identified with pantomime, one can thus see reflected a divine theme, a theme onlookers have to be acquainted with in order to judge its accomplishment and beauty:

> Pantomime is thus an imitation of Pan, an imitation of Mother Nature, Creatrix, God, and of the Eternal Reasons, and not of anything visible to the naked eye. Indian dancing is primarily sacer-

---

[13] Coomaraswamy, "Uday Shankar's Indian Dancing" 611 (see Chap.2, footnote 137).
[14] Ibid.
[15] Ibid.
[16] Ibid.
[17] Ibid.

dotal art [...]: an imitation of what was done by the Gods in the beginning. To understand and be nourished by it, then, we must know, not merely what it looks like, but what it is about: we must have had some inkling of its theme before we can ask if the theme has been accurately or beautifully expressed; apart from which we can only say that we do or do not like what has been done, which is a manner of speaking that describes ourselves, and not the art before us.[18]

Coomaraswamy hence qualifies Indian dance as a spiritual, sophisticated form of art not easily accessible for outsiders. Its demanding character, quite distinct from simple entertainment, is further stressed when he announces that "this is not an art for tired business men, but for active intelligences."[19] He then once more makes use of the then-common link between Indian and ancient Greek art when he compares their aesthetic effects on the side of the spectator:

Alike from the Indian and the ancient Greek point of view the drama effects a *katharsis* or purgation: the pure and disinterested aesthetic experience of the flavor (*rasa*) of the work of art, as distinguished from pleasures directly experienced through the perception of its parts, is called the very twin of perfect experience, or "rapture" in the contemplative sense.[20]

Moving away from the discussion of Indian and ancient Greek aesthetics, Coomaraswamy then arrives at Uday Shankar. He strives to integrate the dancer and his work into the earlier-established system of modern and traditional arts, straightforwardly opening up this section with the question: "Now what has Shankar done?"[21] The classification of Shankar, however, has strong critical undercurrents:

---

[18] Ibid. 611ff.
[19] Ibid. 612.
[20] Ibid.
[21] Ibid.

Much of Shankar's training has been European, and he is much more individually the "artist" in a modern sense than is the Indian virtuoso whose art is one of fixed ends and ascertained means of operation, not to be arbitrarily modified in accordance with any personal taste.[22]

Coomaraswamy further mentions that Shankar's company does not consist entirely of Indians, but contains the French dancer Simkie, who, although a European, is "qualified by a remarkable adaptability."[23] He then apparently takes up a point of criticism that targets Shankar's authenticity, a quality upon which Shankar's success had until then often been built on: "But if Shankar's performances are not just what could still be seen in India, neither would it be fair to say that his art is not authentically Indian dancing or acting. Shankar is after all an Indian, and a man of artistic integrity."[24] Having shown certain essentialism, he lists Uday Shankar's achievements and his efforts to gain a stronger artistic basis in classical Indian dance, while at the same time presenting his readers with information on the traditional arts in India and their continuous existence:

His training in Europe represents only a part of his resources; he has studied obediently and patiently as the disciple (we use the word advisedly) of Indian professionals, and has assimilated rather than merely observed. In recent years he has studied with particular devotion the dramatic practice of Southern India, particularly in Malabar, where the art of the Kathakalis [sic], of which an account was recently published in the *Illustrated London News*, has preserved better than anywhere else both the technique and the quality of the ancient drama. He uses an Indian technique to give expression to Indian themes, derived as in India from the inexhaustible material of the Epics, which are really Myths. He has brought with him groups of hereditary musicians,

---

[22] Ibid.
[23] Ibid.
[24] Ibid.

and enabled Americans to hear the instrumental music of India for the first time.[25]

In the following, Coomaraswamy comes to the conclusion that the adjusted character of Shankar's Indian dance performance in the West, its deviation from the classical ideal, is not the fault of the latter, but has to be ascribed to the circumstances of Western commercial art stages. He also establishes a comparison between current Indian artistic conditions and those of the European Baroque and classical period:

> Bearing in mind that Indian acting, dancing and music are performed under conditions of patronage more like those under which European chamber music has developed than like those of the modern commercial stage, one may say that he has brought the Indian theatre to America as sincerely and as really as was perhaps at all possible; and that he deserves all the credit for this, and all the appreciation, that he has received. Whatever compromises have been made, or suggested by fulsome programmes overloaded with allusions to the "mysterious and sensuous East," have not been so much his fault, as necessitated by the conditions under which even the most sincere performances have to be presented in this country.[26]

According to Coomaraswamy, Shankar apparently did the best possible under the existing conditions of his time in the United States. Yet the criticism is profound; Shankar and his dance pieces are portrayed as lacking the authenticity of classical dance performances in India, particularly of the South. This portrayal, especially coming from Coomaraswamy who has been cited before as a reference for the religious and symbolical background of Shankar's dances, deprives the dancer of important attributes on which his reception in Europe and the United States was strongly built. While denouncing clichés of a mystical East associated with Shankar as Western fantasies, Coomaraswamy at the same time

---

[25] Ibid.
[26] Ibid. 612, 645.

introduces his readers to an existing tradition of authentic spiritual dance primarily in South India.

A corresponding critique of Shankar had in fact already been uttered a few years earlier as summarized in an article published by John Martin in the *New York Times*. In the article, "The Dance: Art of India. Shankar Criticized as Departing From Canons of the Indian Classical Dance," the author had given an account of an Indian correspondence between G.K. Seshagiri from the South Indian magazine *Sound and Shadow* and a following rejoinder by Shankar himself published in *The Bombay Chronicle*. The two articles had been sent by Seshagiri himself to John Martin, obviously in order to make his claim of a lack of classicism in Shankar's art known in the West.

The Indian critic especially attacked the dancing itself, particularly Shankar's use of movements and gestures that Western audiences had already perceived with exaltation and marveled at for their traditional symbolism. Martin echoed:

> He [Mr. Seshagiri] is distressed because audiences in India as well as in the West have flocked to Shan-Kar's performances and acclaimed them with enthusiasm, when he feels that they are "a typical example of the present-day decadence in one of our arts due mainly to the deterioration on our taste." "Uday Shan-Kar's dance," he writes, "considered as some kind of dance, was tolerable. But considered as Indian dance, either as Bharata Natya, or Nritya, or Nritta, is [sic] was absolutely unconvincing except for the costumes, the décor and the music.["][27]

Shankar defended himself by claiming a right to progress and stating that his aim "was to adopt the best from the past and mold it to the requirements of our present-day life," a position Martin in fact sided with, but this early criticism would show the direction which the reception of Uday

---

[27] John Martin, "The Dance: Art of India. Shan-Kar Criticized as Departing From Canons of the Indian Classical Dance," *New York Times* (New York), April 2, 1934; reprinted in: Khokar, *His Dance, His Life* 78 (see Introduction, footnote 8).

Shankar, especially in independent India, would tend towards.[28] About the time when Shankar celebrated his successes with audiences in Europe, the United States, and India, a renaissance of Indian dance primarily known as the Indian dance revival came into being.[29] This led to a renewed appreciation of traditional or classical dance forms in India, especially among the high castes. According to his biographer Khokar, Shankar was a major initiator of the revival of dance in India due to his pioneering role as Indian dancer in the West.[30] In India there were, however, certain dancers and advocates of dance often coming from the more traditional South who took the renaissance of Indian dance into their hands. Among these were E. Krishna Iyer, who was originally trained as a lawyer and one of the first secretaries of the Music Academy of Madras founded in 1928;[31] the Malayalam poet Vallathol, an admirer of the Kathakali dance style since his childhood and who also was able to establish the Kerala Kala Mandalam (The Kerala Institute of Arts) near Shoranur in 1930;[32] Rukmini Devi, founder of the International Institute of the Arts (1936), renamed as *Kalakshetra* (Place of Arts) in 1938, who overtook a leading role in the renaming of *sādir* or *nautch* as *Bharata Nātyam*;[33] and the Bengali poet and Nobel Prize winner Rabindranath Tagore who from the early 1920s on incorporated dance classes in his Visva-Bharati University ("world university" or "place of universal knowledge").[34] Whereas Tagore with his humanist approach welcomed the study of European and other Asian styles at his school, the majority of the main agents of the dance renaissance focused on reviving the classical Indian dance traditions, partly relying on hereditary practitioners,

---

[28] Ibid.

[29] See Allen 63ff (see Chap.2, footnote 127).

[30] Khokar writes: "Indeed it is he [Shankar] who initiated the revival of Indian dance and brought respect to the art at a time when polite society whole-heartedly shunned it." Khokar, *His Dance, His Life* 75.

[31] See *E. Krishna Iyer: Centenary Issue*, Music Academy: Madras, August 9, 1997: 2ff.

[32] See Reginald Massey, *India's Dances. Their History, Technique and Repertoire*, New Delhi: Abhinav Publications 2004: 116.

[33] See Allen 63, 73.

[34] See Martin Kämpchen, *Rabindranath Tagore*, Reinbek bei Hamburg: Rowohlt 1997 (1992): 52, 84 and Mandakranta Bose, *Speaking of Dance. The Indian Critique*, New Delhi: D.K. Printworld 2001: 109ff.

such as the South Indian *devadāsīs* or temple dancers, partly building on the Sanskrit tradition of writing, most importantly Bharata's *Nātyaśāstra* and Nandikesvara's *Abhinaya Darpana*.[35] In the course of the advancing reacceptance of dance in India, which in many ways coincided with the growing nationalist movement, Shankar's style of dancing gained currency under designations such as "Indian 'modern dance'" or "modern Indian ballet."[36]

While his younger brother Ravi Shankar probably remains the most famous Indian musician in the world, Uday seems almost forgotten worldwide, in spite of his enormous successes in Western countries in the 1930s. Although he is sometimes referred to in India as the "Twentieth Century's Nataraja"[37] for his outstanding performances as Shiva onstage, it is with regard to this development that Joan L. Erdman questioned whether his memory had endured at all. Indeed, in 1997 she posed the apt and simple question: "Who Remembers Uday Shankar?"[38] The icon of Shiva as the dancing deity *Natarāja* and the associated image of Indian spiritual arts, however, still capture international audiences and will continue to exert their influence well into the foreseeable future.

---

[35] Shankar himself apparently also made an effort to revive Indian classical dance and music by integrating corresponding classes into the curriculum of his India Art Centre in Almora which opened in 1939. In a booklet from 1937, which gives an outline of the center, the aim to rekindle the traditional arts is formulated: "To-day the great semi-religious occasions for dance and music have been replaced by the cinema and revues, and Western instruments are being introduced which are totally unsuited to the subtleties of Indian music. In the vastness of India are still to be found excellent musicians and dancers, and a large amount of uncorrelated material which would be sufficient to form a firm foundation for an Indian renaissance. But how long will these traditions linger unless a determined und systematic effort is made to save them." "India and the Dance. The Need for Action" n.p. (see Chap. 4, footnote 142).

[36] Khokar, *His Dance, His Life* 151; Projesh Banerjee denominates Shankar as the "father of modern Indian ballet." Projesh Banerjee, *Indian Ballet Dancing*, New Delhi: Abhinav Publications 1983: 120.

[37] See Ashoke Kumar Mukhopadhyay, *Uday Shankar. Twentieth Century's Nataraja*, Kolkata: Rupa & Co. 2004.

[38] Erdman, "Who Remembers Uday Shankar?" n.p. (see Introduction, footnote 1).

Bibliography

Primary Sources

A., S., "The Dance – International Dance Festival Opens at New Yorker Theater – Shan-Kar makes American Debut," *New York City Post* (New York), December 27, 1932: n.p.; printed in: "Press Comments" 40-41.

Abraham, Otto & Erich Moritz von Hornbostel, "Indian melodies recorded on the phonograph," transl. by Bonnie Wade, in: Wachsmann 115-182.

Acocella, Joan and Lynn Garafola (eds.), *André Levinson on Dance. Writings from Paris in the Twenties*, Hanover & London: Wesleyan University Press 1991.

Adams, Paul, Dr., "Indisches Theater. Theater des Westens," *Germania. Zeitung für das deutsche Volk* (Berlin), April 21, 1932: n.p.

"Adolf Bolm Gives His Exotic Dances. [...] Roshanara and Ratan Devi in East India Nautch [...]," *The New York Times* (New York), August 21, 1917: n.p.

"Aid France's Fine Arts. Roshanara and Ratan Devi in Dances and Songs of India," *The New York Times* (New York), March 17, 1917: n.p.

a.l., "Indischer Tanzabend," *Hamburger Fremdenblatt* (Hamburg), September 30, 1931, evening edition: 3.

"A l'Exposition Coloniale," *L'Oeuvre* (Paris), November 7, 1931: 6.

"Arts Theatre Club," *The Times* (London), October 8, 1930: n.p.

"Arts Theatre Club," *The Times* (London), November 13, 1934: n.p.

Arvey, Verna, "Religious Dance – And How It is Used to Express Sacred Themes," *The American Dancer* (Los Angeles), June 1936: 13, 40.

Aubel, Hermann & Marianne, *Die Bedeutung der alten indischen Tanzkultur. Betrachtungen und Bilder zum Auftreten der Hindu-Tanzgruppe Uday Shan-Kar*, [Celle:] Verlag der Arbeitsgemeinschaft für Natur- und Völkerkunde 1932.

Bassoe, Henriette, "Flights Beyond the Horizon with La Meri," *The American Dancer* (Los Angeles), April 1941: 11; 32.

Bentley, Eric, "Martha Graham's Journey" (1952), in: Copeland & Cohen 197-202.

Boas, Franz, *The Mind of Primitive Man*, New York: The Macmillan Company 1911.

Bode, Rudolf, *Rhythmus und Körpererziehung. Fünf Abhandlungen*, Jena: Eugen Diederichs 1925 (1923).

Böhme, Fritz, "Indische Tänze. Theater des Westens," *Deutsche Allgemeine Zeitung* (Berlin), April 20, 1932, evening edition: n.p.

_____, *Der Tanz der Zukunft*, München: Delphin-Verlag 1926.

Boehn, Max von, *Der Tanz*, Berlin: Wegweiser-Verlag 1925.

Boner, Alice, "Der Indische Tanz," in: "Gastspiel der Brahmanischen Inder (Hindus) mit Uday Shan-Kar" n.p. Also published in: *Der Kreis. Zeitschrift für Künstlerische Kultur* (Hamburg), vol. 8, 1931: 524-526.

_____, *Indien, mein Indien. Tagebuch einer Reise*, ed. by G. Boner & H. David, Zürich: Werner Classen Verlag 1984.

Brunck, "Gastspiel indischer Tänzer und Musiker im Opernhaus," *Fränkische Tagespost* (Nürnberg-Fürth), November 7, 1932: n.p.

Brunel, Raoul, "Danses et musique hindoues d'Uday Shan-Kar," *L'Oeuvre* (Paris), May 16, 1932: 5.

c.a.l., "Indischer Tanzabend," *Hamburger Fremdenblatt* (Hamburg), September 30, 1931, evening edition: 3.

Casadesus, Jules, "Les Concerts," *L'Oeuvre* (Paris), March 6, 1931: 5.

Cassirer, Ernst, *Philosophie der Symbolischen Formen. Zweiter Teil: Das Mythische Denken*, Oxford: Bruno Cassirer 1954 (1923).

"Concert to Aid Indian Poor of East London," *The Times* (London), October 25, 1938.

Coomaraswamy, Ananda Kentish, "The Cave Paintings of Ajanta," *Vanity Fair* (New York), Septermber 1916: 67.

_____, *The Dance of Shiva. Fourteen Indian Essays*, Munshiram Manoharlal Publishers: New Delhi 1982.

_____, "The Influence of Greek on Indian Art," in: *Mediaeval Sinhalese Art*, New York: Pantheon Books 1956; originally published: Norman Chapel: Essex House Press 1908: 256-261.

_____, *The Mirror of Gesture. Being the Abhinaya Darpana of Nandikeśvara*, New Delhi: Munshiram Manoharlal 2003^6.

_____, "Oriental Dances in America. And a Word or Two in Explanation of the Nautch," *Vanity Fair* (New York), May 1917: 61.

_____, *The Transformation of Nature in Art*, New York: Dover Publications 1956 (1934).

_____, "Uday Shankar's Indian Dancing," *Magazine of Art* (New York), vol. 30 no. 10, 1937: 611-612, 645.

Crawfurd, John, "Music and Dancing," in: *History of the Indian Archipelago*, vol. 1 (1820); excerpt in: Tagore, *Hindu Music from Various Authors* 297-312.

D., "Die Hindu-Tanzgruppe im Landestheater. Uday Shan-Kar und Simkie mit einem Hindu-Orchester," *Stuttgarter Neues Tageblatt* (Stuttgart), morning edition, November 21, 1931: 2.

"La danse," *Figaro Artistique Illustré* (Paris), November 1931: n.p.

Das, Nirmal A., "The Hindu Dance," *Theatre Arts Monthly* (New York), December 1938: 904.

Daumal, René, "Dance Chronicle: Uday Shan-Kar and the Hindu Dance," translated by Vera Milanova, *Hound & Horn* (Cambridge), vol .4 no. 2, January-March 1933: 288-292.

Devi, Ragini, "Living Traditions of the Hindu Dance," *The American Dancer* (Los Angeles), June 1941: 14, 32.

Duncan, Isadora, "The Dance," *Theatre Arts Magazine. An Illustrated Quarterly* (New York), vol. 2, 1917-1918: 21-22.

_____, "The Dance of the Future" (1902/03), in: Copeland & Cohen 262-264.

_____, "Richard Wagner" (1921), in: Copeland & Cohen 266.

Ellis, Havelock, *The Dance of Life*, New York: The Modern Library 1923/1929.

Emroch, Edna, "Dance of the Orient. A general survey of the philosophy and the art of the dance in the East," *The American Dancer* (Los Angeles), January 1937: 24, 26.

_____, "The Noh Dance of Japan," *The American Dancer* (Los Angeles), March 1937: 16, 40.

"L'exposition. Les danses de Bali à Vincennes," *Je suis partout* (Paris), no. 30, June 20, 1931: 10.

"Fine Art in India," *The Times* (London), February 28, 1910: 6.

Fokine, Michel, "Letter to 'The Times,' July 6th, 1914," in: Copeland & Cohen 257-261.

Fox Strangways, Arthur Henry, *The Music of Hindostan*, Munshiram Manoharlal Publishers: New Delhi 1975 (originally published by Clarendon Press: Oxford 1914).

French, P.T., "Catalogue of Indian Musical Instruments," in: Tagore, *Hindu Music from Various Authors* 243-273.

Fuller, Loïe, "Light and the Dance," in: Brown et al. 13-19.

G., A., "Tanzberichte Berlin," *Der Tanz* (Berlin), vol. 8 no. 3, March 1935: 4.

Gangoly, O.C., "Classical Indian Dancing. Ragini Devi's Interpretation," Reprint from *Amrita Bazar Patrika* (Kolkata), September 23, 1934: n.p.

"Gastspiel der Brahmanischen Inder (Hindus) mit Uday Shank-Kar," program, Theater des Westens, Berlin, April 1932: n.p.

Ghosh, Manomohan, *The Natyaśāstra. A Treatise on Hindu Dramaturgy and Histrionics. Ascribed to Bharata-Muni*, Calcutta: The Royal Asiatic Society of Bengal 1950.

"Give Japanese 'Noh' Dance. Michio Itow in Novelty 'Tamura' at Neighbourhood Playhouse," *The New York Times* (New York), January 9, 1921: 2.

Glasenapp, Helmuth von, *Die Literaturen Indiens von ihren Anfängen bis zur Gegenwart*, Wildpark-Potsdam: Akademische Verlagsgesellschaft Athenaion 1929.

Hegel, Georg Wilhelm Friedrich, *The Philosophy of History*, New York: Cosimo 2007.

Henderson, W.J., "Hindu Dances Performed Here. Shan-Kar and Assisting Group Appear in Exhibition at New Yorker Theater," *The New York Sun* (New York), December 27, 1932; printed in: "Press Comments" 41-42.

Hi., "Hindu-Tänze," *Berliner Tageblatt und Handels-Zeitung* (Berlin), April 20, 1932, evening edition: n.p.

"Hindu Music and Dance. Programme at Arts Theatre," *The Times* (London), April 5, 1933: 12.

"Hindu-Tänze," *Berliner Tageblatt und Handels-Zeitung* (Berlin), April 20, 1932, evening edition: n.p.

Holmes, Olive (ed.), *Motion Arrested. Dance Reviews of H.T. Parker*, Middletown: Wesleyan University Press 1982.

Hornbostel, Erich Moritz von, "The Problems of Comparative Musicology," transl. by Richard Campbell, in: Wachsmann 247-270.

_____, "Vorwort des Übersetzers," in: Stumpf & Hornbostel, *Sammelbände für vergleichende Musikwissenschaft*, vol. 1: 3.

_____ & Curt Sachs, "Systematik der Musikinstrumente," *Zeitschrift für Ethnologie* (Berlin), vol. 46 no. 4-5, 1914: 553-590.

Houville, Gérard d', "Chronique des Théatres de Paris. Théatre des Arts: Salomé, drame en un acte d'Oscar Wilde. Représentations de la Compagnie Pitoëff. – Danses hindoues," *Le Figaro* (Paris), June 8, 1931: n.p.

Huntington, Harriet, "The Balinese Live For Art. Dancers On a Magic Island," *The American Dancer* (Los Angeles), June 1937: 22-23, 62.

hw., "Tanzabend Dini von Essen," *Schwäbischer Merkur* (Stuttgart), November 21, 1931: 5.

"India and the Dance. The Need for Action," in: *Uday Shankar's Project for an Art Centre in India*, 1937: n.p.

"Indian Dances at the Ballet Club. Miss Ishvani Goolbano," *The Times* (London), December 27, 1933: 6.

"Indian Dances at the Tivoli," *The Times* (London), September 30, 1913: n.p.

"Informations Internationales. Allemagne," *Archives Internationales de la Danse* (Paris), initial issue, unnumbered, 1932: 20ff.

"Informations Internationales. France," *Archives Internationales de la Danse* (Paris), no. 1, January 15, 1933: 37.

Jones, William, "On the Musical Modes of the Hindoos," (1784) in: Tagore, *Hindu Music from Various Authors* 123-160.

K., F., "Kultur der Gegenwart: Bühne und Musik: Der Gott und die Bajadere. (Tanzabend der Brahmanen-Gruppe Udaj-Schan-Kars im Weinberger Stadttheater)," *Prager Presse* (Prague), March 24, 1932: 8.

"Kenji Hinoki," *The American Dancer* (Los Angeles), January 1937: 20, 26.

Krüll, Joseph, "Tanzberichte Wien," *Der Tanz* (Berlin), vol. 8 no. 1, January 1935: 13.

L-r., "Indische Tänzer," *Prager Tagblatt* (Prague), March 23, 1932: 7.

Laban, Rudolf, *The Mastery of Movement on the Stage*, London: Macdonald & Evans 1950.

_____, *Die Welt des Tänzers. Fünf Gedankenreigen*, Stuttgart: Verlag von Walter Seifert 1920.

Lambert, Constant, "Music and Action" (1936), in: Copeland & Cohen 203-210.

Learned, Annabel, "Hindu Music," in: "S.Hurok Presents Uday Shan-Kar and His Hindu Ballet," [season 1937/38b]: n.p.

_____, "The Hindu Dance," in: "S.Hurok presents Uday Shan-Kar and His Hindu Ballet," [season 1937/38b]: n.p.

Lepage, Édouard, "Les Danses Brahmaniques au Musée Guimet," undated, unknown source: n.p.

Levinson, André, "Javanese Dancing. The Spirit and The Form," *Theatre Arts Monthly* (London), vol. 14, December 1930: 1056-1065.

_____, "La Danse: Mirages d'Orient," *Candide* (Paris), November 13, 1930: 15.

_____, "Les Danseurs de Bali," *Candide* (Paris), no.385, July 30, 1931: 10.

_____, "The Spirit of the Spanish Dance," *Theatre Arts Monthly* (New York), vol. 9 no. 5, May 1925: 307-320.

Lewitan, J., "Der erste internationale Solotanz-Wettbewerb. Warschau (9.-16. Juni 1933)," *Der Tanz* (Berlin), vol. 6 no. 7, July 1933: 8.

_____, "Tanzaufführungen: Uday Shan-Kar, Simkie und Hindu-Tanzgruppe, Theater des Westens, 19.-25. April 1932," *Der Tanz* (Berlin), vol. 5, June 1932: 13.

_____, "Tanzberichte. Berlin," *Der Tanz* (Berlin), vol. 6 no. 3, March 1933: 5.

_____, "The Month in Berlin," *The Dancing Times* (London), vol. 23, 1932: 257-259.

M., A., "Indische Tänzer. Theater des Westens," *Vossische Zeitung. Berlinische Zeitung von Staats- und gelehrten Sachen* (Berlin), morning edition, April 20, 1932: n.p.

M., v., "Indische Tänze. Uday Shan-Karr [sic], Simkie und ihr indisches Orchester," *Hamburgischer Correspondent* (Hamburg), morning edition, October 10, 1931: 6.

Malmerse, Henry, "Au Théatre des Arts: danses hindoues de M. Unday

[sic] Shankar et de Mlle Simkie," *Le Temps* (Paris), June 10, 1931: 3.

Martin, John, "The Dance: Art of India. Its Culture Is Interpreted by Shan-Kar and His Group of Hindu Performers," *The New York Times* (New York), September 4, 1932: n.p.

_____, "The Dance: Ballet Union; Massine and de Basil Companies Merged—Programs of the Week," *New York Times* (New York), April 24, 1938: 8.

_____, "The Dance: Hindu Art for the Western World. Uday Shan-kar Interprets a Culture Far Different From Ours – Other Programs," *The New York Times* (New York), January 1, 1933: X2.

_____, "The Dance. Its March from Decadence To a Modern 'Golden Age'," *The New York Times Magazine* (New York), December 12, 1937: 10-11, 30.

Mehta, Nanalal Chamanlal, "The Dance of Uday-Shankar," *Roopa Lekha* (New Delhi), vol. 4 no. 13, 1934: 10-14.

Meri, La, *The Gesture Language of the Hindu Dance*, New York: Benjamin Blom 1941.

Milanova, Vera, "The Secret of Hindu Music," reprint from *The New York Times*, in: "S.Hurok Presents Uday Shan-Kar and his Hindu Ballet," [season 1937/38a]: n.p.

Mk., R., "Indischer Tanz. Hamburger Bühne (Besprechung beim ersten Auftreten der Inder in Deutschland)," *Hamburger Nachrichten* (Hamburg), September 29, 1931: n.p.

Modell, Samuel S., "Hindu Dancers win applause in Debut," *New York City American* (New York), undated; printed in: "Press Comments" 39-40.

Müller, Ernst, "Von Tanz und Eurhythmie," *Musikblätter des Anbruch* (Vienna), no. 7, April 1921: 125-127.

_____, "Von Tanz und Eurhythmie. Schluß," *Musikblätter des Anbruch* (Vienna), no. 9-10, May 1921: 161-163.

Müller-Rau, Elli, "Tanzberichte. Misao und Takaya Egutschi. Bach-Saal, 26. Oktober 1933," *Der Tanz* (Berlin), vol. 6 no. 12, December 1933: 10.

"Music: Radio Favorites … Dancer from Hindustan," *Time* (New York), January 9, 1933 (http://www.time.com/time/magazine/article/0,9171,753594,00.html).

Mussy, Georges, "Concerts et récitals. La danse: Uday Shan-Kar et sa compagnie," *Le Figaro* (Paris), March 13, 1931: n.p.

Narghis, Shirada, "India's Dance in America," *Dance Magazine* (New York), no. 19, August 1945: 10ff.

Neuberger, Heinz, "Der Tänzer. Zum Tänzer geboren," *Singchor und Tanz. Fachblatt für Theatersingchor und Kunsttanz* (Berlin), vol. 49 no. 23, 1932: 193.

Nietzsche, Friedrich, "The Birth of Tragedy," in: F. Nietzsche, *The Birth of Tragedy and Other Writings*, edited by R. Geuss & R. Speirs, transl. by R. Speirs, Cambridge: Cambridge University Press 1999.

_____, "The Birth of Tragedy," in: W. Kaufmann, *Basic Writings of Nietzsche*, New York: The Modern Library 2000: 1-144.

_____, *Human, All Too Human. A Book For Free Spirits*, transl. by Marion Faber, with Stephen Lehmann, Lincoln: University of Nebraska Press 1996.

"Nyota-Inyoka et l'enchantement de son ballet Indou," *Archives Internationales de la Danse* (Paris), no. 1, January 15, 1934: 43.

"Old Ladies from Bali," *Time* (New York), November 6, 1939 (http://www.time.com/time/magazine/article/0,9171,762762,00.html)

P., R., *Münchner Neueste Nachrichten* (Munich), July 18, 1932: n.p.

Parker, H.T., "Dancing Arts From India As Far As Boston," *Boston Evening Transcript* (Boston), January 20, 1933; printed in: Holmes 263-266.

_____, "Shankar at Peak of Old-New Powers," *Boston Evening Transcript* (Boston), October 28, 1933; in: Holmes 266-268.

"People [...]," *The Illustrated Weekly of India* (Bombay), September 17, 1933: 38ff; here 38.

"Petites nouvelles," *L'Oeuvre* (Paris), November 7, 1931: 6.

Pierre, Dorathi Bock, "Dance Events Reviewed. Bali and Java Dancers with Devi Dja," *The American Dancer* (Los Angeles), March 1940: 37.

_____, "Dance Events Reviewed. California. Ram Gopal," *The American Dancer* (Los Angeles), May 1938: 46.

_____, "Dance Events Reviewed. Critiques and News from the East, Mid-West and West: California: The Dance Theatre, May 17, Gould Studios, L.A.," *The American Dancer* (Los Angeles), July 1936: 31.

_____, "Ram Gopal. Young Hindu Dancer," *The American Dancer* (Los Angeles), July 1938: 25-26.

Polak, Herbert A., "Tanzbriefe: Den Haag," *Der Tanz* (Berlin), vol. 5 no. 7, July 1932: 12.

"Pola Negri praises Uday Shan-Kar," *The International Literary Exchange* (New York), undated; printed in: "Press Comments" 43-44.

"Press Comments," *Roopa-Lekha* (New Delhi), vol.4 no.13, 1934: 26-44.

Purdom, C.B., "Mystic East and Psychic West," *Everyman* (London), April 15, 1933: 457.

"Ragini Devi Sings and Dances," *The New York Times* (New York), April 29, 1922: n.p.

"Ratan Devi's Indian Songs," *The Times* (London), November 27, 1915: 11.

"Roshanara Dances at Palace," *The New York Times* (New York), January 6, 1914: n.p.

Roy, Basanta Koomar, "Bronze God," in: "S.Hurok Presents Uday Shan-Kar and his Hindu Ballet," [season 1937/38a]: n.p.

"S.Hurok Presents Uday Shan-Kar and his Hindu Ballet," in: *Playbill* (New York), [season 1937/38a]: n.p.

"S.Hurok Presents Uday Shan-Kar and His Hindu Ballet," in: *Playbill* (New York), [season 1937/38b]: n.p.

"S.Hurok presents Uday Shan-Kar with Simkie, Kanak-Lata, Debendra, Robindra," in: *S.Hurok Announces: International Dance Festival*, program, New York Theatre, December 25, 1932 to January 8, 1933: 4-5.

Sachs, Curt, *Eine Weltgeschichte des Tanzes*, Dietrich Reimer & Ernst Vohsen: Berlin 1933 / *World History of the Dance*, translated by Bessie Schönberg, New York: W.W. Norton & Company 1937.

Schelling, Friedrich W.J., *The Philosophy of Art*, ed. and trans. with an introduction by Douglas W. Stott, Minneapolis: University of Minnesota Press 1989.

Scheuer, Franc, "Uday Shan-Kar and Simkie. At the Théâtre des Champs-Elysées," *Dancing Times* (London), April 1931: 15.

Schikowski, John, *Geschichte des Tanzes*, Berlin: Büchergilde Gutenberg 1926.

Schillo, Marion, "Dance Events Reviewed. Critiques and News from the East, Mid-West and West. Chicago," *The American Dancer* (Los Angeles), May 1937: 27.

Sdt., "Indische Musik, indischer Tanz. Uday Shan-Kar und Simkie mit Indischem Orchester. – Abend der Hamburger Bühne," *Hamburger Anzeiger* (Hamburg), September 30, 1931: n.p.

Sée, Edmond, "Première au Theatre des Arts. Salomé d'Oscar Wilde. Danses Hindoues," *L'Œuvre* (Paris), June 6, 1931: 6.

Sen, Gertrude Emerson, "A Beacon on the Himalayas," *ASIA* (New York), December 1941: 690-694.

Shankar, Rajendra, "Uday Shankar – Personal Reminiscences," in: *Nartanam* (Mumbai), no. 4, October – December 2001: 12-28.

Shankar, Ravi, *My Music, My Life*, Vikas Publishing House: New Delhi 1968.

_____, *Raga Mala. The Autobiography of Ravi Shankar*, Edited and introduced by George Harrison, New York: Welcome Rain Publishers, 2nd edition, 1999.

Shankar, Uday, "Reawakening of India's Classical Dance," *The Illustrated Weekly of India* (Bombay), June 30, 1935: 19, 59.

Shawn, Ted, "Constants – What Constitutes a Work of Art in the Dance," in: Brown 27-32.

_____, "Gods Who Dance. 'Now There Danceth a God in Me ......' Nietzsche," undated, unknown source: n.p.

_____, "Hindu Temple Dances. Of the Rites and Customs of the Nautch Dancers of Southern India," undated, unknown source: n.p.

_____ (with Gray Poole), *One Thousand and One Night Stands*, New York: Da Capo 1979 (1960).

"Spectacles," *L'Oeuvre* (Paris), March 3, 1931: 6.

"Spectacles," *L'Oeuvre* (Paris), June 4, 1931: 6.

Stafford, William C., "Oriental Music. The Music of Hindustan or India" in: Tagore, *Hindu Music from Various Authors* 219-228.

St. Denis, Ruth, "The Dance as an Art Form," *Theatre Arts Magazine* (Detroit), vol. 1 no. 1, November 1916: 75-77.

_____, "The Dance as Life Experience" (1924/25), in: Brown 22-25.

_____, "Religious Manifestations in the Dance," in: W. Sorell (ed.), *The Dance Has Many Faces*, Pennington: A cappella books 1992[3]: 3-9.

_____, *An Unifinished Life: An Autobiography*, New York: Harper & Brothers 1939.

Stumf, Carl, "Lieder der Bellakula-Indianer," *Vierteljahrsschrift für Musikwissenschaft* (Leipzig), vol. 2, 1886: 405-426.

_____ & Erich Moritz von Hornbostel (eds.), *Sammelbände für vergleichende Musikwissenschaft*, vol. 1, Georg Olms Verlag: Hildesheim & New York 1975 (Reprint from the original, 1922-23).

_____, "Tonsystem und Musik der Siamesen," *Beiträge zur Akustik und Musikwissenschaft* (Leipzig), vol. 3, 1901: 69-138.

Szamba, Eduard, "Tanzbriefe: Paris," *Der Tanz* (Berlin), vol. 4 no. 4, April 1931: 14.

_____, "Tanzbriefe. Paris," *Der Tanz* (Berlin), vol. 6 no. 1, January 1933: 11-12.

_____, "Tanzbriefe. Paris," *Der Tanz* (Berlin), vol. 6 no. 2, Februar 1933: 8-10.

_____, "Tanzberichte. Paris, " *Der Tanz* (Berlin), vol. 6 no 4, April 1933: 15.

_____, "Paris," *Der Tanz* (Berlin), vol. 7 no. 1, January 1934: 8.

Tagore, Sourindro Mohun (compiler/ed.), *Hindu Music from Various Authors* (1875/1882), Chowkhamba Sanskrit Series Office: Varanasi 1965.

_____, "Hindu Music," in: Tagore, *Hindu Music from Various Authors* 339-387.

Thompson, Oscar, "Music – Shan-Kar's Hindu Dancers in First events of International Festival," *Brooklyn New York Eagle* (New York), December 27, 1932; printed in: "Press Comments" 37-39.

Tidemann, Wilhelm, "Zu den Hindu-Tänzen," *Der Kreis. Zeitschrift für künstlerische Kultur* (Hamburg), vol. 9 no. 10, October 1932: 595-598.

"Uday Shankar and His Hindu Ballet and Musicians," program, Barn Theatre, Dartington Hall, Totnes, Devon, November 15, 1937: n.p.

Vuillermoz, Emile, "Les événements musicaux," *Candide* (Paris), March 12, 1931: n.p.

W., H., "Württembergisches Landestheater. Gastspiel der indischen Hindu-Tanzgruppe. Stuttgart. 21. Nov.," *Schwäbischer Merkur* (Stuttgart), November 22, 1931: 6.

Wachsmann, Klaus P. et al. (eds.), *Hornbostel Opera Omnia*, vol. 1, Martinus Nijhoff: The Hague 1975.

Wagner, Richard, "Art and Revolution," in: *The Art-Work of the Future and Other Works*, transl. by William Ashton Ellis, Lincoln & London: University of Nebraska Press 1993: 23-65; reprint from *Richard Wagner's Prose Works*, vol.1, London: Kegan Paul, Trench, Trübner & Co. 1895.

_____, "The Art-Work of the Future," in: *The Art-Work of the Future and Other Works*, transl. by William Ashton Ellis, Lincoln & London: University of Nebraska Press 1993: 69-213; reprint from *Richard Wagner's Prose Works*, vol.1, London: Kegan Paul, Trench, Trübner & Co. 1895.

_____, "The Music of the Future," in: Edward L. Burlingame (ed. and trans.), *Art Life and Theories of Richard Wagner*, New York: Henry Holt & Company 1904: 132-189.

_____, "Religion and Art," transl. by William Ashton Ellis, Lincoln: University of Nebraska Press 1994: 213-252; originally published: London: K. Paul, Trench, Trübner 1897.

Waker, M., "Internationaler Tanz-Wettbewerb und Volkstanz-Treffen Wien 1934. 27. Mai bis 16. Juni 1934," *Der Tanz* (Berlin), vol. 7 no.7, July 1934: 6.

Watkins, Mary F., "Five Facets of the Dance," *Theatre Arts Monthly* (London), February 1934: 135-143.

_____, "Uday Shan-Kar and troupe offer Program of ancient rituals at New Yorker," *New York City Herald* (New York), December 27, 1932: n.p.; printed in: "Press Comments" 35-36.

Wiesenthal, Grete, "Tänze der Nationen. Freier und gebundener Tanz. Der Wiener Walzer," in: *Der Tanz* (Berlin), vol.8 no.5, May 1935: 19-21.

Wigman, Mary, "Tänzerische Wege und Ziele," *Die Neue Rundschau*, vol. 2, Berlin & Leipzig: S. Fischer Verlag 1923: 1021-1024.

Willard, N. Augustus, "A Treatise on the Music of Hindoostan, Comprising a Detail of the Ancient Theory and Modern Practice," in: Tagore, *Hindu Music from Various Authors* 1-122.

"The World and the Theatre," *Theatre Arts Monthly* (London), January 1933: 94-95.

"Württ. Landestheater. Großes Haus," program announcement, *Stuttgarter Neues Tageblatt* (Stuttgart), morning edition, November 20, 1931: 4.

"Zum Gastspiel des Indischen Balletts," *Hamburger Fremdenblatt* (Hamburg), September 26, 1931, evening edition: 3.

Secondary Sources

Allen, Matthew Harp, "Rewriting the Script for South Indian Dance," *The Drama Review* (Cambridge, Mass.), vol. 41 no. 3, Fall 1997: 63-100.

Anderson, Jack, *Art Without Boundaries. The World of Modern Dance*, Iowa City: University of Iowa Press 1997.

Antliff, Mark & Patricia Leighten, "Primitive," in: R.S. Nelson & R. Shiff, *Critical Terms For Art History*, Chicago & London: The University of Chicago Press, 2003[2]: 217-233.

Ball, Terrence, "James Mill," *Stanford Encyclopedia of Philosophy*, first published November 30, 2005 (http://plato.stanford.edu/entries/james-mill/).

Banerjee, Projesh, *Indian Ballet Dancing*, New Delhi: Abhinav Publications 1983.

Barck, Karlheinz et al. (eds.), *Ästhetische Grundbegriffe*, vol. 1-7, Stuttgart / Weimar: Metzler 2000-2005.

Baxmann, Inge (ed.), *Körperwissen als Kulturgeschichte. Die Archives Internationales de la Danse (1931-1952)*, München: Kieser 2008.

Berman, Nina, *Orientalismus, Kolonialismus und Moderne. Zum Bild des Orients in der deutschsprachigen Kultur um 1900*, Stuttgart: M&P 1997.

Blum, Stephen, "European Musical Terminology and the Music of Africa," in: Nettl & Bohlman 3-36.

Böger, Astrid, "The Princess Rajah Dance and the Popular Fascination with Middle Eastern Culture at the St. Louis World's Fair," in: Heike Schaeffer (ed.), *America and the Orient*, Heidelberg: Universitätsverlag Winter 2006: 203-216.

Boer, Inge, "Orientalism," in: Kelly, vol. 3: 406-408.

Boisits, Barbara, "Hugo Riemann – Guido Adler. Zwei Konzepte von

Musikwissenschaft vor dem Hintergrund geisteswissenschaftlicher Methodendiskussionen um 1900," in: T. Böhme-Mehner & K. Mehner (eds.), *Hugo Riemann (1849-1919). Musikwissenschaftler mit Universalanspruch*, Köln: Böhlau 2001: 17ff.

Bollenbeck, Georg, *Eine Geschichte der Kulturkritik. Von Rousseau bis Günther Anders*, München: Beck 2007.

Bose, Mandakranta, *Speaking of Dance. The Indian Critique*, New Delhi: D.K. Printworld 2001.

Brandstetter, Gabriele, "Ausdruckstanz," in: Kerbs & Reulecker 451-463.

_____, *Tanz-Lektüren. Körperbilder und Raumfiguren der Avantgarde*, Frankfurt am Main: Fischer Taschenbuch Verlag 1995.

_____ & Brygida Maria Ochaim, *Loïe Fuller. Tanz – Lichtspiel – Art Nouveau*, Freiburg: Verlag Rombach 1989.

Brenscheidt gen. Jost, Diana, "Den neuen Menschen tanzen. Tanz und Kulturkritik zu Beginn des 20. Jahrhunderts," in: G. Rebane et al. (eds.), *Humanismus polyphon. Menschlichkeit im Zeitalter der Globalisierung*, Bielefeld: transcript 2009: 55-70.

Brinkmann, Charlotte, "Claire Holt und die Anfänge einer modernen Tanzethnologie im Umfeld der A.I.D.-Expeditionen nach Niederländisch-Indien," in: Baxmann 116-136.

Brown, Jean Morrison et al. (eds.), *The Vision of Modern Dance. In the Words of Its Creators*, London: Dance Books 1998[2].

Burns, Judy Farrar, "La Meri," in: Cohen, *International Encyclopedia of Dance*, vol.4: 354-355.

Capwell, Charles, "Marginality and Musicology in Nineteenth-Century Calcutta: The Case of Sourindro Mohun Tagore," in: Nettl & Bohlman 228-243.

Çelik, Zeynep & Leila Kinney, "Ethnography and Exhibitionism at the Expositions Universelles," *Assemblage. A Critical Journal of Architecture and Design Culture* (Cambridge, Mass.), vol. 13, 1990: 35-59.

Christensen, Dieter, "Erich M. von Hornbostel, Carl Stumpf, and the Institutionalization of Comparative Musicology," in: Nettl & Bohlman 201-209.

Clarke, John James, *Oriental Enlightenment. The Encounter between Asian and Western Thought*, London: Routledge 1997.

Cohen, Marshall "Primitivism, Modernism, and Dance Theory," in: Copeland & Cohen 161-187.

Cohen, Selma Jeanne (ed.), *International Encyclopedia of Dance*, vol. 1-6, New York & Oxford: Oxford University Press 1998.

Connelly, Frances S., "Primitivism," in: Kelly, vol. 4: 88-92.

Conner, Lynne, *Spreading the Gospel of Modern Dance: Newspaper Dance Criticism in the United States, 1850-1934*, Pittsburgh: University of Pittsburgh Press 1997.

Copeland, Roger, "The Dance Medium," in: Copeland & Cohen 103-111.

_____, "The search for origins: Roger Copeland looks at primitivism in modern dance," *Dance Theatre Journal* (London), vol. 12 no. 1, summer 1996: 8-14.

_____ & Marshall Cohen (eds.), *What Is Dance? Readings in Theory and Criticism*, New York: Oxford University Press 1983.

Cramer, Franz Anton, "Die Erfindung der Tanzwissenschaft. Die Archives Internationales de la Danse in Paris," *tanz journal* (München), no. 5, October 2006: 11-13.

Dörr, Evelyn, "Rudolf von Laban. Tänzerische Identität im Spannungsfeld von Kunst, Wissenschaft und Politik," in: S. Karoß & L. Welzin (eds.), *Tanz – Politik – Identität*, Hamburg: LIT Verlag 2001: 103- 132.

_____, "Wie ein Meteor tauchte sie in Europa auf ..." / "She suddenly appeared in Europe like a meteor ...," in: F.-M. Peter (ed.), *Isadora & Elizabeth Duncan in Deutschland / Isadora & Elizabeth Duncan in Germany*, Köln: Wienand Verlag 2000: 31-49.

E. Krishna Iyer: Centenary Issue, Music Academy: Madras, August 9, 1997.

Erdman, Joan L., "Blurred Boundaries: Androgyny and Gender in the Dance of Uday Shankar," in: *Border Crossings: Dance and Boundaries in Society, Politics, Gender, Education and Technology*, Proceedings Society of Dance History Scholars, Toronto, 10-14 May 1995: 117-124.

_____, "Dance Discourses. Rethinking the History of the 'Oriental Dance'," in: Gay Morris (ed.), *Moving Words: Re-Writing Dance*, London: Routledge 1996: 288-305.

_____, "Performance as Translation. Uday Shankar in the West," *The*

Drama Review (New York), vol. 31 no. 1, spring 1987: 64-88.

_____, "Performance as Translation II: Shankar, the Europeans, and the Oriental Dance," S. Hoeber Rudolph et al (ed.), *Institute For Culture and Consciousness. Occasional Papers* vol.1, Chicago: University of Chicago 1993: 34-47.

_____, "Towards Authenticity: Uday Shankar's First Company of Hindu Dancers and Musicians," in: Waterhouse 69-97.

_____, "Who Remembers Uday Shankar?" (http://www.muktomona.com/new_site/mukto-mona/Articles/jaffor/uday_shanka2.htm).

Farrell, Gerry, *Indian Music and the West*, New York: Oxford University Press 2004.

Friedman, Michael, "Ernst Cassirer," *Stanford Encyclopedia of Philosophy*, 2004, (http://plato.stanford.edu/entries/cassirer/).

Fröböse, Eva (ed.), *Rudolf Steiner über Eurythmische Kunst*, Köln: DuMont 1983.

Gaiger, Jason, "Lebensphilosophie," *Routledge Encyclopedia of Philosophy* (http://www.texttribe.com/routledge/L/Lebensphilosophie.html).

Garafola, Lynn, "Serge Diaghilev," in: Cohen, *International Encyclopedia of Dance*, vol. 2: 406-412.

Gaston, Anne-Marie, *Śiva in Dance, Myth and Iconography*, New Delhi: Oxford University Press 1982.

Germana, Nicholas A., *The Orient of Europe: The Mythical Image of India and Competing Images of German National Identity*, Newcastle upon Tyne: Cambridge Scholars Publishing 2009.

Glasenapp, Helmuth von, *Das Indienbild deutscher Denker*, Stuttgart: Köhler 1960.

Goodman, Russell, "Transcendentalism," *Stanford Encyclopedia of Philosophy*, 2008 (http://plato.stanford.edu/entries/transcendentalism/).

Gopal, Ram, "Pavlova and the Indian dance," in: A.H. Franks (ed.), *Pavlova. A Biography*, New York: Da Capo Press 1979: 98-110.

Greenhalgh, Paul, *Ephemeral vistas: The Expositions Universelles, Great Exhibitions and World's Fairs, 1851-1939*, Manchester: Manchester University Press 1988.

Guest, Ann Hutchinson, "Labanotation," in: Cohen, *International Encyclopedia of Dance*, vol. 4: 95-98.

Guha-Thakurta, Tapati, *The Making of a New 'Indian' Art. Artists, aesthetics and nationalism in Bengal, c. 1850-1920*, Cambridge: Cambridge University Press 1992.

_____, *Monuments, Objects, Histories. Institutions of Art in Colonial and Postcolonial India*, New York: Columbia University Press 2004.

Hanna, Judith L., "Feminist Perspectives on Classical Indian Dance: Divine Sexuality, Prostitution, and Erotic Fantasy," in: Waterhouse 193-231.

Hood, Mantle, "Ethnomusicology," in: W. Apel (ed.), *Harvard Dictionary of Music*, Cambridge: Harvard University Press 1969[2]; printed in: Kaufman Shelemay 134-136.

Huschka, Sabine, *Moderner Tanz. Konzepte, Stile, Utopien*, Reinbek bei Hamburg: Rowohlt 2002.

Huxley, M. & N. Witts (eds.), *The Twentieth-Century Performance Reader*, London & New York: Routledge 2002.

Jeschke, Claudia & Gabi Vettermann, "François Delsarte," in: Oberzaucher-Schüller, *Ausdruckstanz* 15-24.

Jones, Amelia, "Body," in: *Critical Terms for Art History*, R.S. Nelson & R. Shiff (eds.), Chicago & London: The University of Chicago Press 2003[2]: 251-266.

Jowitt, Deborah, "Modern Dance" in: "Modernism," in: Kelly, vol. 3: 259-263.

Kämpchen, Martin, *Rabindranath Tagore*, Reinbek bei Hamburg: Rowohlt 1997 (1992).

Kaufman Shelemay, Kay (ed.), *Ethnomusicology. History, Definitions, and Scope*, Garland: New York & London 1992.

Kelly, Michael (ed.), *Encyclopedia of Aesthetics*, vol. 1-4, New York & Oxford: Oxford University Press 1998.

Kerbs, Diethart & Jürgen Reulecke (eds.), *Handbuch der deutschen Reformbewegungen 1880-1933*, Wuppertal: Peter Hammer Verlag 1998.

Kermode, Frank, "Loïe Fuller And the Dance Before Diaghilev," *Theatre Arts* (New York), September 1962: 6-21.

_____, "Poet and Dancer Before Diaghilev," in: Copeland & Cohen 145-160.

Kirstein, Lincoln, "Classical Ballet: Aria of the Aerial," *Playbill* (New York), May 1976; in: Copeland & Cohen 238-243.

Khokar, [Ashish] Mohan "Uday Shankar: An Appraisal," in: *Nartanam* (Mumbai), no. 4, October-December 2001: 39-42.

_____, *His Dance, His Life. A Portrait of Uday Shankar*, New Delhi: Himalayan Books 1983.

Knapman, Gareth, "Race, Empire and Liberalism: Interpreting John Crawfurd's History of the Indian Archipelago," paper for the 17th Biennial Conference of the Asian Studies Association of Australia in Melbourne, 1-3 July 2008 (http://arts.monash.edu.au/mai/asaa/garethknapman.pdf).

Koch, Lars-Christian, *Zur Bedeutung der Rasa-Lehre für die zeitgenössische nordindische Kunstmusik. Mit einem Vergleich mit der Affektenlehre des 17.und 18. Jahrhunderts*, Bonn: Holos Verlag 1995.

Kopf, David, *British Orientalism and the Bengal Renaissance. The Dynamics of Indian Modernization 1773-1835*, Calcutta: Firma K.L. Mukhopadhyay 1969.

_____, "Hermeneutics versus History," in: A.L. Macfie (ed.), *Orientalism. A Reader*, New York University Press: New York 2000: 194-207.

Koritz, Amy, "Dancing the Orient for England. Maud Allan's 'The Vision of Salome'," in: Jane C. Desmond (ed.), *Meaning in Motion. New Cultural Studies of Dance*, Durham: Duke University Press 1997: 133-152.

Levin, David Michael, "Balanchine's Formalism" (1973), in: Copeland & Cohen 123-145.

Lipsey, Roger, *Coomaraswamy. Vol. 3: His Life and Work*, Princeton: Princeton University Press 1977.

Macdonald, Nesta, "Isadora Re-examined. Lesser known aspects of the great dancer's life, 1877-1900," *Dance Magazine* (New York), vol. 51 no. 7, July 1977: 50-65.

MacKenzie, John M., *Orientalism. History, theory and the arts*, Manchester & New York: Manchester University Press 1995.

Manning, Susan A., "Mary Wigman," in: Cohen, *International Encyclopedia of Dance*, vol. 6: 389-396.

Massey, Reginald, *India's Dances. Their History, Technique and Repertoire*, New Delhi: Abhinav Publications 2004.

"Mata Hari," in: *Encyclopedia Britannica* (http://www.britannica.com/EBchecked/topic/368879/Mata-Hari).

"Maud Allan," Dance Collection Danse, Toronto, Canada (http://www.dcd.ca/pih/maudallan.html).

Michaels, Axel, *Der Hinduismus. Geschichte und Gegenwart*, München: Beck 1998.

Mitter, Partha, *Art and Nationalism in Colonial India 1850-1922. Occidental Orientations*, Cambridge: Cambridge University Press 1994.

_____, *Much Maligned Monsters. History of European Reactions to Indian Art*, Oxford: Clarendon Press 1977.

Mukhopadhyay, Ashoke Kumar, *Uday Shankar. Twentieth Century's Nataraja*, Kolkata: Rupa & Co. 2004.

Nectoux, Jean-Michel, "*Schéhérazade* – Musik und Tanz," in: C. Jeschke et al (eds.), *Spiegelungen. Die Ballets Russes und die Künste*, Berlin: Verlag Vorwerk 1997: 105-112.

Nettl, Bruno & Philip V. Bohlman (eds.), *Comparative Musicology and Anthropology of Music. Essays on the History of Ethnomusicology*, Chicago: University of Chicago Press 1991.

Nochlin, Linda, "The Imaginary Orient," in: L. Nochlin, *The Politics of Vision. Essays on Nineteenth-Century Art and Society*, London: Thames and Hudson 1991: 33-59.

Nürnberger, Marianne, *Tanz / Ritual: Integrität und das Fremde*, Habil., April 2010 (http://homepage.univie.ac.at/marianne.nuernberger/ Nuernb_Habil.pdf).

Oberzaucher-Schüller, Gunhild (ed.), *Ausdruckstanz. Eine mitteleuropäische Bewegung der ersten Hälfte des 20. Jahrhunderts*, Florian Noetzel: Wilhelmshaven 1992.

_____, "Vorbilder und Wegbereiter. Über den Einfluß der 'prime movers' des amerikanischen Modern Dance auf das Werden des Freien Tanzes in Mitteleuropa," in: Oberzaucher-Schüller, *Ausdruckstanz* 347-366.

Preston-Dunlop, Valerie: "Rudolf Laban," in: Cohen, *International Encyclopedia of Dance*, vol. 4: 89-95.

Ramnarayan, Gowri, "Rukmini Devi: A Quest For Beauty. A Profile (Part I)," in: *Sruti* (Madras), June 1984, vol. 8: 17-29.

Rincón, Carlos, "Exotisch / Exotismus," in: Barck, vol. 2, 2001: 338-366.

Robinson, Jacqueline, *Modern Dance in France. An Adventure 1920 – 1970*, Amsterdam: Harwood Academic Publishers 1997.

Rössler, Martin, "Die deutschsprachige Ethnologie bis ca. 1960: Ein historischer Abriss," *Cologne Working Papers in Cultural and Social Anthropology*, no. 1, April 2007 (http://kups.ub.uni-koeln.de/volltexte/2007/1998/pdf/kae0001.pdf).

Ruyter, Nancy Lee Chalfa, "Antique longings: Genevieve Stebbins and American Delsartean performance," in: Susan L. Foster (ed.), *Corporealities*, London & New York: Routledge 1996: 70-89.

_____, "Delsarte System of Expression," in: Cohen, *International Encyclopedia of Dance*, vol. 2: 370-372.

_____, *The Cultivation of Body and Mind in Nineteenth-Century American Delsartism*, Westport & London: Greenwood Press 1999.

Said, Edward, *Musical Elaborations*, New York: Columbia University Press 1991.

_____, *Orientalism*, New York: Pantheon Books 1978.

Schlundt, Christena L., "Into the mystic with Miss Ruth," *Dance Perspectives* (New York), no. 46, summer 1971: 1-54.

Schneider, Albrecht, *Musikwissenschaft und Kulturkreislehre. Zur Methodik und Geschichte der Vergleichenden Musikwissenschaft*, Bonn: Verlag für systematische Musikwissenschaft 1976.

Schneider, Norbert, *Geschichte der Ästhetik von der Aufklärung bis zur Moderne*, Stuttgart: Reclam 2005[4].

Schwarz, Hans-Günther, *Der Orient und die Ästhetik der Moderne*, München: Iudicium 2003.

Scott, Trudy, "Orientalism," in: Cohen, *International Encyclopedia of Dance*, vol. 5: 44-47.

Shawn, Ted, *Every Little Movement. A Book About François Delsarte*, Dance Horizons: New York 1963.

Shelton, Suzanne, *Divine Dancer: A Biography of Ruth St. Denis*, New York: Doubleday 1981.

Simon, Artur, *Ethnomusikologie: Aspekte, Methoden und Ziele*, Berlin: Simon Verlag für Bibliothekswesen 2008.

_____, "Probleme, Methoden und Ziele der Ethnomusikologie," in: *Jahrbuch für Musikalische Volks- und Völkerkunde* (Köln), vol. 9, 1978; printed in: Kaufman Shelemay 252-296.

Sommer, Sally R., "Loie Fuller," in: Cohen, *International Encyclopedia of Dance*, vol. 3: 90-96.

Storch, Wolfgang, "Gesamtkunstwerk," in: Barck, vol.2, 2001: 730-791.

Subramaniam, Lakshmi, "Negotiating Orientalism: The *Kaccheri* and the Critic in Colonial South India," in: Martin Clayton & Bennett Zon (eds.), *Music and Orientalism in the British Empire, 1780s-1940s: Portrayal of the East*, Hampshire: Ashgate Publishing Limited 2007: 189-206.

Subramaniam, V. (ed.), *The Sacred and the Secular in India's Performing Arts: Ananda K. Coomaraswamy Centenary Essays*, New Delhi: Ashish Publishing House 1980.

Sünderhauf, Esther Sophia, *Griechensehnsucht und Kulturkritik. Die deutsche Rezeption von Winckelmanns Antikenideal 1840-1945*, Berlin: Akademie Verlag 2004.

Tarapor, Mahrukh, "Art Education in Imperial India: the Indian Schools of Art," in: K. Ballhatchet & D. Taylor (eds.), *Changing South Asia. Vol. III: City and Culture*, London: Asian Research Service 1984: 91-98.

Thapar, Romila, *Cultural Pasts. Essays in Early Indian History*, New Delhi: Oxford University Press 2000.

Waterhouse, David (ed.), *Dance of India*, Mumbai: Popular Prakashan 1998.

Weber, Max, "Wissenschaft als Beruf" (1919), Berlin: Duncker & Humblot 1967[5].

Williamson, George S., *The Longing for Myth in Germany. Religion and Aesthetic Culture from Romanticism to Nietzsche*, Chicago & London: The University of Chicago Press 2004.

Willson, A. Leslie, *A Mythical Image: The ideal of India in German Romanticism*, Durham, N.C.: Duke University Press 1964.

Youngerman, Suzanne, "Curt Sachs and His Heritage: A Critical Study of 'World History of the Dance' with a Survey of Recent Studies

That Perpetuate His Ideas," *CORD News*, vol. 6, 1974: 6-19.

Zon, Benett, "From 'very acute and plausible' to 'curiously misinterpreted': Sir William Jones's 'On the Musical Modes of the Hindus' (1792) and its reception in later musical treatises," in: M.J. Franklin, *Romantic Representations of British India*, London & New York: Routledge 2006: 197-219.